PLATO ON LOVE

LYSIS
SYMPOSIUM
PHAEDRUS
ALCIBIADES
with selections from
REPUBLIC
LAWS

PLATO ON LOVE

LYSIS
SYMPOSIUM
PHAEDRUS
ALCIBIADES
with selections from
REPUBLIC
LAWS

Edited by
C. D. C. Reeve

Hackett Publishing Company, Inc.
Indianapolis/Cambridge

For
Sunny
at last!

For further information, please address
Hackett Publishing Company, Inc.
P.O. Box 44937
Indianapolis, IN 46244-0937

www.hackettpublishing.com

Cover design by Abigail Coyle
Text design by Elizabeth Wilson
Composition by Professional Book Compositors
Printed at Edwards Brothers, Inc.

Library of Congress Cataloging-in-Publication Data

Plato.
    [Selections. English. 2006]
    Plato on love : Lysis—Symposium—Phaedrus—Alcibiades, with selections
from Republic and Laws / edited by C.D.C. Reeve.
        p. cm.
    Includes bibliographical references and index.
    ISBN 0-87220-789-7 (cloth) — ISBN 0-87220-788-9 (pbk.)
    1. Love.   I. Reeve, C. D. C., 1948–   II. Title.
    B358.R44 2006
    177'.7—dc22
                                                                2005022218

ISBN-13: 978-0-87220-789-9 (cloth)
ISBN-13: 978-0-87220-788-2 (pbk.)

CONTENTS

PREFACE

This book brings together all of Plato's major writings about love. It includes the *Symposium* and *Phaedrus*, but also the less well known *Lysis*, the (perhaps spurious) *Alcibiades*, and selections from the *Republic* and *Laws*. The Introduction provides a guide to these works, together with a brief account of Plato's larger philosophical enterprise and its Socratic roots. The translations of the selections from the *Republic* and *Laws* are my own, as are such footnotes as I have not borrowed from the other translators. Translations of the *Symposium* and *Phaedrus* are the work of Alexander Nehamas and Paul Woodruff; that of the *Lysis*, of Stanley Lombardo; that of the *Alcibiades*, of D. S. Hutchinson. I am grateful to these skilled Platonists for allowing me to make use of their work. Finally, I renew my gratitude to a dear friend, John Cooper, this time for his detailed comments on the Introduction and the translation of the *Laws*; to Janet Zweig for introducing me to the photography of Sally Gall; to my beloved editor and ally, Deborah Wilkes, for suggesting this project and helping me carry it out; and to Hackett Publishing Company for its ongoing support of my work.

Introduction

Before beginning to read Plato's dialogues about love, it is useful to know something about Plato himself and his philosophical work more generally, about Socrates, who is the protagonist in these dialogues, and about the sexual norms of classical Athens that provide an essential backdrop to them.

Plato

Plato was born in Athens in 429 BCE and died there in 348–347. His father, Ariston, traced his descent to Codrus, who was supposedly king of Athens in the eleventh century; his mother, Perictione, was related to Solon, architect of the Athenian constitution (594/3). While Plato was still a boy, his father died and his mother married Pyrilampes, a friend of the great Athenian statesman, Pericles.[1] Hence Plato was familiar with Athenian politics from childhood and was expected to enter it himself. Partly in reaction to the execution of his mentor and teacher Socrates in 399, he turned instead to philosophy, thinking that only it could bring true justice to human beings and put an end to civil war and political upheaval (see *Seventh Letter* 324b–326b).

Plato's works, which are predominantly dialogues, all seem to have survived. Few ancient writings have been so lucky. They are customarily divided into four chronological groups, though the precise ordering (especially within groups) is controversial:

> EARLY: *Apology, Charmides, Crito, Euthyphro, Hippias Minor, Hippias Major, Ion, Laches, Lysis, Menexenus*
> TRANSITIONAL: *Euthydemus, Gorgias, Meno, Protagoras*
> MIDDLE: *Cratylus, Phaedo, Symposium, Republic, Phaedrus, Parmenides, Theaetetus*
> LATE: *Timaeus, Critias, Sophist, Statesman, Philebus, Laws*

Plato also contributed to philosophy by founding the Academy, arguably the first university. This was a center of research and teaching,

---

[1] See *Symposium* 215e4 note.

both in theoretical subjects and in more practical ones. Eudoxus, who gave a geometrical explanation of the presumed revolutions of the sun, moon, and planets around the earth, brought his own students with him to join Plato, and studied and taught in the Academy; Theaetetus developed solid geometry there. But cities also invited members of the Academy to help them in the practical task of developing new political constitutions.

The Academy lasted for some centuries after Plato died, ending around 80 BCE. Its early leaders, including Plato's own nephew, Speusippus, who succeeded him as head, all modified his teachings in various ways. Later, influenced by the early dialogues, which end in puzzlement (*aporia*), the Academy, under Arcesilaus, Carneades, and other philosophers, practiced skepticism; later still, influenced by different dialogues, Platonists were more dogmatic, less unsure. Platonism of one sort or another—Middle or Neo- or something else— remained the dominant philosophy in the pagan world of late antiquity, influencing St. Augustine among others, until the emperor Justinian closed the pagan schools at Athens in 529 CE. Much of what passed for Plato's thought until the nineteenth century, when German scholars pioneered a return to Plato's writings themselves, was a mixture of these different "Platonisms."

Given the vast span and diversity of Plato's writings and the fact that they are dialogues, not treatises, it is little wonder that they were read in many different ways, even by Plato's ancient followers. In this respect nothing has changed: different schools of philosophy and textual interpretation continue to find profoundly different messages and methods in Plato. Doctrinal continuities, discontinuities, and outright contradictions of one sort or another are discovered, disputed, rediscovered, and redisputed. Neglected dialogues are taken up afresh, old favorites reinterpreted. New questions are raised, old ones resurrected and reformulated: is Plato's Socrates really the great ironist of philosophy, or is he a largely nonironic figure? Is Plato a systematic philosopher with answers to give, or is he an explorer of philosophical ideas only? Is he primarily a theorist about universals, a moralist, or a mystic with an otherworldly view about the nature of reality and the place of the human psyche in it? Or is he all of these at once? Does the dramatic structure of the dialogues undermine their apparent philosophical arguments? Should Plato's negative remarks about the efficacy of written philosophy (*Phaedrus* 274b–278b, below) lead us to look behind his dialogues for what Plato's student Aristotle refers to as the "so-called unwritten doctrines" (*Physics* 209^{b}14–15)?

Besides this continued engagement with Plato's writings, there is, of course, the not entirely separate engagement with the problems Plato brought to philosophy, the methods he invented to address them, and the solutions he suggested and explored. So many and various are these, however, that they constitute not just Plato's philosophy, but much of philosophy proper. Part of his heritage, they are also what we inevitably bring to our reading of him.

Socrates

In some of Plato's dialogues, Socrates is thought to be—and probably is—based to some extent on the historical Socrates. These are often called "Socratic" dialogues. In the so-called transitional, middle, and late dialogues, however, he is thought to be increasingly a mouthpiece for ideas that go well beyond Plato's Socratic heritage.

In the Socratic dialogues, philosophy consists almost exclusively in the philosophically pointed questioning of people about the conventionally recognized moral virtues. What is piety (*Euthyphro*)? Socrates asks, or courage (*Laches*)? Or temperance (*Charmides*)? He seems to take for granted, moreover, that there are correct answers to these questions—that piety, courage, and temperance are each some definite characteristic or form (*eidos, idea*). He does not discuss the nature of these forms, however, nor develop any explicit theory of them or our knowledge of them. He does not, for that matter, explain his interest in definitions, nor justify his claim that if we do not know what, for example, justice is, we cannot know whether it is a virtue, whether it makes its possessor happy, or anything else of any significance about it (*Republic* 354b–c).

Despite this silence on Socrates' part, however, there is ample evidence that he sought definitions of forms because he thought of forms as epistemic first principles, and that he did so because his model of genuine or expert knowledge was that of craft (*technê*). As a shoemaker, for instance, treats a well-made shoe as a pattern or paradigm in making another, so the moral expert, if he existed, would look to the form of piety (or whatever) in order to decide what actions or people were pious, and what it was that made them so (*Euthyphro* 6d–e). Of the dialogues included here, it is especially in the

Phaedrus, with its attempt to say what a properly scientific rhetoric would look like, that we see these ideas being developed.

Socrates' style of questioning is called (by us, not him) an *elenchus*—from the Greek verb *elengchein,* meaning to examine or refute: he asks what justice is; his interlocutor puts forward a definition he sincerely believes to be correct, at least for the moment; Socrates refutes this definition by showing that it conflicts with other beliefs the interlocutor sincerely holds and does not think he can reasonably abandon. In the ideal situation, which is never actually portrayed in the Socratic dialogues, this process continues until a satisfactory definition emerges—one that is not inconsistent with other sincerely held beliefs, and so can withstand elenctic scrutiny.

The goal of an elenchus is not just to reach adequate definitions of the virtues, however. Its primary aim is *moral reform.* For Socrates believes that, by curing people of the hubris of thinking they know when they do not, leading the elenctically examined life makes them happier and more virtuous than anything else. Philosophizing is so important for human welfare, indeed, that Socrates is willing to accept execution rather than give it up (*Apology* 29b–d, 30a, 36c–e, 38a, 41b–c).

Platonic Philosophy

In a number of dialogues, Plato connects the relativist doctrines he attributes to the some of the sophists[2] with the metaphysical theory of Heraclitus,[3] according to which the perceptible things or characteristics we see around us are in constant flux or change—always *becoming,* never *being.* In the *Theaetetus,* he argues that Protagoras' claim that "man is the measure of all things" presupposes that the world is in flux; in the *Cratylus,* he suggests that the theory of flux may itself be the result of projecting Protagorean relativism onto the world (411b–c).[4] Nonetheless, Plato seems to accept some version of this theory himself. In the *Symposium,* for example, Diotima argues that "everything mortal is preserved, not, like the divine, by always being

---

[2] See *Symposium* 177b2 note.

[3] See *Symposium* 187a5 note.

[4] See *Phaedrus* 267c4 note.

the same in every way, but because what is departing and aging leaves behind something new, something such as it had been" (208a–b).

The theory of flux has clear repercussions for the Socratic elenchus. If perceptible things and characteristics are always in flux, how can justice or love be a stable form? How can there be stable definitions of them to serve as correct answers to Socrates' questions? And if there are no stable definitions, how can there be such a thing as knowledge of them? More generally, if perceptible things and characteristics are always in flux, always *becoming*, how can anything *be* anything? How can one know or say what anything *is?* Aristotle tells us that it was reflection on these fundamental questions that led Plato to "separate" the forms from perceptible things and characteristics (*Metaphysics* 987ª29–ᵇ1). The famous ladder of love in the *Symposium* seems to reflect this separation (210a–212b).

Conceived in this way, forms seemed to Plato to offer solutions to the metaphysical and epistemological problems to which the elenchus and flux give rise. As intelligible objects, set apart from the perceptible world, they are above the sway of flux, and so are available as stable objects of knowledge, stable meanings or referents for words. As real and unchanging entities that are independent of the mind, they provide the basis for the definitions Socrates seeks.

Like many proposed solutions to philosophical problems, however, Plato's raises new problems of its own. If forms really are separate from the world of flux our senses reveal to us, how can we know them? How can our words connect with them? If items in the perceptible world really are separate from forms, how can they owe what share of being they have to forms? In the *Meno, Phaedo,* and *Phaedrus,* Plato answers the first of these questions by appeal to the doctrine of recollection (*anamnêsis*). We have knowledge of forms through our souls' having had prenatal direct contact with them; we forget this knowledge when our souls become embodied at birth; then we "recollect" it in this life when our memories are appropriately jogged. He answers the second question by saying that items in the world of flux "participate" in forms by resembling them. Thus perceptible objects possess the characteristic of beauty because they resemble the form of beauty, which is itself beautiful in a special and basic way (*Symposium* 210b–211e).

The doctrine of recollection presupposes the immortality of the soul—something Plato argues for in *Phaedrus* (245c ff) and elsewhere (*Phaedo* 69e ff; *Republic* 10). It also presupposes some method of jogging our memories in a reliable way. This method is dialectic, which is a descendant of the Socratic elenchus. The "method of division" discussed in the *Phaedrus* (265d–266b) is part of dialectic, since it explains how correct definition must proceed.

Once acquired, such correct definitions are available as first principles or starting points for the various sciences. But if these are treated as "absolute"—that is, as to be accepted without argument—there is a problem: if the starting points are false, the entire system collapses (*Republic* 510c–d). It is here that dialectic comes in again. It defends these starting points—it renders them "unhypothetical"—not by deriving them from something yet more primitive (which is impossible, since they are "starting" points), but by defending them against all objections; by solving all the *aporiai*, or problems, to which they give rise (534b–c, 437a). With the objections solved, our intellectual vision is cleared and we are able then to see the forms these definitions define in something like the way we did before our souls became embodied (540a–b).

In the process of their dialectical defense, the definitions themselves undergo conceptual revamping, so that their consistency with one another—and hence their immunity to dialectical (elenctic) refutation—is revealed and assured. This enables the philosopher (to whom the craft of dialectic belongs) to knit them all together into a single unified science of everything and so to "see things as a whole" (*Republic* 557c; cf. *Symposium* 210d–e). It is this unified science that provides the philosopher—and him alone—with genuine knowledge (533d–534a).

Love in Ancient Athens

The ancient Greeks had two words corresponding to the English word "love," *erôs* (verb, *eran*) and *philia* (verb, *philein*). The former refers primarily to erotic love, the sort that makes one person passionately desire another as a sexual partner. The second refers primarily to friendship, or to the sort of love we have for our parents, children, and siblings. Nonetheless, if one wanted to declare one's love for a sexual partner, one would normally use *philein* and say, *"Philô se"* ("I love you"). Hence words alone are not always a reliable guide to what sort of love is under discussion. Even when, as in Plato, *erôs* is the focus, *philia* is bound, even if only nominally, to come in.

Ancient Greek sexual customs were markedly different from our own. A "normal," upper-class Athenian male, for example, typically had sex both with other males and with females. As an adolescent, he would be the boyfriend (*erômenos*) of an adult male (*erastês*) and would serve as his passive partner in sexual intercourse. In theory, such intercourse was intercrural (between the thighs) and the boy neither solicited nor enjoyed it. (We might think here of Victorian ideas about the sexual desires of respectable women.) In reality, as Greek comedy makes plain and common sense suggests, anal intercourse was common and boys often did solicit and enjoy it. Once a boy reached manhood, however, once his beard grew, he had to change his behavior. On pain of losing his citizen's rights, he could no longer allow himself to be a passive partner. Instead, he typically married, had children, and became an *erastês* in his turn. At the same time, he would likely have sex with other women besides his wife, whether his own female slaves or other (typically non-Greek) women who worked in the sex industry, as we call it. Courtesans were numerous; female prostitution, legal.

Among such men, there probably were some who were homosexual in our sense—that is to say, men whose erotic desires were exclusively for other males. There were some, no doubt, who wished to be the passive partner only, and who found the most intense satisfactions involved being penetrated. Equally well, there were some who were heterosexual or bisexual in our sense. But the socially sanctioned, normal form of sexual life for a male in Athens simply cut across our characterizations. In that respect, it was like our own marriage laws. We cannot infer from the fact that a man is married that he is a heterosexual: Oscar Wilde, to cite a famous example, was married with children, but was homosexual. By the same token, we cannot infer from the fact that a man has sex with other men that he is homosexual; he may, like men in prison or boys in boarding school, simply be making do with what is available.

At a yet higher level of ideological idealization, a relationship between an *erastês* and an *erômenos* was represented as primarily educative rather than sexual. By associating with someone who was already a man, a boy learned *aretê*—civic virtue or excellence. He learned how to be a man himself. We might think here of rites of passage in primitive warrior societies, some of which also involve sex between men and boys. (In the Sambia Tribe of Papua, New Guinea, for example, boys must have oral sex with men as part of becoming men themselves.) It is often suggested, indeed, that Greek *paiderasteia* had its roots in a warrior past.

Adding to the complexity of an already complex situation is the dimension of *romance*. Various factors in ancient Greece contrived to prevent the romanticizing of heterosexual courtship and marriage among the upper classes: marriages were typically arranged for social or economic reasons; brides were often much younger than their husbands; women were sequestered in the household, excluded from the public world in which men primarily worked out their destinies. As a result, it was relationships between men and courtesans or between men and boys that took the form of romance, with its rituals of pursuit and avoidance, the giving of love gifts, and the writing of love songs and poems.

The erotic world of Plato's dialogues is in part, of course, just that of his society. But it is also, recognizably, the world of homoerotic romance—even if, as an ideal, at least, it is one transformed almost beyond recognition by philosophy. Plato's own attitudes toward sexual intercourse between men, as opposed to sublimated romantic attachment, are negative, but also—if somewhat reluctantly—tolerant (see, e.g., *Phaedrus* 352c ff; *Laws* 841a–c).

PLATO ON LOVE[1]

Plato discusses love primarily in two dialogues, the *Lysis* and the presumably later *Symposium*, with the presumably still later *Phaedrus* significantly enhancing his views.[2] A few passages from the *Republic* and the *Laws* complete the picture. The *Alcibiades*, which many scholars think not to be by Plato himself, but by a member of his school, is interesting more for what it *shows* about Platonic love than for what it says about it. It is included here as a companion piece to the *Symposium*, in which Alcibiades figures prominently, and as a nice introduction to Socratic philosophical practice.

In *Lysis*, *Symposium*, and *Phaedrus*, Socrates as the quintessential philosopher is in two ways at center stage: first, as a lover of wisdom (*sophia*) and discussion (*logos*), and, second, as himself an inverter or disturber of Athenian erotic norms. Plato's views on love, indeed, are largely a meditation on Socrates and the power his philosophical conversations have to mesmerize, obsess, and educate.

Socrates and the Art of Love

"The only thing I say I know," Socrates tells us in the *Symposium*, "is *ta erôtika*" (177d8–9). What is he claiming to know? Like *ta phusika* ("physics"), *ta politika* ("statesmanship"), and other similar neuter plurals, *ta erôtika* refers to "the art or craft of love (*hê erôtikê technê*)," which Socrates acknowledges as a gift from the god *Erôs* in the *Phaedrus* (257a3–9). And that raises a problem. Are we really to believe that the man who affirms, when on trial for his life, that he knows himself to be wise "in neither a great nor a small way" (*Apology* 21b4–5) knows something as significant as the art of love? No. The claim is a nontrivial play on words facilitated by the fact that the noun *erôs* ("love") and the verb *erôtan* ("to ask questions") seem to be etymologically connected—something explicitly mentioned in the

---

[1] Readers new to Plato might want to return to this essay after reading the relevant dialogues themselves. Translations may differ slightly from those in the body of the text.

[2] Some scholars think, however, that *Symposium* is later than *Phaedrus*.

Cratylus (398c5–e5). Socrates knows about the art of love in that—but just insofar as—he knows how to ask questions, how to converse elenctically.

Just how far that is, we discover in the *Lysis*, in which Socrates makes a similar claim. Hippothales, like Socrates, loves beautiful boys and philosophical discussions (203b6–204a3). But he does not know the art of love and so does not know how to talk to Lysis—the boy he loves. What Hippothales does is sing eulogies to Lysis, and that, Socrates argues, no skilled lover would ever do: if your suit succeeds, "everything you've said and sung turns out to eulogize yourself as victor in having won such a boyfriend," but if it fails, then "the greater your praise of his beauty and goodness, the more you will seem to have lost and the more you will be ridiculed." Consequently, someone "who is wise in the art of love (*ta erôtika*) doesn't praise his beloved until he has him: he fears how the future may turn out" (205e2–206a2). Convinced, Hippothales asks Socrates to tell him "what one should say or do to get his prospective boyfriend to love him?" (206c1–3). Unlike in the *Symposium,* in which he is gnomic, Socrates is here willing to explain what he means: "if you're willing to have him talk with me, I might be able to give you a demonstration of how to carry on a conversation with him" (c4–6). What follows is an elenctic examination of Lysis. Socrates' lessons in love, we may infer, are elenctic lessons—lessons in how to ask and answer questions.

At the end of the examination, Socrates describes what he has accomplished: "This is how you should talk with your boyfriends, Hippothales, cutting them down to size and putting them in their place, instead of swelling them up and spoiling them, as you do" (210e2–5). It sounds simply chastening when put like that. But in the overall context of the *Lysis,* where love is a desire and desire is an unpleasant emptiness, it is much more. It is a step in the creation of the canonical lover—the philosopher:

> Those who are already wise no longer love wisdom (*philosophein*), whether they are gods or men. Nor do those who are so ignorant that they are bad, for no bad and stupid man loves wisdom. There remain only those who have this bad thing, ignorance, but have not yet been made ignorant and stupid by it. They are conscious of not knowing what they don't know (218a2–b1).

So, by showing Lysis that he is not already wise, by getting him to recognize that he does not know, Socrates sets him on the road to philosophy (cf. *Sophist* 231b3–8).

The elenchus is important to love, then, because it creates a hunger for wisdom—albeit a hunger that it cannot itself assuage. So, even though Lysis is already something of a philosopher when he meets Socrates and receives a rare accolade from him—"I was pleased with his love of wisdom (*philosophia*)" (213d6)—he, too, is left in puzzlement (*aporia*). He is made aware of his desire by Socrates, but the desire itself remains unsatisfied. Socrates may be the master of foreplay, of arousing desire; and he may, to that extent, be a master of the art of love; but when it comes to satisfying desire, he is a failure. In the *Clitophon*—perhaps spurious, but arguably by Plato—this criticism is raised to Socrates' face and receives no answer. If we are not already persuaded to pursue virtue, Clitophon claims, Socrates "will wake us up from our sleep" (408c3–4). But if we are so persuaded, and now want to know what virtue is and what benefit it, in particular, brings to its possessor, he "is pretty much a stumbling block for reaching complete virtue and becoming happy" (410e7–8).

The connection—amounting to an identification—between the art of discussion and the art of loving boys, as explored in the *Lysis,* allows us to see why Plato's own explorations of love invariably involve an exploration of discussion, too—love talk in the *Lysis,* symposiastic speechmaking and drama in the *Symposium,* oratory and rhetoric in the *Phaedrus.* Loving boys correctly, after all, is—in part at least—just a matter of knowing how to talk to them, of how to persuade them to love the right things.

Socrates and Athenian Paiderastia

As a man who loves boys in an idiosyncratic, because elenctic, way, Socrates is placed in potential conflict with the norms of a peculiar Athenian social institution, that of *paiderastia*—the socially regulated intercourse between an older Athenian male (*erastês*) and a teenage boy (*erômenos, pais*), through which the latter was supposed to learn virtue. And this potential, as we know, was realized with tragic consequences—in 399, Socrates was found guilty of corrupting the young men of Athens and condemned to death. The effect on Plato is palpable in his works, turning very many of them into defenses—not always uncritical—of Socrates, and of what he represented to the young men he encountered. His account in the *Symposium* of one such relationship—that with the brilliant and beautiful Alcibiades—is an illuminating case in point.

Alcibiades was so in love with Socrates—"it was obvious," the *Symposium* (222c1–2) tells us—that when asked to speak of love, he speaks of his beloved. No general theories of love for him, just the vividly remembered stories of the times he spent with a man so extraordinary that there has never been anyone like him—a man so powerfully erotic that he turned the conventional world of love upside down by "seeming to be a lover (*erastês*) while really establishing himself as a beloved boy (*pais*) instead" (222b3–4).

The list of characters (all of them historical figures) present at Agathon's dinner party may seem more or less accidental—these are just the people who happened to be there. But, as is always true of Plato's dialogues, the list is in fact carefully chosen to further the purposes of the dialogue itself. In this case, most are representatives of the various kinds of people from whom Athenians (or Athenian men, at any rate) acquired their views about erotic love. We have a tragic poet (Agathon), a comic poet (Aristophanes), a doctor (Eryximachus), an *erastês* (Pausanias), and an *erômenos* (Phaedrus).[3] These are the ancient equivalents of the erotic authorities from whom we, today, learn about love: novelists, journalists, movie-makers (Agathon, Aristophanes), and doctors (Eryximachus). We lack an exact equivalent for Pausanias and Phaedrus, but the sometimes recommended "older man" or "younger woman" are perhaps rough analogues.

The stories these people tell about love, though independently interesting, seem to be intended to show how inadequate the views of these representatives of conventional erotic wisdom actually are. And as theories of love they are, indeed, pretty comical. Nonetheless, most of them contain some grain of what Plato takes to be the truth about love. Phaedrus claims that "love is the most ancient of the gods, the most honored, and the most powerful in helping men gain virtue and happiness" (180b6–8), and this, appropriately modified, is endorsed by Socrates and Diotima. Pausanias introduces the distinction between

---

[3] The dramatic date of the *Symposium* is 416, the year of Agathon's first victory. The historical Phaedrus was then probably in his mid-thirties, rather old for an *erômenos*. But Phaedrus' speech suggests that this is his preferred erotic identity.

same-sex boy-love and love between the sexes, which is also endorsed by Diotima. Eryximachus broadens the field of love—"it occurs everywhere in the universe" (186b1)—and connects it specifically to the good—the power of love "is far greater when love is directed, in temperance and justice, toward the good" (188d5–6). Again, both elements are preserved in Diotima's story. Aristophanes introduces the idea of the incompleteness of the lover, which is endorsed by Socrates in his questioning of Agathon. Finally, Agathon introduces the crucial distinction between what love itself is and what its effects or consequences are, which is also endorsed by Socrates.

So, the acknowledged authorities on erotic love have grasped something of its real nature; they have grasped what Diotima will later refer to as "images" of love, but they have mistaken these images for love itself. Moreover, it is clearly the particular brand of love that each of them favors or suffers from that has caused him to settle, not just for any old image of love, but for one that matches his brand.[4] Thus, for Agathon and Pausanias, the canonical image of true love— the quintessential love story—features the right sort of *erastês* and the right sort of *erômenos* (the latter is more prominent in Phaedrus' version, the former in Pausanias'). For Eryximachus, the image of true love is painted in the languages of his own beloved medicine and of all the other crafts and sciences. For Aristophanes, it is painted in the language of comedy (albeit a comic language tinged with tragic hues). For Agathon, it is painted in the loftier tones of tragedy (and the very loftiness of these tones make us laugh). In ways that these interlocutors are unaware of, then, but that Plato knows, their love stories are themselves manifestations of their loves, as well as the inversions or perversions expressed and embodied in them—hence the unmistakable aura of parody that surrounds Plato's presentation of their views. These men think their stories are the truth about love, but these are really love's delusions. As such, however, they are of course essential parts of that truth. For the power of love to engender delusive images of the beautiful is as much a part of the truth about it as its power to lead to the beautiful itself. "Eyes' falsehoods," as Shakespeare calls them in *Sonnet* 137, are name players in the theater of *erôs*.

---

[4] As David Halperin (*One Hundred Years of Homosexuality* [New York: Routledge, 1990], p. 117) and others have noticed.

Love stories like that of Alcibiades and the others, however inadequate they may be as theories of love, are nonetheless stories, *logoi*, items that admit of analysis. But because they are manifestations of our loves, not mere, cool bits of theorizing, we—our deepest feelings—are invested in them. They are therefore tailor-made, in one way at least, to satisfy the Socratic sincerity condition, the demand that you say what you believe (*Crito* 49c11–d2; *Protagoras* 331c4–d1). Under the cool gaze of the elenctic eye, they are tested for consistency with other beliefs that lie just outside love's controlling and often distorting ambit. Under such testing, a lover may be forced to say with Agathon, "I didn't know what I was talking about in that story" (201b11–12). The love that expressed itself in his love story meets then another love: his rational desire for consistency and intelligibility; his desire to be able to tell and live a coherent story; his desire—to put it the other way around—not to be endlessly frustrated and conflicted, because he is repetitively trying to live out an incoherent love story.

In Alcibiades' love story, in particular, these two desires are self-consciously in play: "Socrates is the only man in the world who has made me feel shame . . . I know perfectly well that I can't prove he's wrong when he tells me what I should do; yet, the moment I leave his side, I go back to my old ways: I cave in to my desire to please the crowd" (216b1–5). Even such awareness of conflict as is manifested here, however, is no guarantee of a satisfactory resolution. For the new love—the one that seems to offer coherence, satisfaction, and release from shame—may turn out just to be the old, frustrating one in disguise.

The famous failed attempt Alcibiades makes to seduce Socrates shows that this is his own situation (218b8–e5). For Alcibiades does not try to win Socrates' love by undertaking the difficult task of self-transformation required to become a more virtuous, and so more truly beautiful and lovable, person. Instead, he takes the easy, familiar path of offering the physical attractions he already has—the ones that have earned him the approval of the crowd. When these fail him, it is to the crowd (in the form of the revelers we meet at the end of the *Symposium*) he will regressively return, having never really succeeded in turning away.

That he has never turned away is made yet more vivid in one of the most intriguing passages in the *Symposium*. Socrates, Alcibiades says, is "ironical (*eirôneuomenos*) and spends his whole life playing with people. Yet, I don't know whether anyone else has seen the figures within (*ta entos agalmata*) when he is serious and opened up, but I saw them once, and I thought that they were so divine and golden, so marvelously beautiful, that I just had to do whatever Socrates told me" (216e4–217a2). For those who think Socrates to be a profoundly ironic figure, it is an amazing moment in which Socrates is seen without his mask of mock modesty. Alas, as is so often the case with love, it is a fantasy with which we are dealing. What Alcibiades thinks he sees in Socrates are embryonic virtues, which—like spermatozoa in the embryology that the *Symposium* implicitly embraces when it portrays forth *the lover* as pregnant and as seeking a beautiful boy in which to beget an offspring—need only be ejaculated into the right receptacle in order to grow into their mature forms (209a5–c2). Sex can lead to virtue, in other words, without the need for hard work. As soon as the illusion is enjoyed, therefore, it gives birth not to a realistic attempt to acquire virtue, but to the sexual seduction fantasy mentioned earlier.

The origins of this fantasy—though, no doubt, partly personal—are predominantly social. It is the complex ideology of Athenian *paiderasteia* that has shaped Alcibiades' own desires. For, according to it, love is really "two things": good Uranian love, the object of which is the soul, and the aim is to instill virtue in the younger male; and bad Pandemotic love, the object of which is the body, and the aim is sexual pleasure for the older lover (180c1–d7). What causes the split is the need Pandemotic love has to mask itself as Uranian love in order to preserve the illusion that the young man's participation in it is compatible with his status as a future male citizen. It cannot, then, be motivated by a reprehensible desire to adopt a passive, slavish, female, pleasure-seeking role. Instead, another motive must be invented for it—a willingness to accept "slavery for the sake of virtue" (184c2–3).

A major cost of preserving this split, however, is that the older male's body-focused, sexual intercourse must itself be refigured as intercourse of a more respectable sort. Alcibiades' later redescription of Socrates' inner figures shows him succumbing to the double vision that inevitably results:

> If you were to listen to his arguments, at first they'd strike you as totally ridiculous; they're clothed in words as coarse as the hides worn by the most vulgar satyrs. He's always going on about pack asses, or blacksmiths, or cobblers, or tanners. . . . But if the arguments are opened and one sees them from the

inside, one will find first that they are the only arguments
with any sense in them, and next that they contain within
themselves utterly divine and multitudinous figures of virtue
(*agalmat' arêtes*; 221e1–222a4).

For Alcibiades, then, Socrates' body is identical to his words; the
virtues that are in him are in them; talking about philosophy is having
sexual intercourse, and vice versa.

Loving Socrates

At the beginning of the *Symposium,* an unidentified man wants to
hear what was said about love by Socrates and the others at Agathon's
house. He has heard a garbled account. Now he wants Apollodorus to
tell him what was really said. But Apollodorus was not there, either.
He got his account of the proceedings secondhand from Aristodemus. Men who ought to be chasing boys are presented as so besotted
with Socrates and his conversations that one of them—Apollodorus—makes it his business to know exactly what Socrates does
and says each day (172c4–6), while another—Aristodemus—is so far
gone in his passion for Socrates that he walks barefoot like his beloved
(173b1–4). One reason for this complex setup is to let us see the in-
verting impact of Socrates—and so of philosophy—on Athenian
paiderastic norms. Another is more subtle. Alcibiades' love for
Socrates focuses on the beautiful figures of virtue that he thinks he
sees lying beneath those "words as coarse as the hides worn by the
most vulgar satyrs," which are the analog for him of Socrates' ugly,
satyrlike body (215b3–4). Aristodemus' love for Socrates, by contrast,
seems to focus on his coarse exterior, so that Aristodemus—whose
very name associates him with Pausanias' body-centered goddess of
love, *Pandêmos*—is himself a sort of inverted Alcibiades. Loving
Socrates, we may infer, is a complex business, since just what someone
loves in loving him is tied to that person's peculiar desires, and the
limits they impose on how like Socrates he can become.

In the dialogue's next few scenes, this point is driven home. When
Aristodemus meets him, Socrates has just bathed and put on his fancy
sandals—"both very unusual events" (174a3–4). Aristodemus remarks
on this because he is naturally sensitive to those aspects of Socrates
which he himself—perhaps because of his own size and appearance
(173b2)—has chosen to emulate. The reason for the departure from

his usual habits, Socrates explains, is that he is going to Agathon's party and wants "beauty to go to beauty" (174a9). Oddly, this does not stop him from bringing Aristodemus—unbathed, unsandaled, unbeautiful—along. But what is odd from the point of view of *Socrates'* self-ascribed motivations is not at all odd from that of *Plato's.* He has now made the complexity of Socrates—his beautiful insides and ugly outsides, or vice versa—as dramatically present to our eyes as to those of Agathon and his other guests.

Socrates is invited to Agathon's—or Goodman's—home. (*Agathon* means "good" in Greek.) He thinks—wrongly as it happens—that Aristodemus is not invited, but offers to take him along anyway. Aristodemus' reply—"I'll do whatever you say" (174b2)—again connects him to Alcibiades: "I just had to do whatever he told me" (217a1–2). "Come with me then," Socrates responds, "and we shall prove the proverb wrong; the truth is, 'Good men go uninvited to Goodman's feast'" (174b4–5).[5] Aristodemus is not convinced. "Socrates, I am afraid. . . . Mine is a case of an obvious inferior arriving uninvited at the table of a wise man" (174c5–7). The familiar Socratic triunity— good, beautiful, wise—is now fully in play.

Despite his reservations, Aristodemus agrees to accompany Socrates—but with an important proviso: "See what defense you're going to make (*apologêsêi*) for bringing me along, because I won't admit I came uninvited, I'll say you brought me!"(174c7–d1). It is this proviso that initiates the next mystifying episode. It begins when Socrates replies by underquoting Homer: "We'll take counsel about what to say 'when two go together along the way'" (174d2–3). What he leaves out is what happens when two *do* go together: namely, "one of them knows before the other" (*Iliad* X.24). The elision of this phrase is matched by an elision of Plato's own. For what happened on the road to Agathon's is that "Socrates began to think about something, lost himself in thought, and kept lagging behind" (174d4–7). Yet we are never told what he thought about—what it was that one knew before the other.

That the match between these two elisions is significant is evidenced by the close parallels between the preamble to Socrates' speech in praise of *Erôs* in the *Symposium,* and that to his speech of

---

[5] The proverb is that "good men go uninvited to an inferior man's feast" (Eupolis, fragment 289).

defense in the *Apology*. There he is "amazed (*ethaumasa*)" by what his accusers say (*Apology* 17a4–5); here Agathon's speech is "amazing (*thaumasta*)" (*Symposium* 198b4). There he isn't a clever (*deinos*) speaker, unless cleverness consists in speaking the truth (*Apology* 17a4–b6)—a standard rhetorical trope. Here he isn't clever in the art of love unless encomia to *Erôs* involve telling the truth about it (*Symposium* 198c5–199a6). There "what the jurors will hear will be spoken extemporaneously (*epituchousin*) in whatever words come to mind" (*Apology* 17c1–2); here the symposiasts will "hear the truth spoken about *Erôs* in such words and arrangements as occur to me extemporaneously (*tuchê epelthousa*)" (*Symposium* 199b3–5). Whatever occupies Socrates on the road to Agathon's, we may infer, ends not in the knowledge that Homer is so confident either he or Aristodemus, as two people going together along the way, will have; but in the aporetic awareness of the absence of knowledge that distinguishes Socrates' "human wisdom" from the "more than human wisdom" claimed by the sophists (*Apology* 20c4–e8).

The result of Socrates' losing his way in thought and ending up stymied on Agathon's neighbor's porch is that Aristodemus, like a proper Socratic paraclete, arrives at Agathon's quite a bit before Socrates. When Socrates finally does arrive *in propria persona,* Agathon says: "Socrates, come lie down next to me. Who knows: if I touch you, I may catch a bit of the wisdom that came to you under my neighbor's porch" (175c7–d1). Socrates replies with an obviously sexual simile, which acknowledges, so as later once again to invert, paiderastic norms: "If only wisdom were like water, which always flows from a full cup into an empty one when we connect them with a piece of yarn. If wisdom were that way too, I value the place beside you very much indeed; for I think I will be filled from you with wisdom of great beauty" (175d4–e2). What actually happens, however, is the very reverse. Socrates responds to Agathon's fancy speech about love with an elenchus, so that his own emptiness, his own lack of knowledge, flows into Agathon, destroying the wisdom of great beauty that had won his tragedy a first prize the day before (175e4–7).

Love and the Ascent to the Beautiful

Though Socrates may be adept at some parts of the art of love, he cannot, as we have seen, take his beloveds all the way. So, he is clearly in need of further instruction in this art. In the *Symposium,* it is provided to him by Diotima, whom he describes as "the one who taught me the art of love" (201d5). And what she teaches him, in a nutshell, is Plato's own philosophy. What the elenchus needs, if it is to satisfy rather than frustrate love, in other words, is the theory of Platonic Forms. What Socrates needs—and so ought to love—is Plato! The story of Platonic love is, one might say, the story of the Platonizing of Socrates.

If what Socrates learned from Diotima was about all love, however, it would be put in question by the very fact of Alcibiades, whose love for Socrates has not led him to love the beautiful itself. It would be equally threatened, indeed, by all the other symposiasts, none of whom has been led there by his love. But Diotima's love story is not so general. It is self-advertised as a story about "loving boys correctly (to orthôs paiderastein)" (211b5–6)—as a lesson in "the correct way to go or to be led by another, into the art of Love" (211b7–c1). To be sure, it does not itself explicitly provide us with a story about how Erôs can act as a force that retards development. But that is not because Plato thought Erôs could not act as such a force—consider Alcibiades. Rather, it is because Diotima's story is a story about successful or correct love.

The credibility of Diotima's love story is another matter, of course. To many, it has seemed both incredible and distasteful, because it seems to say that beautiful individuals have only instrumental value. When one has climbed the ladder, of which beautiful people are merely the first rung, one should kick it—and them—away. But is this message really Diotima's?

What we all love, according to Diotima, is the good—that is to say, we want good things to be ours forever. But because we are mortal, the closest we can come to satisfying this desire is to initiate an endless cycle of reproduction in which each new generation has good things. We achieve this, in a famous phrase, by "giving birth in beauty (tokos en kalôi)" (206b7–8, e5). What does this mean? Like Pausanias, Diotima recognizes two fundamentally different kinds of love, two fundamentally different varieties of the desire to give birth in beauty. In the case of lovers of opposite sexes, who are "pregnant in body," such birthing consists in producing children who resemble, and so share in the beauty of, their parents (209a3–4). Lovers of the same sex, however, are a different story. What they give birth to is "wisdom and the rest of virtue" (209b8). When a man who is pregnant in soul finds a beautiful boy, Diotima says, it "makes him instantly teem with accounts of virtue" (209b8), or "beautiful accounts" (210a8). Giving birth to virtue and giving birth to accounts of it are obviously different. But some of the other phrases Diotima uses show us how to mitigate the difference. For what such lovers want is to give birth to accounts of virtue of a particular sort—ones that can be used in "the proper ordering of cities and households" (209a6–7), and so can "make young men better" (210c1–3).

If the lover's accounts are to achieve this goal, however, they must not be the product of distorting fantasy, as Nietzsche thinks so many of our moral concepts are, and as some feminists think our concept of romantic love itself is. What is intended to insure that they will not is their openness to reality—an openness guaranteed by the fact that, in the course of his ascent, the lover must study the beauty of ways of life and laws (210c3–5), and the beauty of the sciences (c6–7). What he gains from these studies are the conceptual resources needed to see the world, including the human world, aright—to gain knowledge of it. This is not the project an analysand takes up in psychoanalysis. Nor is it the one that we less formally undertake when we reflect on our own love stories in hopes of understanding them (often a project provoked, alas, by an unhappy ending). It is instead the project of philosophy, as Plato conceives of it. That is why it culminates in "the birth of many gloriously beautiful accounts and theories in unstinting love of wisdom (*philosophia*)" (210d5–6). Yet the grander project intersects with the analysand's project, and with ours, in an interesting way. The terms or concepts we use to tell our love stories must themselves be coherent if the stories we use them to tell are themselves to be coherently livable.

In Plato's view, this means that they must be the concepts the true lover uses once he has seen the beautiful itself—the concepts of which the ontological correlates are forms. If they are not, they will be incoherent, and the lover who employs them will find himself embroiled in a love story he cannot fully understand, a love story whose incoherence the elenchus, or psychoanalysis, or just plain critical scrutiny will reveal. It is this incoherence, indeed, encountered at lower stages in the ascent, that leads the correct lover, under pressure from his rational desire for truth and consistency, and from the pain of inconsistency, to climb to the next stage.

We can see Diotima, then, not only as revealing the other, more abstract loves that a true lover of boys must have, but also as exploring the conditions concepts must meet if they are to figure in genuinely coherent love stories. Her story is not about a lover who abandons the individual boys he loves, but about someone who comes to love boys correctly by coming to love something else as well.

Like Diotima herself, we have been concentrating on what other things a correct lover is led to love by his love for his beloved boy. We have said nothing about the changes that explorations in this enlarged erotic field effect in the desires and feelings of the lover himself. But these, too, help us to see what happens to his love for his boy in the course of his explorations. What hooks the lover, to begin with, is love for a particular body: "First, if the leader leads aright, he should love one body and beget beautiful accounts there" (210a6–8). At this stage, what the boy engages in the lover is his sexual desire for physical beauty, albeit one which, in firm keeping with the norms of Athenian *paiderastia*, is supposedly aim-inhibited: instead of sexual intercourse, it leads to discussions about beauty, and to accounts of it. Here the beauty at issue is, in the first instance, the boy *who represents beauty itself to the lover.* That is why, when the lover finally comes to see the beautiful itself, "beauty will no longer seem to you to be measured by gold or raiment or beautiful boys and youths, which now you look upon dumbstruck" (211d3–5). One effect of generating *accounts* of this beauty, however, is that the lover comes to see his beloved's beautiful body as one among many: if it is beautiful, so are any other bodies the accounts fit. And this initially cognitive discovery leads to a conative change: "Realizing this, he is established as a lover of all beautiful bodies and relaxes this excessive preoccupation with one, thinking less of it and believing it to be a small matter" (210b4–6).

It is important in reading Diotima's description of this change that we see it as comparative and contrastive: the lover used to *overvalue* his beloved (211d5–8, quoted below)—now he *values him appropriately.* But valuing appropriately is still valuing. The boy is still included in the class of beautiful bodies that the lover now loves. It is also important to notice that cognitive and conative changes are going hand in hand. To recognize that his beloved is one among many, the lover's love for him has to change. And that means that psychological resources within the lover—beyond his sexual responsiveness to physical beauty—are coming into play. More of the lover is now involved in his love. Hence what his beloved might be thought to lose in exclusivity, he gains in richness—and no doubt in endurance and reliability—of response. When his physical bloom fades, he will now still be loved (see *Alcibiades* 131c5–d2).

But love that is to escape frustration cannot stop with bodies. The attempt to formulate an account of love free from puzzles and immune to elenctic refutation must lead on from beautiful bodies to beautiful souls, and so to the beautiful laws and practices that will improve souls and make young men better. Again this cognitive achievement is matched by a conative one. When the lover sees that all these beautiful things are somehow akin in the beauty, he comes to think that "bodily beauty is a small thing" (*Symposium* 210c5–6), and so, as before, becomes less obsessed with it.

At the top of the *scala amoris* lies the beautiful itself, the first loved object that—like the "primary object of love (*próton philon*) in the *Lysis* (219d2–e4)—is not in any way gone beyond. Here, it seems, the lover at last finds something worthy of the obsessive attention he once lavished on his beloved boy (211d8–212a7). Nonetheless, obsession is out of place even here. For the beautiful itself can no more satisfy the lover's desires to eat and drink than his beloved can. Here—as there—what he would do if it were possible must not be confused with what he can and does do. After all, the lover himself cannot become immortal, except by giving birth in the beauty he has at last found. He does that, however, precisely by arranging for his beloved to grow up, become truly virtuous, and be with him in the contemplation of—and, to the extent that it is possible, the possession of—true beauty.

The Art and Psychology of Love Explained

In the *Phaedrus* (chiefly in Socrates' second speech in praise of love), we find a more detailed account of the psychology and art of love than in the *Symposium*. This account will be the exclusive focus of our discussion. The soul, whether divine or human, Socrates claims, is like "the natural union of a team of winged horses and their charioteer" (246a6–7). But whereas in a divine soul all three elements are "good and come from good stock," in a human soul, the white horse (familiar from *Republic* 4 as the honor-loving, spirited element) is "beautiful and good, and of similar stock," while the black one (the *Republic*'s appetitive element) is "the opposite and of the opposite stock," so that "the chariot-driving, in our case, is necessarily difficult and troublesome" (a7–b4). When spirit together with the charioteer (the *Republic*'s rational element, there too identified with what is truly human rather than bestial in us (588b10–589a4)) "leads us toward what is best and is in control," we possess moderation (*sôphrosunê*)

(237e2–3). But when "appetite drags us irrationally towards pleasures and rules in us, its rule is called excess or lewdness (*hubris*)" (238a1–2). Of this excess, gluttony is one species, but erotic love another (238b7–c4). This is the bad kind of love—Pandemotic in the *Symposium*—that Lysias rightly disparages in the speech Phaedrus admires and reads to Socrates (230e6–234c5).

In Socrates' view, however, there is also another kind of love; namely, "the madness of a man who, on seeing beauty here on earth, and being reminded of true beauty, becomes winged, and fluttering with eagerness to fly upward, but unable to leave the ground, looks upwards like a bird, and takes no heed of things below—and that is what causes him to be regarded as mad" (249d5–e1). This madman is the philosopher of the *Symposium*, who, when he falls in love with a boy, is led by his love to ascend by stages to the Platonic form of the beautiful. What makes his madness a divine gift, however, is that the ascent is now revealed as involving recollection of a prior prenatal ascent taken in the company of a god.

From the rich literary account of this ascent, we need take away just one idea: souls have different psychological structures depending on which god they followed in this life, since this sets an upper limit on how much of the forms they see, and so how much they can subsequently recollect. Since gaining access to forms nourishes and strengthens the rational element in the soul (248b5–c2), this also helps determine that soul's overall motivational structure: the stronger reason is, the more likely it will be to succeed in controlling the other elements.

Followers of Zeus (the king of the gods), for example, choose someone to love whose soul resembles their patron god. So, they seek someone who is "naturally disposed to philosophy and leadership, and when they have found him and fall in love they do everything to make him philosophical" (252e1–5). Nonetheless, the falling itself involves a huge psychological upheaval. The black horse of appetite immediately urges toward sexual intercourse. The white horse—"constrained then as always, by its sense of shame" (254a2)—holds itself and the chariot of the soul back. Eventually, however, the black horse forces both the charioteer and the white horse "to move toward the beloved and mention to him the delights of sex" (a5–7). Again they balk, "indignant at being forced to do terrible and improper things" (b1). But finally, "when there is no limit to their plight, they follow its lead, giving in and agreeing to do what it tells them" (b2–3). As they come close to the beloved, however, to initiate intercourse, the flashing face of the beloved reminds the charioteer of the beautiful itself, so that his memory "again sees it standing together with temperance on a holy pedestal" (b5–7). He becomes frightened and "in sudden reverence falls on his back, and is forced at the same time to pull back the reins so violently as to bring the horses down on their haunches, the one willingly, because of its lack of resistance to him, but the unruly horse much against its will" (b7–c3). Eventually, "when the same thing happens to the evil horse many times, it allows the charioteer with his foresight to lead" (e5–7). If this control of appetite by reason and spirit continues—even when the boy has accepted his lover and embraces, kisses, and lies down with him—and draws them to "a well-ordered life and to philosophy," they are blessedly happy here on earth, and, if they live such a life for three successive incarnations, they regrow their wings and rejoin the entourage of their god (255e2–b7).

When followers of Ares (the god of war) fall in love, on the other hand, they "adopt a lower way of living, not philosophical, but honor-loving" (256b7–c1). When they are drinking together, for example, or are careless in some other way, "the licentious horses in the two of them catch their souls off guard," and since the man's recollection of beauty is dimmer and is not rekindled by philosophical conversation, they end up having sex together—something "the masses regard as the happiest choice of all" (c1–5). Nonetheless, they do not have sex very often, because "what they are doing has not been approved by their whole mind" (c6–7). So, while the degree of their love and happiness is less than that of the philosophical pair and, on their death, "they leave the body without wings," still they have an impulse, coming from love, to try to gain them. Hence they are not punished in the next life, but helped on the way to future happiness together (c7–e2).

The love that is divine madness is a good thing, therefore, especially when, "accompanied by philosophical discussions (*erôta meta philosophôn logôn*)" (257b6), it leads to the beautiful itself and the other forms, which are what we—as most of all the rational element in our souls—truly love and crave. The question is what makes a discussion philosophical? What makes it of the sort to be included in the true art of love that the philosopher, who loves the beautiful itself, practices? The answer now proposed is that it must be a *technê*, or craft, and so must have the defining characteristics of one. As applied to love itself, for example, it must begin with a definition of love, and reach its conclusions by ordering its discussion in relation to it (263d5–e3). And this definition, in turn, must be established by what Socrates refers to as collection and division (266b3–4).

Collection is a process of "perceiving together and bringing into one form items that are scattered in many places" (265d3–4). It is a process that we, unlike other animals, are able to engage in, because our souls include a rational element that has prior acquaintance with forms: "a soul that never [prenatally] saw the truth cannot take a human shape, since a human being must understand what is said by relation to a form that is reached from many sense-perceptions being collected into one by reasoning" (249b5–c1).[6]

Once a form has been reached in this way, division begins. This is a matter of "cutting the form up again, by relation to [sub]forms, by relation to its natural joints" (265e1–2). As an example, Socrates cites the case of love itself:

> just as a single body naturally has its parts in pairs, with both members of each pair having the same name, and labeled respectively left and right, so the two speeches regarded madness as naturally a single form in us. The one [Socrates' reorganized version of Lysias' attack on love] cut off the part on the left side, then cutting it again, and not giving up until it had found among the parts a love that is, as we say, "left-handed," and abused it with full justice, while the other speech [Socrates' own defense of love] led us to the parts of madness on the right-hand side, and discovering and exhibiting a love that shares the same name as the other, but is divine, it praised it as a cause of our greatest goods. (265e4–266b1)

Thus, while each speech tells only half the story, the two together show how correct division should proceed. The goal, however, is not just truth or correctness, but explanatory adequacy. Thus if the form in question "is simple, we should consider. . . what natural capacity it has for acting and on what, or for being acted upon and by what," and

---

[6] It is useful to compare this description with the one given in Aristotle, *Posterior Analytics* II.19.

if it is complex, we should count its subforms and consider the same things about them as about the simple ones (270d3–7). That Socrates—the archetypal searcher for explanatory definitions (*Euthyphro* 6d9–e6)—should pronounce himself "a lover of these divisions and collections" is no surprise, therefore (266b3–4).

Philosophy aims at true definitions and true stories based on them. But it also aims at persuasion, since the philosophical lover wants to persuade his boy to follow him on the path to the forms. Philosophy and rhetoric must thus go together, which means that rhetoric, too, must be developed as a *technê*. It must, first, distinguish and give definitions of the various kinds of souls and kinds of speeches, revealing their respective capacities and susceptibilities; and, second, "coordinate each kind of soul with the kind of speech appropriate to it, explaining why one kind of soul is necessarily convinced by one kind of speech, while another is not" (271b1–5). Mastery of such a science, however, requires one further thing: "the student must observe these things as they are in real life, and actually being put into practice, and be able to follow them with keen perception" (d8–e1). It is not enough, in other words, to know what kinds of speeches affect what kinds of souls; the philosophical rhetorician must also know that this man in front of him is of such-and-such a kind, and be able to talk in the kind of way that will prove convincing to him (e2–272b2).

Writing about Love

At the end of the *Symposium,* Alcibiades has gone off, presumably with the throng of Bacchic revelers, who burst into his life as representatives of his overpowering love for the approval and flattery of the crowd. Socrates, Aristophanes, and Agathon are left behind discussing tragedy and comedy: "the main point was that Socrates was trying to prove to them that the same man knows (*epistasthai*) how to write both comedy and tragedy: that someone who is by craft (*technê*) a tragic poet is a comic poet too" (223d2–6).

The key words here, as we learn in the *Ion,* are *epistasthai* and *technê.* Ordinary poets cannot write both comedy and tragedy, because they do not write out of knowledge and craft (*technê*), but out of divine inspiration (*Ion* 534c5–6). If they did write out of craft and knowledge, if they were *craftsmen poets,* they would be able to write both comedy and tragedy, because opposites are always studied by the same craft. Thus the comedic craft and the tragic craft would have to be one and the same, just as one and the same craft, medicine, deals with both sickness and health.

Socrates tells us what a craftsman poet would *be able to* write; he does not tell us what he *would* write. Other Platonic spokesmen are somewhat more forthcoming. "We ourselves are poets," the Athenian tells us in the *Laws*, "who have to the best of our ability created a tragedy that is the finest and the best; at any rate, our entire constitution is constructed as an imitation of the finest and best way of life—the very thing which we claim is the truest tragedy" (817b1–5). Earlier in the same discussion, the Athenian is equally explicit that this same constitution, though not a comedy, does nonetheless embody comedic knowledge:

> Someone who is going to gain practical wisdom can't learn serious matters without learning ridiculous ones, nor anything else, for that matter, without its opposite. But if we intend to acquire virtue, even on a small scale, we can't be serious and comic, too; and this is precisely why we must learn to recognize what is ridiculous, to avoid being trapped by our ignorance of it into doing or saying something ridiculous, when we don't have to. (816d5–e5)

The *Laws* is a tragedy, then, because it is "an imitation of the finest and best way of life."

The *Symposium* is a tragedy for an analogous reason: it contains an imitation of one part of such a life, namely, what the *Protagoras* terms a "symposium of beautiful and good men" who "test each other's mettle in mutual argument" by asking and answering questions (347d3–348a9). This is how Socrates responds to Agathon's speech. It is how Diotima converses with Socrates. It is the type of symposium Socrates tries to reestablish when Alcibiades' "satyr play" is finished, and the throng of Bacchic revelers has left.

Unlike the *Laws*, however, the *Symposium* is a comedy too, since it also contains an imitation of the second-best kind of symposium described in the *Protagoras*. This is one in which poets figure as authorities, either by being present themselves (as Aristophanes is), or by being quoted by the participants, without being there to be questioned (as Homer and Hesiod are by Phaedrus), and where the participants "argue over points that can't be established with any certainty" (347e1–7).

Finally, Alcibiades arrives with—significantly enough—a flute-girl (*Symposium* 212c5–e3; compare 176e6–7). And though she does not play, her arrival inaugurates the further decline of the symposium into something even more like the kind of symposium reviled in the *Protagoras* as "a symposium of common, vulgar fellows . . . who, unable to entertain one another with their own conversation, put up the price of flute-girls, and pay large sums to hear the sound of the flute instead of their own talk" (347c4–d2). This is the element of satyr play in the *Symposium*—satyr imagery is frequent in Alcibiades' speech.

The idea is the one mentioned earlier. Some love stories—the good ones—are tragedies (as these are understood in the *Laws*): they involve the kind of love found in the best kind of life, a life that comes as close as possible to the divine—one in which we achieve happiness by having good things be ours forever (205d1–206a12). Other love stories are comedies: they involve a lesser kind of love. Others still are satyr plays: genital farces. But the true story of love, the story that is Plato's *Symposium* itself, is the story of all these stories. In the *Symposium,* the story takes the form appropriate to its genre and audience. But in the *Phaedrus,* we learn of the longer, more technical road it might take in the future, when, armed with a scientific psychology and rhetoric, it becomes a matter for experts.

SELECT BIBLIOGRAPHY

Allen, R. E. *Plato: The Symposium*. New Haven: Yale University Press, 1991.

Bartsch, Shadi, and Thomas Bartscherer, eds. *Erotikon: Essays on Eros, Ancient and Modern*. Chicago: University of Chicago Press, 2005.

Bobonich, Christopher. *Plato's Utopia Recast*. Oxford: Clarendon Press, 2002.

Bury, R. G. *The Symposium of Plato*, 2nd ed. Warminster: Aris and Phillips, 1973.

Clay, Diskin. " The Tragic and Comic Poet of the Symposium." In *Essays in Ancient Greek Philosophy, v. 2*, edited by John P. Anton and Anthony Preus. Albany: State University of New York Press, 1983: 186–202.

Cohen, David. *Law, Sexuality, and Society: The Enforcement of Morals in Classical Athens*. Cambridge: Cambridge University Press, 1991.

Davidson, James. *Courtesans and Fishcakes: The Consuming Passions of Classical Athens*. London: St. Martin's Press, 1998.

Denyer, Nicholas. *Plato: Alcibiades*. Cambridge: Cambridge University Press, 2001.

Dorter, Kenneth M. "The Significance and Interconnection of the Speeches in Plato's Symposium." *Philosophy and Rhetoric* 2 (1969): 315–34.

Dover, K. J. *Greek Homosexuality*. Cambridge, MA: Harvard University Press, 1978.

———. *Plato: The Symposium*. Cambridge: Cambridge University Press, 1980.

Dyson, Michael. "Immortality and Procreation in Plato's Symposium." *Antichthon* 20 (1986): 59–72.

Ferrari, G. *Listening to the Cicadas: A Study of Plato's Phaedrus*. Cambridge: Cambridge University Press, 1987.

———. "Platonic Love." In *The Cambridge Companion to Plato*, edited by Richard Kraut. Cambridge: Cambridge University Press, 1992: 248–76.

Frede, Dorothea. "Out of the Cave: What Socrates Learned from Diotima." In *Nomodeiktes: Greek Studies in Honor of Martin Oswald*, edited by Ralph M. Rosen and Joseph Farrell. Ann Arbor: University of Michigan Press, 1993: 397–422.

Gill, Christopher. "Platonic Love and Individuality." In *Polis and Politics: Essays in Greek Moral and Political Philosophy*, edited by Andros Loizou and Harrey Lesser. Aldershot: Avebury, 1990.

———. *Plato: The Symposium*. Harmondsworth: Penguin Books, 1999.

Gould, Thomas. *Platonic Love*. London: Routledge and Kegan Paul, 1973.

Griswold, Charles L. *Self-Knowledge in Plato's Phaedrus*. New Haven: Yale University Press, 1986.

Hackforth, R. *Plato's Phaedrus*. Cambridge: Cambridge University Press, 1952.

Halperin, David. *One Hundred Years of Homosexuality*. New York: Routledge, 1990.

Hunter, Richard. *Plato's Symposium*. Oxford: Oxford University Press, 2004.

Irwin, Terence. *Plato's Ethics*. New York: Oxford University Press, 1995.

Kahn, Charles. "Plato's Theory of Desire." *Review of Metaphysics* 41 (1987–1988): 77–103.

Kosman, L. A. "Platonic Love." In *Facets of Plato's Philosophy*, edited by W. H. Werkmeister. Assen: Van Gorcum, 1976: 53–69.

Lear, Jonathan. *Open Minded: Working Out the Logic of the Soul*. Cambridge, MA: Harvard University Press, 1998.

———. *Happiness, Death, and the Remainder of Life*. Cambridge, MA: Harvard University Press, 2000.

Moravcsik, J. M. E. "Reason and Eros in the Ascent Passage of the *Symposium*." In *Essays in Ancient Greek Philosophy*, edited by John P. Anton and G. L. Kustas. Albany: State University of New York Press, 1972: 285–302.

Nehamas, Alexander. *The Virtues of Authenticity: Essays on Plato and Socrates*. Princeton: Princeton University Press, 1999.

Nightingale, Andrea Wilson. "The Folly of Praise: Plato's Critique of Encomiastic Discourse in the *Lysis* and *Symposium*." *Classical Quarterly* 43 (1993): 112–30.

Nussbaum, Martha C. *The Fragility of Goodness*. Cambridge: Cambridge University Press, 1986.

O' Brien, Michael. "Becoming Immortal in Plato's Symposium." In *Greek Poetry and Philosophy: Studies in Honour of Leonard Woodbury*, edited by Douglas E. Gerber. Chica, CA: Scholars Press, 1984: 185–205.

Pender, Elizabeth E. "Spiritual Pregnancy in Plato's Symposium." *Classical Quarterly* 42 (1992): 72–86.

Penner, Terry, and Christopher Rowe. *Plato's Lysis*. Cambridge: Cambridge University Press, 2005.

Price, A. W. *Love and Friendship in Plato and Aristotle*. Oxford: Clarendon Press, 1989.

Reeve, C. D. C. "Telling the Truth about Love: Plato's *Symposium*." *Proceedings of the Boston Area Colloquium in Ancient Philosophy* VIII (1992): 89–114.

Rowe, C. J. *Plato: Phaedrus.* Warminster: Aris and Phillips, 1986.

————. *Plato: Symposium.* Warminster: Aris and Phillips, 1998.

Teçusan, Manuela. *"Logos Sympotikos:* Patterns of the Irrational in Philosophical Drinking: Plato Outside the *Symposium."* In *Sympotica: A Symposium on the Symposion,* edited by Oswin Murray. Oxford: Clarendon Press, 1990: 238–62.

Thompson, Wayne N. "The *Symposium:* A Neglected Source for Plato's Ideas on Rhetoric." In *Plato: True and Sophistic Rhetoric,* edited by Keith V. Erickson. Amsterdam: Rodopi, 1979: 325–38.

Tuana, Nancy, ed. *Feminist Interpretations of Plato.* University Park: The Pennsylvania State University Press, 1994.

Vlastos, Gregory. "The Individual as the Object of Love in Plato." In *Platonic Studies,* 2nd ed. Princeton: Princeton University Press, 1981: 3–42.

Warner, Martin. "Love, Self, and Plato's Symposium." *Philosophical Quarterly* 29 (1979): 329–39.

LYSIS

I was on my way from the Academy[1] straight to the Lyceum,[2] following the road just outside and beneath the wall;[3] and when I got to **203a** the little gate by Panops spring, I happened to meet Hippothales, Hieronymus' son,[4] and Ctesippus of Paeania,[5] and with them some other young men standing together in a group. Seeing me coming, 5 Hippothales said,

"Hey, Socrates, where are you coming from and where are you going?" **203b**

"From the Academy," I said, "straight to the Lyceum."

"Well, come straight over here to us, why don't you? You won't come? It's worth your while, I assure you."

"Where do you mean, and who all are you?" 5

"Over here," he said, showing me an open door and an enclosed area just facing the wall. "A lot of us spend our time here. There are quite a few besides ourselves—and they're all good-looking."

"What is this, and what do you do here?" **204a**

"This is a new wrestling school," he said, "just built. But we spend most of our time discussing things, and we'd be glad to have you join in."

"How very nice," I said. "And who is the teacher here?"

"Your old friend and admirer, Mikkos."[6] 5

"Well, God knows, he's a serious person and a competent instructor."

"Well, then, won't you please come in and see who's here?"

Translated by Stanley Lombardo

[1] A gymnasium and park northwest of Athens, where Plato later founded his famous school.

[2] A gymnasium northeast of Athens, where Aristotle (Plato's most famous student) founded his school. See Introduction, pp. xi–xiii

[3] The wall surrounding the city of Athens.

[4] Otherwise largely unknown.

[5] Ctessipus also appears in the *Euthydemus* and was present at the death of Socrates (*Phaedo* 59b). Paenania was a *deme*, or administrative unit, southwest of Athens.

[6] Otherwise unknown.

204b   "First I'd like to hear what I'm coming in for—and the name of the best-looking member."

"Each of us has a different opinion on who that is, Socrates."

"So tell me, Hippothales, who do you think it is?"

5   He blushed at the question, so I said, "Aha! You don't have to answer that, Hippothales, for me to tell whether you're in love with any of these boys or not—I can see that you are not only in love but pretty far gone, too. I may not be much good at anything else, but I

204c   have this god-given ability to tell pretty quickly when someone is in love, and with whom he's in love."

When he heard this he really blushed, which made Ctesippus say, "O very cute, Hippothales, blushing and too embarrassed to tell

5   Socrates the name. But if he spends any time at all with you he'll be driven to distraction hearing you say it so often. We're all just about deaf, Socrates, from all the 'Lysis' he's poured into our ears. And if

204d   he's been drinking, odds are we'll wake up in the middle of the night thinking we hear Lysis' name. As bad as all this is in normal conversation, it's nothing compared to when he drowns us with his poems and

5   prose pieces. And worst of all, he actually sings odes to his beloved in a weird voice, which we have to put up with listening to. And now when you ask him the name he blushes!"

204e   "Lysis must be pretty young," I said. "I say that because the name doesn't register with me."

"That's because they don't call him by his own name much. He still goes by his father's name, because his father is so famous. I'm sure you

5   know what the boy looks like; his looks are enough by which to know him."

"Tell me whose son he is," I said.

"He's the oldest son of Democrates of Aexone."[7]

"Well, congratulations, Hippothales, on finding someone so spir-

10   ited and noble to love! Now come on and perform for me what you've performed for your friends here, so that I can see if you know

205a   what a lover ought to say about his boyfriend to his face, or to others."

"Do you think what *he* says really counts for anything, Socrates?"

"Are you denying that you are in love with the one he says you are?"

---

[7] Democrates was the lover of Alcibiades (see *Symposium* 212c–223b). Aexone was a deme southeast of Athens.

"No, but I am denying that I write love poems about him and all."   5
"The man's not well, he's raving," Ctesippus hooted.
"O.K., Hippothales," I said. "I don't need to hear any poems or
songs you may or may not have composed about the boy. Just give me   205b
the general sense, so I'll know how you deal with him."
"Well why don't you ask Ctesippus? He must have total recall of it
all, from what he says about it being drummed into his head from
listening to me."   5
"You bet I do," Ctesippus said, "and it's pretty ridiculous, too,
Socrates. I mean, here he is, completely fixated on this boy and totally
unable to say anything more original to him than any child could say.   205c
How ridiculous can you get? All he can think of to say or write is
stuff the whole city goes around singing—poems about Democrates
and the boy's grandfather Lysis and all his ancestors; their wealth and
their stables and their victories at the Pythian, Isthmian, and Nemean
Games[8] in the chariot and horseback races. And then he gets into the   5
really ancient history. Just the day before yesterday, he was reciting
some poem to us about Heracles[9] being entertained by one of their
ancestors because he was related to the hero—something about him
being a son of Zeus[10] and the daughter of their deme's founding   205d
father—old women's spinning-songs, really. This is the sort of thing
he recites and sings, Socrates, and forces us to listen to."
When I heard that, I said, "Hippothales, you deserve to be
ridiculed. Do you really compose and sing your own victory ode be-   5
fore you've won?"
"I don't compose or sing victory odes for myself, Socrates."
"You only think you don't."
"How is that?" he asked.   10
"You are really what these songs are all about," I said. "If you make   205e
a conquest of a boy like this, then everything you've said and sung
turns out to eulogize yourself as victor in having won such a
boyfriend. But if he gets away, then the greater your praise of his
beauty and goodness, the more you will seem to have lost and the   5
more you will be ridiculed. This is why the skilled lover doesn't praise   **206a**

---

[8] The Pythian Games took place at Delphi; the Isthmian at Corinth; the Nemean
near Argolis; the more famous Olympian Games at Olympia in Elis.

[9] Or Hercules; a hero of legendary strength.

[10] The greatest of the Greek gods.

his beloved until he has him: he fears how the future may turn out. And besides, these good-looking boys, if anybody praises them, get swelled heads and start to think they're really somebody. Doesn't it seem that way to you?"

5 "It certainly does," he said.

"And the more swell-headed they get, the harder they are to catch."

"So it seems."

"Well, what do you think of a hunter who scares off his game and
10 makes it harder to catch?"

206b "He's pretty poor."

"And isn't it a gross misuse of language and music to drive things wild rather than to soothe and charm?"

"Well, yes."

5 "Then be careful, Hippothales, that you don't make yourself guilty of all these things through your poetry. I don't imagine you would say that a man who hurts himself by his poetry is at all a good poet—after all, he does hurt himself."

"No, of course not," he said. "That wouldn't make any sense at all. But that's just why I'm telling you all this, Socrates. What different
206c advice can you give me about what one should say or do so that his prospective boyfriend will like him?"

"That's not easy to say. But if you're willing to have him talk with
5 me, I might be able to give you a demonstration of how to carry on a conversation with him instead of talking and singing the way your friends here say you've been doing."

"That's easy enough," he said. "If you go in with Ctesippus here and sit down and start a conversation, I think he will come up to you
10 by himself. He really likes to listen, Socrates. And besides, they're celebrating the festival of Hermes,[11] so the younger and older boys are
206d mingled together. Anyway, he'll probably come up to you; but if he doesn't, he and Ctesippus know one another because Ctesippus'
5 nephew is Menexenus, and Menexenus is Lysis' closest companion. So have Ctesippus call him if he doesn't come by himself."

"That's what I'll have to do," I said, and, taking Ctesippus with me,
206e I went into the wrestling school, followed by the others. When we got inside we found that the boys had finished the sacrifice and the

---

[11] God of gymnasia, among other things.

ritual and, still all dressed up, were starting to play knucklebones.[12] Most of them were playing in the courtyard outside, but some of them were over in a corner of the dressing room playing with a great many knucklebones, which they drew from little baskets. Still others were standing around watching this group, and among them was Lysis. He stood out among the boys and older youths, a garland on his head, and deserved to be called not only a beautiful boy but a well-bred young gentleman. We went over to the other side of the room, where it was quiet, sat down, and started up a conversation among ourselves. Lysis kept turning around and looking at us, obviously wanting to come over, but too shy to do so alone. After a while Menexenus, taking a break from his game in the court, came in, and, when he saw Ctesippus and me, he came to take a seat beside us. Lysis saw him and followed him over, sitting down together with Menexenus next to him, and then all the others came, too. When Hippothales (let's not forget about him) saw that a small crowd had gathered, he took up a position in the rear where he thought Lysis wouldn't see him—afraid he might annoy him—and listened from his outpost.

Then I looked at Menexenus and asked him, "Son of Demophon, which of you two is older?"

"We argue about that," he said.

"Then you probably disagree about which one has the nobler family, too," I said.

"Very much so," he said.

"And likewise about which one is better looking." They both laughed.

"Naturally, I won't ask which of you two is richer. For you two are friends, isn't that so?"

"Definitely," they said.

"And friends have everything in common, as the saying goes; so in this respect the two of you won't differ, that is, if what you said about being friends is true."

They agreed.

I was about to ask them next which of them was more just and wiser, when somebody came in to get Menexenus, saying that the trainer was calling him. It seemed he still had some part to play in the

---

[12] A game like that of dice.

5 ceremony, and so off he went. I asked Lysis then, "Am I right in assuming, Lysis, that your father and mother love you very much?"

"Oh, yes," he said.

"Then they would like you to be as happy as possible, right?"

"Naturally."

207e "Well, do you think a man is happy if he's a slave and is not permitted to do whatever he likes?"

"No, by Zeus, I don't think so."

"Well, then, if your father and mother love you and want you to be happy, it's clear that they must be extremely concerned to make sure 5 that you *are* happy."

"Well, of course," he said.

"So they allow you to do as you please, and they never scold you or stop you from doing whatever you want to do."

"Not true, Socrates. There are a whole lot of things they don't let me do."

"What do you mean?" I said. "They want you to be happy but 208a they stop you from doing what you want? Well, tell me this. Suppose you have your heart set on driving one of your father's chariots and holding the reins in a race. You mean they won't let you?"

"That's right," he said. "They won't let me."

"Well, whom do they let drive it?"

5 "There's a charioteer who gets a salary from my father."

"What? They trust a hired hand instead of you to do whatever he likes with the horses, and they actually pay him for doing that?"

208b "Well, yes."

"But I suppose they trust you to drive the mule team, and if you wanted to take the whip and lash them, they would let you?"

"Why ever would they?" he said.

"Is anyone allowed to whip them?"

5 "Sure," he said, "the muleteer."

"A slave or free?"

"A slave."

"It seems, then, that your parents think more even of a slave than they do their own son, and trust him rather than you with their property, and let him do what he wants, but prevent you. But tell me one 208c more thing. Do they allow you to be in charge of your own life, or do they not trust you even that far?"

"Are you kidding?"

"Who is in charge of you, then?"

"My tutor[13] here."

"He's a slave, isn't he?"

"What else? He's ours, anyway."

"Pretty strange, a free man directed by a slave. How does this tutor direct you; I mean, what does he do?"

"Mostly he takes me to school."

"And your schoolteachers, they're not in charge of you too, are they?"

"They sure are!"

"It looks like your father has decided to put quite a few masters and dictators over you. But what about when you come home to your mother, does she let you do whatever it takes to make you happy, like playing with her wool or her loom when she's weaving? She doesn't stop you from touching the blade or the comb or any of her other wool-working tools, does she?"

"Stop me?" he laughed. "She would beat me if I laid a finger on them."

"Good gracious!" I said. "You must have committed some kind of terrible offense against your father or mother."

"No, I swear!"

"Then why in the world do they so unaccountably prevent you from being happy and doing what you like? And why are they raising you in a perpetual condition of servitude to someone or other, day in and day out? Why do you hardly ever get to do what you want to do? The upshot is, it seems, that your many and varied possessions do you no good at all. Everybody but you has charge of them, and this extends to your own person, which, well born though it is, somebody else tends and takes care of—while you, Lysis, control nothing, and get to do nothing you want to do."

"Well, Socrates, that's because I haven't come of age yet."

"That can't be it, son of Democrates, since there are *some* things, I imagine, that your father and mother trust you with, without waiting for you to come of age. For instance, when they want someone to read or write for them, I'll bet that you, of everyone in the household, are their first choice for the job. Right?"

"Right."

---

[13] *Paidagôgos:* a household slave who served as a sort of chaperone, caretaker, and tutor.

"And nobody tells you which letter to write first and which second, and the same goes for reading. And when you take up your lyre, I'll bet neither your father nor your mother stops you from tightening or loosening whatever string you wish, nor from using a plectrum or just your fingers to play."

"No, they don't."

"Then what's going on? What's the reason why they let you have your way here, but not in all the cases we've been talking about?"

"I suppose it's because I know about these things but not those."

"Aha!" I said. "So your father isn't waiting for you to come of age before he trusts you with everything; but come the day when he thinks that you know more than he does, he'll trust you with himself and everything that belongs to him."

"I guess so," he said.

"Well, then," I said, "what about your neighbor? Would he use the same rule of thumb as your father about you? When he thinks you know more about managing his estate than he does, will he trust you to do it, or will he manage it himself?"

"I suppose he will trust me to do it."

"And how about the Athenians? Do you think they will trust you with their affairs when they perceive that you know enough?"

"I sure do."

"Well, by Zeus, let's not stop here," I said. "What about the Great King?[14] Would he trust his eldest son, crown prince of Asia, to add whatever he likes to the royal stew, or would he trust us, provided we went before him and gave him a convincing demonstration of our superior culinary wisdom?"

"Why, us, of course."

"And he wouldn't let his son put the least little bit into the pot, but we could throw in fistfuls of salt if we wanted."

"Right."

"What about if his son had something wrong with his eyes; would he let him treat his own eyes, knowing he wasn't a doctor, or would he prevent him?"

"Prevent him."

---

[14] Darius, King of Persia (died 486 BCE). Represented by Plato as an ideal lawgiver at *Laws* 695c–d.

"But, if he thought we were doctors, he wouldn't stop us even if we pried his eyes open and smeared ashes in them, because he would think we knew what we were doing."

"True."

"So . . . he would trust us, rather than himself or his son, with all his business, as long as we seemed to him wiser than either of them." 5

"He would have to, Socrates," he said.

"Then this is the way it is, my dear Lysis: in those areas where we're really wiser, everybody—Greeks and barbarians, men and women—will trust us, and there we will act just as we choose, and nobody will want to get in our way. There we will be free ourselves, and in control of others. There things will belong to us, because we will derive some advantage from them. But in areas where we haven't got any understanding, no one will trust us to act as we judge best, but everybody will do their best to stop us, and not only strangers, but also our mother and father and anyone else even more intimate. And there we are going to be subject to the orders of others; there things are not going to be ours because we are not going to derive any advantage from them. Do you agree this is how it is?" 210b 5 210c

"I agree."

"Well, then, are we going to be anyone's friend, or is anyone going to love us as a friend in those areas in which we are good for nothing?" 5

"Not at all," he said.

"So it turns out that your father does not love you, nor does anyone love anyone else, so far as that person is useless."

"It doesn't look like it."

"But if you become wise, my boy, then everybody will be your friend; everybody will feel close to you, because you will be useful and good. If you don't become wise, though, nobody will be your friend, not even your father or mother or your close relatives." 210d

"Now, tell me, Lysis, is it possible to be really wise in areas in which one hasn't yet acquired wisdom?"

"How could it be?" he said. 5

"And if you need a teacher, you haven't yet acquired wisdom."

"True."

"Then you're not really wise either—since you lack wisdom."

"You've got me there, Socrates!"

Hearing his last answer I glanced over at Hippothales and almost made the mistake of saying: "This is how you should talk with your 210e

boyfriends, Hippothales, cutting them down to size and putting them in their place, instead of swelling them up and spoiling them, as you
5 do." But when I saw how anxious and upset he was over what we were saying, I remembered how he had positioned himself so as to escape Lysis' notice, so I bit my tongue. In the middle of all this,
211a Menexenus came back and sat down next to Lysis, where he had been before. Then Lysis turned to me with a good deal of boyish friendliness and, unnoticed by Menexenus, whispered in my ear: "Socrates,
5 tell Menexenus what you've been saying to me."

I said to him: "Why don't you tell him yourself, Lysis? You gave it your complete attention."

"I certainly did," he said.

"Then try as hard as you can to remember it, so that you can tell it
211b all to him clearly. But if you forget any of it, ask me about it again the next time you run into me."

"I will, Socrates; you can count on it. But talk to him about some-
5 thing else, so I can listen too until it's time to go home."

"Well, I guess I'll have to, since it's you who asks. But you've got to come to my rescue if he tries to refute[15] me. Or don't you know what a debater[16] he is?"

"Sure I do—he's very much one. That's why I want you to have a
211c discussion with him."

"So that I can make a fool of myself?"

"No, so you can teach him a lesson!"

"What are you talking about? He's very clever, and Ctesippus' stu-
5 dent at that. And look, Ctesippus himself is here!"

"Never mind about anybody else, Socrates. Just go on and start discussing with him."

"Discuss we shall," I said.

Our little tête-à-tête was interrupted by Ctesippus' asking: "Is this a private party between you two, or do we get a share of the
211d conversation?"

"Of course you get a share!" I said. "Lysis here doesn't quite understand something I've been saying, but he says he thinks Menexenus knows and wants me to ask him."

---

[15] *Elengchein:* As in the Socratic *elenchus.* See Introduction, p. xiv.

[16] *Eristikos:* Someone who practices the sort of argument that aims at scoring points against an opponent, rather than discovering the truth. See *Republic* 537e–540c.

"Why don't you ask him then?"

"That's just what I'm going to do," I said. "So, Menexenus, tell me something. Ever since I was a boy, there's a certain thing I've always wanted to possess. You know how it is, everybody is different: one person wants to own horses, another dogs, another money, and another fame. Well, I'm pretty lukewarm about those things, but when it comes to having friends I'm absolutely passionate, and I would rather have a good friend than the best quail or gamecock known to man, and, I swear by Zeus above, more than any horse or dog.[17] There's no doubt in my mind, by the Dog,[18] that I would rather possess a friend than all Darius' gold,[19] or even than Darius himself. That's how much I value friends and companions. And that's why, when I see you and Lysis together, I'm really amazed; I think it's wonderful that you two have been able to acquire this possession so quickly and easily while you're still so young. Because you have in fact, each of you, gotten the other as a true friend—and quickly, too. And here I am, so far from having this possession that I don't even know how one person becomes the friend of another, which is exactly what I want to question you about, since you have experience of it.

"So tell me: when someone loves someone else, which of the two becomes the friend of the other, the one who loves or the one who is loved? Or is there no difference?"

"I don't see any difference," he said.

"Do you mean," I said, "that they both become each other's friend when only one of them loves the other?"

"It seems so to me," he said.

"Well, what about this: isn't it possible for someone who loves somebody not to be loved by him in return?"

"Yes, it's possible."

"And isn't it possible for him even to be hated? Isn't this how men are often treated by the young boys they are in love with? They are deeply in love, but they feel that they are not loved back, or even that they are hated. Don't you think this is true?"

"Very true," he said.

"In a case like this, one person loves and the other is loved. Right?"

---

[17] Aviaries and hunting dogs were common in wealthy Greek households.

[18] Probably the dog-headed Egyptian god Anubis. See *Gorgias* 482b5.

[19] See 209d6 note.

"Yes."

"Then which is the friend of the other? Is the lover the friend of
the loved, whether he is loved in return or not, or is even hated? Or is
the loved the friend of the lover? Or in a case like this, when the two
do not both love each other, is neither the friend of the other?"

"That's what it looks like, anyway," he said.

211d   "So our opinion now is different from what it was before. First we
thought that if one person loved another, they were both friends. But
now, unless they both love each other, neither is a friend."

"Perhaps."

"So nothing is a friend of the lover unless it loves him in return."

"It doesn't look like it."

5   "So there are no horse-lovers unless the horses love them back, and
no quail-lovers, dog-lovers, wine-lovers, or exercise-lovers. And no
lovers of wisdom, unless wisdom loves them in return. But do people
really love them even though these things are not their friends, mak-
212e   ing a liar of the poet who said,

> Happy the man who has as friends his children and solid-hoofed
> horses, his hunting hounds and a host abroad?"[20]

"I don't think so," he said.

5   "Then you think he spoke the truth?"

"Yes."

"So what is loved is a friend to the person who loves it, or so it
seems, Menexenus, whether it loves him or hates him. Babies, for
example, who are too young to show love but not too young to hate,
213a   when they are disciplined by their mother or father, are at that moment, even though they hate their parents then, their very dearest
friends."

"It seems so to me."

"So by this line of reasoning it is not the lover who is a friend, but
the loved."

"It looks like it."

5   "And so the hated is the enemy, not the hater."

"Apparently so."

---

[20] Solon fragment 23 (Edmonds).

"Then many people are loved by their enemies and hated by their friends, and are friends to their enemies and enemies to their friends—if the object of love, rather than the lover, is a friend. But this doesn't make any sense at all, my dear friend; in fact I think it is simply impossible to be an enemy to one's friend and a friend to one's enemy." 213b

"True, Socrates, I think you're right."

"Then if this is impossible, that would make the lover the friend of 5 the loved."

"Apparently so."

"And the hater the enemy of the hated."

"That must be."

"Then we are going to be forced to agree to our previous statement, that one is frequently a friend of a nonfriend, and even of an 213c enemy. This is the case when you love someone who does not love you, or even hates you. And frequently one is an enemy to a nonenemy, or even to a friend, as happens when you hate someone who does not hate you, or even loves you."

"Perhaps," he said.

"Then what are we going to do," I said, "if friends are not those 5 who love, nor those who are loved, nor those who love and are loved? Are there any others besides these of whom we can say that they become each other's friends?"

"By Zeus," he said, "I certainly can't think of any, Socrates."

"Do you think, Menexenus," I said, "that we may have been going about our inquiry in entirely the wrong way?" 213d

"I certainly think so, Socrates," said Lysis. And as he said it, he blushed. I had the impression that the words just slipped out unintentionally because he was paying such close attention to what was being said, which he clearly had been all along. 5

Well, I wanted to give Menexenus a break anyway, and I was pleased with the other's fondness for philosophy, so I turned the conversation toward Lysis, and said: "I think you're right, Lysis, to say that 213e if we were looking at things in the right way, we wouldn't be so far off course. Let's not go in that direction any longer. That line of inquiry looks like a rough road to me. I think we'd better go back to where we turned off, and look for guidance to the poets, the ancestral voices 5 of human wisdom. What they say about who friends are is by no 214a means trivial: that God himself makes people friends, by drawing them together. What they say goes something like this: 5

God always draws the like unto the like[21]

214b   and makes them acquainted. Or haven't you come across these lines?"
He said he had.

"And haven't you also come across writings of very wise men
saying the same thing, that the like must always be friend to the like?
You know, the authors who reason and write about Nature and the
5   Universe?"[22]

"Yes, I have," he said.

"And do you think what they say is right?" I asked.

"Maybe," he said.

"Maybe half of it," I said, "maybe even all of it, but we don't understand it. To our way of thinking, the closer a wicked man comes
214c   to a wicked man and the more he associates with him, the more he
becomes his enemy. Because he does him an injustice. And it's impossible for those who do an injustice and those who suffer it to be
friends. Isn't that so?"

"Yes," he said.

"Then that would make half the saying untrue, if we assume the
wicked are like each other."

5   "You're right," he said.

"But what I think they're saying is that the good are like each other
and are friends, while the bad—as another saying goes—are never
alike, not even to themselves. They are out of kilter and unstable.
214d   And when something is not even like itself and is inconsistent with itself, it can hardly be like something else and be a friend to it. Don't
you agree?"

"Oh, I do," he said.

"Well, my friend, it seems to me that the hidden meaning of those
who say 'like is a friend to like' is that only the good is a friend, and
5   only to the good, while the bad never enters into true friendship with
either the good or the bad. Do you agree?"

He nodded yes.

"So now we've got it. We know what friends are. Our discussion
indicates to us that whoever are good are friends."

---

[21] Homer, *Odyssey* 17.218.

[22] Empedocles fragment B22; Democritus fragment B164 (Diels-Kranz).

"That seems altogether true to me."   214e

"To me also," I said. "But I'm still a little uneasy with it. By Zeus, let's see why I'm still suspicious. Is like friend to like insofar as he is like, and as such, is he useful to his counterpart? I can put it better this way: when something, anything at all, is like something else, how can   5 it benefit or harm its like in a way in which it could not benefit or harm itself? Or what could be done to it by its like that could not be done to it by itself? Can such things be prized by each other when   215a they cannot give each other assistance? Is there any way?"

"No, there isn't."

"And how can anything be a friend if it is not prized?"

"It can't."

"All right, then, like is not friend to like. But couldn't the good still be friend to the good insofar as he is good, not insofar as he is like?"

"Maybe."   5

"What about this, though? Isn't a good person, insofar as he is good, sufficient to himself?"

"Yes."

"And a self-sufficient person has no need of anything, just because of his self-sufficiency?"

"How could he?"

"And the person who needs nothing wouldn't prize anything."

"No, he wouldn't."

"What he didn't prize, he wouldn't love."   215b

"Definitely not."

"And whoever doesn't love is not a friend."

"It appears not."

"Then how in the world are the good going to be friends to the good? They don't yearn for one another when apart, because even then they are sufficient to themselves, and when together they have no   5 need of one another. Is there any way people like that can possibly value each other?"

"No."

"But people who don't place much value on each other couldn't be   215c friends."

"True."

"Now, Lysis, consider how we have been knocked off course. Are we somehow completely mistaken here?"

"How?" he asked.

"Once I heard someone say—I just now remembered this—that
5   like is most hostile to like,[23] and good men to good men. And he cited
Hesiod[24] as evidence:

215d
> *Potter is angry with potter, poet with poet*
> *And beggar with beggar.*[25]

And he said that it had to be the same with everything else: things
that are most like are filled with envy, contentiousness, and hatred for
each other, and things most unlike with friendship. The poor man is
5   forced to be friends with the rich, and the weak with the strong—for
the sake of assistance—and the sick man with the doctor, and in general every ignorant person has to prize the man who knows and love
215e   him. Then he went on to make a very impressive point indeed, saying
that the like is totally unqualified to be friend to the like; that just the
opposite is true; that things that are completely in opposition to each
other are friends to the highest degree, since everything desires its op-
5   posite and not its like. Dry desires wet, cold hot, bitter sweet, sharp
blunt, empty full, full empty, and so forth on the same principle. For
the opposite, he said, is food for its opposite, whereas the like has no
216a   enjoyment of its like. Well, my friend, I thought he was quite clever
as he said this, for he put it all so well. But you two, what do you
think of what he said?"

"It sounds fine," said Menexenus, "at least when you hear it put like
that."

"Then should we say that the opposite is its opposite's best friend?"

"Absolutely."

5   "But Menexenus," I said, "this is absurd. In no time at all those vir-
tuosos, the contradiction mongers,[26] are going to jump on us gleefully
and ask us whether enmity is not the thing most opposite to friend-
216b   ship. How are we going to answer them? Won't we have to admit that
what they say is true?"

"Yes, we will."

---

[23] Heraclitus fragment B51 (Diels-Kranz). See *Symposium* 187a5 note.

[24] Early (c. 700 BCE) epic poet from Boeotia; author of *Works and Days* and
Theogony.

[25] *Works and Days* 25–6.

[26] *Antilogikoi*: synonym of *eristikoi*. See 211b8 note.

"So then, they will continue, is the enemy a friend to the friend, or the friend a friend to the enemy?"

"Neither," he answered.

"Is the just a friend to the unjust, or the temperate to the licentious, or the good to the bad?"

"I don't think so."

5

"But if," I said, "something is a friend to something because it is its opposite, then these things must be friends."

"You're right, they must."

"So like is not friend to like, nor is opposite friend to opposite."

"Apparently not."

"But there's this too that we still ought to consider. We may have overlooked something else, the possibility that the friend is none of these things, but something that is neither bad nor good and becomes the friend of the good just for that reason."

216c

"What do you mean?" he asked.

"By Zeus," I said, "I hardly know myself. I'm getting downright dizzy with the perplexities of our argument. Maybe the old proverb is right, and the beautiful is a friend. It bears a resemblance, at any rate, to something soft and smooth and sleek, and maybe that's why it slides and sinks into us so easily, because it's something like that. Now I maintain that the good is beautiful. What do you think?"

5

216d

"I agree."

"All right, now, I'm going to wax prophetic and say that what is neither good nor bad is a friend of the beautiful and the good. Listen to the motive for my mantic utterance. It seems to me that there are three kinds of things: the good, the bad, and the neither good nor bad. What about you?"

5

"It seems so to me, too," he said.

"And the good is not a friend to the good, nor the bad to the bad, nor the good to the bad. Our previous argument disallows it. Only one possibility remains. If anything is a friend to anything, what is neither good nor bad is a friend either to the good or to something like itself. For I don't suppose anything could be a friend to the bad."

216e

"True."

"But we just said that like is not friend to like."

5

"Yes."

"So what is neither good nor bad cannot be a friend to something like itself."

"Apparently not."

"So it turns out that only what is neither good nor bad is friend to
217a the good, and only to the good."

"It seems it must be so."

"Well, then, boys, are we on the right track with our present statement? Suppose we consider a healthy body. It has no need of a doc-
5   tor's help. It's fine just as it is. So no one in good health is friend to a
doctor, on account of his good health. Right?"

"Right."

"But a sick man is, I imagine, on account of his disease."

"Naturally."

217b "Now, disease is a bad thing, and medicine is beneficial and good."

"Yes."

"And the body, as body, is neither good nor bad."

"True."

"And because of disease, a body is forced to welcome and love
medicine."

"I think so."

"So what is neither good nor bad becomes a friend of the good be-
5   cause of the presence of something bad."

"It looks like it."

"But clearly this is before it becomes bad itself by the bad with
which it is in contact. Because once it has become bad, it can no
longer desire the good or be its friend. Remember we said it was im-
217c possible for the bad to befriend the good."

"It *is* impossible."

"Now consider what I'm going to say. I say that some things are of
the same sort as what is present with them, and some are not. For ex-
5   ample, if you paint something a certain color, the paint is somehow
present with the thing painted."

"Definitely."

"Then is the thing painted of the same sort, as far as color goes, as
217d the applied paint?"

"I don't understand," he said.

"Look at it this way," I said. "If someone smeared your blond hair
with white lead, would your hair then *be* white or *appear* white?"

"Appear white," he said.

"And yet whiteness would surely be present with it."

"Yes."

"But all the same your hair would not yet be white. Though
5   whiteness would be present, your hair would not be white any more
than it is black."

"True."

"But when, my friend, old age introduces this same color to your hair, then it will become of the same sort as what is present, white by the presence of white."

"Naturally."

"Here at last is my question, then. When a thing has something present with it, will it be of the same sort as what is present? Or only when that thing is present in a certain way?" 217e

"Only then," he said.

"And what is neither good nor bad sometimes has not yet become bad by the presence with it of bad, but sometimes it has." 5

"Certainly."

"And when it is not yet bad although bad is present, that presence makes it desire the good. But the presence that makes it be bad deprives it of its desire as well as its love for the good. For it is no longer neither good nor bad, but bad. And the bad can't be friend to the good." 218a

"No, it can't."

"From this we may infer that those who are already wise no longer love wisdom,[27] whether they are gods or men. Nor do those love it who are so ignorant that they are bad, for no bad and stupid man 5 loves wisdom. There remain only those who have this bad thing, ignorance, but have not yet been made ignorant and stupid by it. They are conscious of not knowing what they don't know. The upshot is 218b that those who are as yet neither good nor bad love wisdom, while all those who are bad do not, and neither do those who are good. For our earlier discussion made it clear that the opposite is not friend to the opposite, nor is like friend to like. Remember?" 5

"Of course," they both answered.

"So now, Lysis and Menexenus, we have discovered for sure what is a friend and to what it is a friend. For we maintain that in the soul and in the body and everywhere, that which is neither good nor bad itself is, by the presence of evil, a friend of the good." 218c

The two of them heartily agreed that this was the case, and I was pretty happy myself. I had the satisfied feeling of a successful hunter and was basking in it, when a very strange suspicion, from where I don't know, came over me. Maybe what we had all agreed to wasn't 5 true after all. What an awful thought. "Oh, no!" I screamed out. "Lysis and Menexenus, our wealth has all been a dream!"

---

[27] *Philosophein:* "philosophize," "engage in philosophy."

218d   "But why?" said Menexenus.

"I'm afraid we've fallen in with arguments about friendship that are no better than con artists."

5   "How?" he asked.

"Let's look at it this way," I said. "Whoever is a friend, is he a friend to someone or not?"

"He has to be a friend to someone," he said.

"For the sake of nothing and on account of nothing, or for the sake of something and on account of something?"

"For the sake of something and on account of something."

"And that something for the sake of which he is a friend, is it a

10   friend, or is it neither friend nor foe?"

"I don't get it," he said.

218e   "Naturally enough," I said. "But perhaps you will if we try it this way—and I think I might better understand what I am saying myself. A sick man, we were just now saying, is a friend to the doctor. Right?"

"Yes."

"And isn't he a friend on account of disease and for the sake of health?"

"Yes."

"And disease is a bad thing?"

"Of course."

5   "And what about health?" I asked. "Is it a good thing or a bad thing or neither?"

"A good thing," he said.

219a   "I believe we also said that the body, which is neither good nor bad, is a friend of medicine on account of disease, that is, on account of something bad. And medicine is a good thing. It is for the sake of health that medicine has received the friendship. And health is a good thing. All right so far?"

"Yes."

"Is health a friend or not a friend?"

5   "A friend."

"And disease is an enemy?"

"Certainly."

"So what is neither good nor bad is friend of the good on account

219b   of what is bad and an enemy, for the sake of what is good and a friend."

"It appears so."

"So the friend is friend of its friend for the sake of a friend, on account of its enemy."

"It looks like it."

"Well, then," I said, "since we have come this far, boys, let's pay close attention so that we won't be deceived. The fact that the friend has become friend of the friend, and so like has become friend of like, which we said was impossible—I'm going to let that pass by. But there is another point that we must examine, so that what is now being said won't deceive us. Medicine, we say, is a friend for the sake of health."

"Yes." 219c

"Health, then, is also a friend?"

"Very much a friend."

"If, therefore, it is a friend, it is for the sake of something."

"Yes."

"And that something is a friend, if it is going to accord with our previous agreement."

"Very much so."

"Will that too, then, also be a friend for the sake of a friend?"

"Yes."

"Aren't we going to have to give up going on like this? Don't we have to arrive at some first principle that will no longer bring us back to another friend, something that goes back to what is the first friend, something for the sake of which we say that all the rest are friends, too?" 219d

"We have to."

"This is what I am talking about, the possibility that all the other things that we have called friends for the sake of that thing may be deceiving us, like so many phantoms of it, and that it is that first thing which is truly a friend. Let's think of it in this way. Suppose a man places great value on something: say, a father who values his son more highly than all his other possessions. Would such a man, for the sake of his supreme regard for his son, also value something else? If, for example, he learned that his son had drunk hemlock, would he value wine if he thought it could save his son?" 219e

"Why, certainly," he said.

"And also the container the wine was in?"

"Very much."

"At that time would he place the same value on the ceramic cup or the three pints of wine as on his son? Or is it the case that all such concern is expended not for things that are provided for the sake of

220a something else, but for that something else for whose sake all the other things are provided? Not that we don't often talk about how much we value gold and silver. But that's not so and gets us no closer to the truth, which is that we value above all else that for which gold and all other

5 provisions are provided, whatever it may turn out to be. Shall we put it like that?"

"Most certainly."

"And isn't the same account true of the friend? When we talk about all the things that are our friends for the sake of another friend,

220b it is clear that we are merely using the word 'friend.' The real friend is surely that in which all these so-called friendships terminate."

"Yes, surely," he said.

"Then the real friend is not a friend for the sake of a friend."

5 "True."

"So much, then, for the notion that it is for the sake of some friend that the friend is a friend. But then is the good a friend?"

"It seems so to me," he said.

"And it is on account of the bad that the good is loved. Look, this is how it stands. There are three things of which we have just been

220c speaking—good, bad, and what is neither good nor bad. Suppose there remained only two, and bad were eliminated and could affect no one in body or soul or anything else that we say is neither good nor bad in and

5 of itself. Would the good then be of any use to us, or would it have become useless? For if nothing could still harm us, we would have no

220d need of any assistance, and it would be perfectly clear to us that it was on account of the bad that we prized and loved the good—as if the good is a drug against the bad, and the bad is a disease, so that without the disease there is no need for the drug. Isn't the good by nature loved

5 on account of the bad by those of us who are midway between good and bad; but by itself and for its own sake, it has no use at all?"

"It looks like that's how it is," he said.

"Then that friend of ours, the one that was the terminal point for all the other things that we called 'friends for the sake of another friend,'

220e does not resemble them at all. For they are called friends for the sake of a friend, but the real friend appears to have a nature completely the opposite of this. It has become clear to us that it was a friend for the sake of an enemy.[28] Take away the enemy and it seems it is no longer a friend."

---

[28] Plato writes "for the sake of (*heneka*) an enemy," when logic requires "because of (*dia*) an enemy." However, *heneka* can also mean "because of," and that is, perhaps, how it should be translated here.

"It seems it isn't," he said, "not, at least, by what we are saying now." 5

"By Zeus," I said, "I wonder, if the bad is eliminated, whether it will be possible to be hungry or thirsty or anything like that. Or if there will be hunger as long as human beings and other animals exist, 221a but it won't do harm. Thirst, too, and all the other desires, but they won't be bad, because the bad will have been abolished. Or is it ridiculous to ask what will be then and what will not? Who knows? But we do know this: that it is possible for hunger to do harm, and 5 also possible for it to help. Right?"

"Certainly."

"And isn't it true that thirst or any other such desires can be felt sometimes to one's benefit, sometimes to one's harm, and sometimes 221b to neither?"

"Absolutely."

"And if bad things are abolished, does this have anything to do with things that aren't bad being abolished along with them?"

"No."

"So the desires that are neither good nor bad will continue to exist, even if bad things are abolished."

"It appears so." 5

"And is it possible to desire and love something passionately without feeling friendly toward it?

"It doesn't seem so to me."

"So there will still be some friendly things even if the bad is abolished."

"Yes." 221c

"It is impossible, if bad were the cause of something's being a friend, that with the bad abolished, one thing could be another's friend. When a cause is abolished, the thing that it was the cause of can no longer exist."

"That makes sense."

"Haven't we agreed that the friend loves something, and loves it on 5 account of something, and didn't we think then that it was on account of the bad that what was neither good nor bad loved the good?"

"True."

"But now it looks like some other cause of loving and being loved 221d has appeared."

"It does look like it."

"Then can it really be, as we were just saying, that desire is the cause of friendship, and that what desires is a friend to that which it desires, and is so whenever it does so? And that what we were saying

5   earlier about being a friend was all just chatter, like a poem that trails
on too long?"

"There's a good chance," he said.

"But still," I said, "a thing desires what it is deficient in. Right?"

"Yes."

221e "And the deficient is a friend to that in which it is deficient."

"I think so."

"And it becomes deficient when something is taken away from it."

"How could it fail to do so?"

"Then it is what belongs to oneself, it seems, that passionate love
and friendship and desire are directed toward, Menexenus and Lysis."

They both agreed.

5   "And if you two are friends with each other, then in some way you
naturally belong to each other."

"Absolutely," they said together.

"And if one person desires another, my boys, or loves him passion-
222a ately, he would not desire him or love him passionately or as a friend
unless he somehow belonged to his beloved, either in his soul or in
some characteristic, habit, or aspect of his soul."

"Certainly," said Menexenus, but Lysis was silent.

"All right," I said, "what belongs to us by nature has shown itself to
5   us as something we must love."

"It looks like it," he said.

"Then the genuine and not the pretend lover must be loved by his
boy."

Lysis and Menexenus just managed a nod of assent, but Hippothales
222b beamed every color in the rainbow in his delight.

Wanting to review the argument, I said, "It seems to me, Lysis and
Menexenus, that if there is some difference between belonging and
being like, then we might have something to say about what a friend
5   is. But if belonging and being like turn out to be the same thing, it
won't be easy to toss out our former argument that like is useless to
like insofar as they are alike. And to admit that the useless is a friend
222c would strike a sour note. So if it's all right with you," I said, "since we
are a little groggy from this discussion, why don't we agree to say that
what belongs is something different from what is like?"

"Certainly."

"And shall we suppose that the good belongs to everyone, while the
5   bad is alien? Or does the bad belong to the bad, the good to the good,
and what is neither good nor bad to what is neither good nor bad?"

They both said they liked this latter correlation.

"Well, here we are again, boys," I said. "We have fallen into the   222d
same arguments about friendship that we rejected at first. For the unjust will be no less a friend to the unjust, and the bad to the bad, as the
good will be to the good."

"So it seems," he said.

"Then what? If we say that the good is the same as the belonging,   5
is there any alternative to the good being a friend only to the good?"

"No."

"But we thought we had refuted ourselves on this point. Or don't
you remember?"

"We remember."

"So what can we still do with our argument? Or is it clear that
there is nothing left? I do ask, like the able speakers in the law courts,   222e
that you think over everything that has been said. If neither the loved
nor the loving, nor the like nor the unlike, nor the good, nor the belonging, nor any of the others we have gone through—well, there   5
have been so many I certainly don't remember them all any more; but
if none of these is a friend, then I have nothing left to say."

Having said that, I had a mind to get something going with one of
the older men there. But just then, like some kind of divine interme-   223a
diaries, the tutors of Menexenus and Lysis were on the scene. They
had the boys' brothers with them and called out to them that it was
time to go home. It actually was late by now. At first our group tried   5
to drive them off, but they didn't pay any attention to us and just got
riled up and went on calling in their foreign accents. We thought they
had been drinking too much at the Hermaea and might be difficult to   223b
handle, so we capitulated and broke up our party. But just as they
were leaving I said, "Now we've done it, Lysis and Menexenus—
made fools of ourselves, I, an old man, and you as well. These people   5
here will go away saying that we are friends of one another—for I
count myself in with you—but what a friend is, we have not yet been
able to find out."

SYMPOSIUM

172a
APOLLODORUS: In fact, your question does not find me unprepared. Just the other day, as it happens, I was walking to the city from my home in Phaleron[1] when a man I know, who was making his way behind me, saw me and called from a distance:

"The gentleman from Phaleron!" he yelled, trying to be funny. "Hey, Apollodorus,[2] wait!"

So I stopped and waited.

5 "Apollodorus, I've been looking for you!" he said. "You know there once was a gathering at Agathon's[3] when Socrates, Alcibiades,
172b and their friends had dinner together; I wanted to ask you about the speeches they made on Love. What were they? I heard a version from a man who had it from Phoenix, Philip's son,[4] but it was badly garbled, and he said you were the one to ask. So please, will you tell me
5 all about it? After all, Socrates is your friend—who has a better right than you to report his conversation? But before you begin," he added, "tell me this: were you there yourself?"

"Your friend must have really garbled his story," I replied, "if you
172c think this affair was so recent that I could have been there."

"I did think that," he said.

"Glaucon,[5] how could you? You know very well Agathon hasn't lived in Athens for many years,[6] while it's been less than three that I've been Socrates' companion and made it my job to know exactly what
173a he says and does each day. Before that, I simply drifted aimlessly. Of

---

Translated by Alexander Nehamas and Paul Woodruff

[1] A port town in Attica, southwest of Athens.

[2] An enthusiastic and emotional follower of Socrates, present at his trial, where he contributes to his fine (*Apology* 34a); and at his death, where he breaks down in tears (*Phaedo* 117d).

[3] Agathon was a Greek tragedian, also present in the *Protagoras* (315e2).

[4] Otherwise unknown.

[5] Possibly the father of Charmides (mentioned at 222b1 below), but most likely Plato's brother and Socrates' interlocutor in the *Republic*.

[6] Agathon left Athens for the court of Archelaus of Phaleron sometime before 405 BCE.

course, I used to think that what I was doing was important, but in fact I was the most worthless man on earth—as bad as you are this very moment: I used to think philosophy was the last thing a man should do."

"Stop joking, Apollodorus," he replied. "Just tell me when the party took place."

"When we were still children, when Agathon won the prize with his first tragedy.[7] It was the day after he and his troupe held their victory celebration."

"So it really was a long time ago," he said. "Then who told you about it? Was it Socrates himself?"

"Oh, for god's sake, of course not!" I replied. "It was the very same man who told Phoenix: a fellow called Aristodemus, from Cydatheneum,[8] a real runt of a man, who always went barefoot. He went to the party because, I think, he was obsessed with[9] Socrates—one of the worst cases at that time. Naturally, I checked part of his story with Socrates, and Socrates agreed with his account."

"Please tell me, then," he said. "You speak and I'll listen, as we walk to the city. This is the perfect opportunity."

So this is what we talked about on our way; and that's why, as I said before, I'm not unprepared. Well, if I'm to tell *you* about it too—I'll be glad to. After all, my greatest pleasure comes from philosophical conversation, even if I'm only a listener, whether or not I think it will be to my advantage. All other talk, especially the talk of rich businessmen like you, bores me to tears, and I'm sorry for you and your friends because you think your affairs are important when really they're totally trivial. Perhaps, in your turn, you think I'm a failure, and, believe me, I think that what you think is true. But as for all of you, I don't just *think* you are failures—I know it for a fact.

FRIEND: You'll never change, Apollodorus! Always nagging, even at yourself! I do believe you think everybody—yourself first of all—is totally worthless, except, of course, Socrates. I don't know exactly

---

[7] In 416 BCE, probably at the Lenaean festival.

[8] Aristodemus is also mentioned as a companion of Socrates in Xenophon, *Memorobilia* 1.4, but is otherwise largely unknown. Cydatheneum is a deme (administrative unit) within the walled city of Athens.

[9] Literally "a lover (*erastês*) of Socrates."

how you came to be called "the maniac,"[10] but you certainly talk like one, always furious with everyone, including yourself—but not with

10   Socrates!

APOLLODORUS: Of course, my dear friend, it's perfectly obvious

173e   why I have these views about us all: it's simply because I'm a maniac, and I'm raving!

FRIEND: It's not worth arguing about this now, Apollodorus. Please

5   do as I asked: tell me the speeches.

APOLLODORUS: All right. . . . Well, the speeches went something like this—but I'd better tell you the whole story from the very begin-

174a   ning, as Aristodemus told it to me.

He said, then, that one day he ran into Socrates, who had just bathed and put on his fancy sandals—both very unusual events. So he

5   asked him where he was going, and why he was looking so good.

Socrates replied, "I'm going to Agathon's for dinner. I managed to avoid yesterday's victory party—I really don't like crowds—but I promised to be there today. So, naturally, I took great pains with my appearance: I'm going to the house of a good-looking man; I had to look my best. But let me ask you this," he added, "I know you haven't

174b   been invited to the dinner; how would you like to come anyway?"

And Aristodemus answered, "I'll do whatever you say."

"Come with me, then," Socrates said, "and we shall prove the proverb wrong; the truth is, 'Good men go uninvited to Goodman's

5   feast.'[11] Even Homer[12] himself, when you think about it, did not much like this proverb; he not only disregarded it, he violated it. Agamemnon, of course, is one of his great warriors, while he de-

174c   scribes Menelaus as a 'limp spearman.'[13] And yet, when Agamemnon

---

[10] *Manikos*. Alternatively, *malakos*—"soft," "emotional," "impressionable"—with connotations of being a bit effeminate.

[11] Agathon's name could be translated "Goodman." The proverb is, "Good men go uninvited to an inferior man's feast" (Eupolis fragment 289 Kock).

[12] Approximately eighth century. Greatest of the Greek epic poets. Author of the *Iliad* and the *Odyssey*.

[13] King of Mycenae. He led the Greek forces in the Trojan War. Menelaus, husband of Helen (whose abduction by Paris caused that war), was Agamemnon's brother.

offers a sacrifice and gives a feast, Homer has the weak Menelaus arrive uninvited at his superior's table."[14]

Aristodemus replied to this, "Socrates, I am afraid Homer's description is bound to fit me better than yours. Mine is a case of an obvious inferior arriving uninvited at the table of a man of letters. I think you'd better figure out a good excuse for bringing me along, because, you know, I won't admit I've come without an invitation. I'll say I'm your guest."   174d

"Let's go," he said. "We'll think about what to say 'as we proceed, the two of us, along the way.'"[15]

With these words, they set out. But as they were walking, Socrates began to think about something, lost himself in thought, and kept lagging behind. Whenever Aristodemus stopped to wait for him, Socrates would urge him to go on ahead. When he arrived at Agathon's, he found the gate wide open, and that, Aristodemus said,   174e caused him to find himself in a very embarrassing situation: a household slave saw him the moment he arrived and took him immediately to the dining room, where the guests were already lying down on their couches, and dinner was about to be served.

As soon as Agathon saw him, he called:

"Welcome, Aristodemus! What perfect timing! You're just in time   5 for dinner! I hope you're not here for any other reason—if you are, forget it. I looked all over for you yesterday, so I could invite you, but I couldn't find you anywhere. But where is Socrates? How come you didn't bring him along?"

So I turned around (Aristodemus said), and Socrates was nowhere to be seen. And I said that it was actually Socrates who had brought   10 *me* along as his guest.

"I'm delighted he did," Agathon replied. "But where is he?"

"He was directly behind me, but I have no idea where he is now."   **175a**

"Go look for Socrates," Agathon ordered a slave, "and bring him in. Aristodemus," he added, "you can share Eryximachus' couch."[16]   5

---

[14] Menelaus calls on Agamemnon at *Iliad* 2.408. Menelaus is called a limp spearman at 17.587–88.

[15] An allusion to *Iliad* 10.224: "When two go together, one has an idea before the other."

[16] Eryximachus of Athens, like his father Acumenus before him, was a doctor and friend of Phaedrus (*Phaedrus* 268a). Two (or three) to a couch was not unusual.

A slave brought water, and Aristodemus washed himself before he lay down. Then another slave entered and said: "Socrates is here, but he's gone off to the neighbor's porch. He's standing there and won't come in, even though I called him several times."

"How strange," Agathon replied. "Go back and bring him in. Don't leave him there."

But Aristodemus stopped him. "No, no," he said. "Leave him alone. It's one of his habits: every now and then he just goes off like that and stands motionless, wherever he happens to be. I'm sure he'll come in very soon, so don't disturb him; let him be."

"Well, all right, if you really think so," Agathon said, and turned to the slaves: "Go ahead and serve the rest of us. What you serve is completely up to you; pretend nobody's supervising you—as if I ever did! Imagine that we are all your own guests, myself included. Give us good reason to praise your service."

So they went ahead and started eating, but there was still no sign of Socrates. Agathon wanted to send for him many times, but Aristodemus wouldn't let him. And, in fact, Socrates came in shortly afterward, as he always did—they were hardly halfway through their meal. Agathon, who, as it happened, was all alone on the farthest couch, immediately called: "Socrates, come lie down next to me. Who knows: if I touch you, I may catch a bit of the wisdom that came to you under my neighbor's porch. It's clear *you've* seen the light. If you hadn't, you'd still be standing there."

Socrates sat down next to him and said, "How wonderful it would be, dear Agathon, if the foolish were filled with wisdom simply by touching the wise. If only wisdom were like water, which always flows from a full cup into an empty one when we connect them with a piece of yarn—well, then I would consider it the greatest prize to have the chance to lie down next to you. I would soon be overflowing with your wonderful wisdom. My own wisdom is of no account—a shadow in a dream—while yours is bright and radiant and has a splendid future. Why, young as you are, you're so brilliant I could call more than thirty thousand Greeks as witnesses."[17]

"Now you've gone *too* far, Socrates," Agathon replied. "Well, eat

---

[17] The theater of Dionysus, where Agathon's plays were staged, actually held between 10,000 and 20,000 people.

your dinner. Dionysus[18] will soon enough be the judge of our claims
to wisdom!"   10

Socrates took his seat after that and had his meal, according to Aris-   **176a**
todemus. When dinner was over, they poured a libation to the god,
sang a hymn, and—in short—followed the whole ritual. Then they
turned their attention to drinking. At that point Pausanias[19] addressed
the group:

"Well, gentlemen, how can we arrange to drink less tonight? To be   5
honest, I still have a terrible hangover from yesterday, and I could
really use a break. I daresay most of you could, too, since you were
also part of the celebration. So let's try not to overdo it."   176b

Aristophanes[20] replied: "Good idea, Pausanias. We've got to make a
plan for going easy on the drink tonight. I was over my head last night
myself, like the others."

After that, up spoke Eryximachus, son of Acumenus: "Well said,   5
both of you. But I still have one question: How do *you* feel, Agathon?
Are you strong enough for serious drinking?"

"Absolutely not," replied Agathon. "I've no strength left for anything."

"What a lucky stroke for us," Eryximachus said, "for me, for Aris-   176c
todemus, for Phaedrus,[21] and the rest—that you large-capacity
drinkers are already exhausted. Imagine how weak drinkers like ourselves feel after last night! Of course I don't include Socrates in my
claims: he can drink or not, and will be satisfied whatever we do. But
since none of us seems particularly eager to overindulge, perhaps it   5
would not be amiss for me to provide you with some accurate information as to the nature of intoxication. If I have learned anything
from medicine, it is the following point: inebriation is harmful to   176d
everyone. Personally, therefore, I always refrain from heavy drinking;
and I advise others against it—especially people who are suffering the
effects of a previous night's excesses."

---

[18] The god of drama and also of wine and drunkenness.

[19] Pausianias of Cerameis (a deme slightly northwest of Athens) is also present in
the *Protagoras*.

[20] The great Athenian comic dramatist (c. 450–385 BCE), whose play, *Clouds*,
presents a hostile portrait of Socrates.

[21] Socrates' interlocutor in the eponymous *Phaedrus*, also present in the *Protagoras*.
He was exiled, as was Alcibiades, after being accused of profaning the Eleusynian
Mysteries. See 212d3 note below.

5   "Well," Phaedrus of Myrrhinus[22] interrupted him, "I always follow
your advice, especially when you speak as a doctor. In this case, if the
others know what's good for them, they too will do just as you say."

176e   At that point they all agreed not to get drunk that evening; they
decided to drink only as much as pleased them.[23]

"It's settled, then," said Eryximachus. "We are resolved to force no
5   one to drink more than he wants. I would like now to make a further
motion: let us dispense with the flute-girl[24] who just made her entrance; let her play for herself or, if she prefers, for the women in the
house. Let us instead spend our evening in conversation. If you are so
10   minded, I would like to propose a subject."

They all said they were quite willing, and urged him to make his
177a   proposal. So Eryximachus said:

"Let me begin by citing Euripides' *Melanippe:* 'Not mine the tale.'
What I am about to tell belongs to Phaedrus here, who is deeply indignant on this issue, and often complains to me about it:

5   "'Eryximachus,' he says, 'isn't it an awful thing! Our poets have
composed hymns in honor of just about any god you can think of;
but has a single one of them given one moment's thought to the god
177b   of love (*Erôs*), ancient and powerful as he is? As for our fancy intellectuals,[25] they have written volumes praising Heracles[26] and other
heroes (as did the distinguished Prodicus[27]). Well, perhaps *that's* not
surprising, but I've actually read a book by an accomplished author
5   who saw fit to extol the usefulness of salt! And you can find hymns of

---

[22] A deme southeast of Athens.

[23] Cf. 223b5–6.

[24] *Aulêtris:* The *aulos* was in fact a reed instrument, like an oboe. "Flute" is the
standard translation.

[25] *Sophistas:* sophists—itinerant professors, who charged sometimes substantial
fees for popular lectures and specialized instruction in a wide variety of fields, including natural science, rhetoric, grammar, ethics, and politics. They did not
constitute a single school or movement, and were neither doctrinally nor organi-
zationally united.

[26] See *Lysis* 205c7 note.

[27] Prodicus of Ceos, about whom little is known, was also a fifth-century teacher
of rhetoric, with an interest in fine distinctions of meaning (*Protagoras* 337a1–c4;
Laches 197d3–5) and the correctness of names (*Euthydemus* 277e4; *Cratylus*
384a8–c2). Socrates is described as attending some of his lectures (*Cratylus*
384b2–c1; *Charmides* 163d3–4), and as being educated by him (*Meno* 96d7).

praise to many other, similar things. How *could* people pay attention to such trifles and never, not even once, write a proper hymn to Love? How could anyone ignore so great a god?'

177c

"Now, Phaedrus, in my judgment, is quite right. I would like, therefore, to take up a contribution, as it were, on his behalf, and gratify his wish. Besides, I think this a splendid time for all of us here to honor the god. If you agree, we can spend the whole evening in discussion, because I propose that each of us give as good a speech in praise of Love as he is capable of giving, in proper order from left to right. And let us begin with Phaedrus, who is at the head of the table and is, in addition, the father of our subject."

5

177d

5

"No one will vote against that, Eryximachus," said Socrates. "How could *I* vote 'No,' when the only thing I say I understand is the art of love?[28] Could Agathon and Pausanias? Could Aristophanes, who thinks of nothing but Dionysus and Aphrodite?[29] No one I can see here now could vote against your proposal.

177e

"And though it's not quite fair to those of us who have to speak last, if the first speeches turn out to be good enough and to exhaust our subject, I promise we won't complain. So let Phaedrus begin, with the blessing of Fortune; let's hear his praise of Love."

5

They all agreed with Socrates, and pressed Phaedrus to start. Of course, Aristodemus couldn't remember exactly what everyone said, and I myself don't remember everything he told me. But I'll tell you what he remembered best, and what I consider the most important points.

178a

5

As I say, he said Phaedrus spoke first, beginning more or less like this:

Love is a great god, wonderful in many ways to gods and men, and most marvelous of all is the way he came into being. We honor him as one of the most ancient gods, and the proof of his great age is this: the parents of Love have no place in poetry or legend. According to Hesiod,[30] the first to be born was Chaos,

178b

---

[28] *Ta erôtika:* A literal translation would be "erotics." The formulation is parallel to that of *ta phusika:* "physics" or the science of nature. See Plato on Love, p. xix.

[29] Goddess of love.

[30] See *Lysis* 215c7 note.

5   . . . *but then came*
                    Earth, broad-chested, a seat for all, forever safe,
                    And Love.[31]

        And Acusilaus[32] agrees with Hesiod: after Chaos came Earth and
10   Love, these two. And Parmenides tells of this beginning:

                    The very first god [she] designed was Love.[33]

178c   All sides agree, then, that Love is one of the most ancient gods. As
        such, he gives to us the greatest goods. I cannot say what greater good
        there is for a young boy than a gentle lover, or for a lover than a boy
        to love. There is a certain guidance each person needs for his whole
5   life, if he is to live well; and nothing imparts this guidance—not high
        kinship, not public honor, not wealth—nothing imparts this guidance
178d   as well as Love. What guidance do I mean? I mean a sense of shame at
        acting shamefully, and a sense of pride in acting well. Without these,
        nothing fine or great can be accomplished, in public or in private.
             What I say is this: if a man in love is found doing something shame-
5   ful, or accepting shameful treatment because he is a coward and makes
        no defense, then nothing would give him more pain than being seen
        by the boy he loves—not even being seen by his father or his com-
178e   rades. We see the same thing also in the boy he loves, that he is espe-
        cially ashamed before his lover when he is caught in something
        shameful. If only there were a way to start a city or an army made up
        of lovers and the boys they love! Theirs would be the best possible
5   system of society, for they would hold back from all that is shameful,
        and seek honor in each other's eyes.[34] Even a few of them, in battle
179a   side by side, would conquer all the world, I'd say.[35] For a man in love
        would never allow his loved one, of all people, to see him leaving
5   ranks or dropping weapons. He'd rather die a thousand deaths! And as
        for leaving the boy behind, or not coming to his aid in danger—why,

---

[31] *Theogony* 116–120, 118 omitted.

[32] Early–fifth-century writer of genealogies.

[33] Parmenides (fifth-century philosopher), B13 (Diels-Kranz.) "She" is probably
the goddess from B12.

[34] Accepting the deletion of *ê* in e5.

[35] The "Sacred Band" established by the Thebans in 379/8 BCE (probably after
the *Symposium* was composed) was an army of just this sort.

no one is so base that true Love could not inspire him with courage, and make him as brave as if he'd been born a hero. When Homer says a god 'breathes might' into some of the heroes, this is really Love's gift to every lover.[36]

179b

Besides, no one will die for you but a lover, and a lover will do this even if she's a woman. Alcestis is proof to everyone in Greece that what I say is true.[37] Only she was willing to die in place of her husband, although his father and mother were still alive. Because of her love, she went so far beyond his parents in family feeling that she made them look like outsiders, as if they belonged to their son in name only. And when she did this her deed struck everyone, even the gods, as nobly done. The gods were so delighted, in fact, that they gave her the prize they reserve for a handful chosen from the throngs of noble heroes—they sent her soul back from the dead. As you can see, the eager courage of love wins highest honors from the gods.

5

179c

5

179d

Orpheus,[38] the son of Oeagrus, however, they sent unsatisfied from Hades, after showing him only an image of the woman he came for. They did not give him the woman herself, because they thought he was soft (he was, after all, a cithara-player[39]) and did not dare to die like Alcestis for Love's sake, but contrived to enter, living, into Hades. So they punished him for that, and made him die at the hands of women.

5

The honor they gave to Achilles,[40] the son of Thetis, is another matter. They sent him to the Isles of the Blest[41] because he dared to stand by his lover Patroclus and avenge him, even after he had learned from his mother that he would die if he killed Hector,[42] but that if he chose otherwise he'd go home and end his life as an old man.[43] Instead he chose to die for his lover Patroclus, and more than that, he did it

179e

5

---

[36] Cf. *Iliad* 10.482, xv.262; *Odyssey* 9.381.

[37] Alcestis was the self-sacrificing wife of Admetus, to whom Apollo gave a chance to live if anyone would go to Hades in his place.

[38] A musician of legendary powers, who charmed his way into the Underworld in search of his dead wife, Eurydice.

[39] A cithara (or box lyre) was a stringed instrument.

[40] The champion of the Greeks in the Trojan War. Patroclus is his friend.

[41] A place where good people live in eternal happiness.

[42] The champion of the Trojans in the Trojan War.

[43] *Iliad* 9.410–6.

180a for a man whose life was already over. The gods were highly delighted at this, of course, and gave him special honor, because he made so much of his lover. Aeschylus talks nonsense when he claims Achilles was the lover;[44] he was more beautiful than Patroclus, more beautiful than all the heroes, and still beardless. Besides he was much younger, as Homer says.

In truth, the gods honor virtue most highly when it belongs to **180b** Love. They are more impressed and delighted, however, and are more generous with a loved one who cherishes his lover, than with a lover who cherishes the boy he loves. A lover is more godlike than his boy, you see, since he is inspired by a god. That's why they gave a higher honor to Achilles than to Alcestis, and sent him to the Isles of the Blest.

Therefore I say Love is the most ancient of the gods, the most honored, and the most powerful in helping men gain virtue and blessedness, whether they are alive or have passed away.

That was more or less what Phaedrus said, according to Aristode- **180c** mus. There followed several other speeches which he couldn't remember very well. So he skipped them and went directly to the speech of Pausanias.

Phaedrus (Pausanias began), I'm not quite sure our subject has been well defined. Our charge has been simple—to speak in praise of Love. This would have been fine if Love himself were simple, too, but as a matter of fact, there are two kinds of Love. In view of this, it might be better to begin by making clear which kind of Love we are to **180d** praise. Let me therefore try to put our discussion back on the right track and explain which kind of Love ought to be praised. Then I shall give him the praise he deserves, as the god he is.

It is a well-known fact that Love and Aphrodite are inseparable. If, therefore, Aphrodite[45] were a single goddess, there could also be a single Love; but, since there are actually two goddesses of that name, there must also be two kinds of Love. I don't expect you'll disagree with me about the two goddesses, will you? One is an older deity, the motherless daughter of Uranus, the god of heaven: she is known as Urania, or Heavenly Aphrodite.[46] The other goddess is younger, the

---

[44] In his play, *The Myrmidons*. In Homer, there is no hint of sexual attachment between Achilles and Patroclus.

[45] See 177e2 note.

[46] Hesiod, *Theogony* 188–206.

daughter of Zeus and Dione: her name is Pandemos, or Common
Aphrodite.[47] It follows, therefore, that there is a Common as well as a   180e
Heavenly Love, depending on which goddess is Love's partner. And
although, of course, all the gods must be praised, we must still make
an effort to keep these two gods apart.

The reason for this applies in the same way to every type of action:
considered in itself, no action is either good or bad, honorable or
shameful. Take, for example, our own case. We had a choice between   5
drinking, singing, or having a conversation. Now, in itself, none of   **181a**
these is better than any other: how it comes out depends entirely on
how it is performed. If it is done honorably and properly, it turns out
to be honorable; if it is done improperly, it is disgraceful. And my
point is that exactly this principle applies to being in love: Love is not
in himself noble and worthy of praise; that depends on whether the   5
sentiments he produces in us are themselves noble.

Now the Common Aphrodite's Love is himself truly common. As   **181b**
such, he strikes wherever he gets a chance. This, of course, is the love
felt by the vulgar, who are attached to women no less than to boys, to
the body more than to the soul, and to the least intelligent partners,
since all they care about is completing the sexual act. Whether they   5
do it honorably or not is of no concern. That is why they do whatever comes their way, sometimes good, sometimes bad; and which
one it is, is incidental to their purpose. For the Love who moves them
belongs to a much younger goddess, who, through her parentage,
partakes of the nature both of the female and the male.   **181c**

Contrast this with the Love of Heavenly Aphrodite. This goddess,
whose descent is purely male (hence this love is for boys), is consider-
ably older and therefore free from the lewdness[48] of youth. That's why
those who are inspired by her Love are attracted to the male: they find   5
pleasure in what is by nature stronger and more intelligent. But, even
within the group that is attracted to handsome boys, some are not
moved purely by this Heavenly Love; those who are do not fall in love
with little boys; they prefer older ones whose cheeks are showing the   **181d**
first traces of a beard—a sign that they have begun to form minds of
their own. I am convinced that a man who falls in love with a young
man of this age is generally prepared to share everything with the one

---

[47] Homer, *Iliad* 5.370–1.

[48] *Hubris.* Here, violent sexual passions of the sort that lead to rape.

he loves—he is eager, in fact, to spend the rest of his own life with
him.[49] He certainly does not aim to deceive him—to take advantage
of him while he is still young and inexperienced and then, after ex-
posing him to ridicule, to move quickly on to someone else.
    As a matter of fact, there should be a law forbidding affairs with
young boys. If nothing else, all this time and effort would not be
wasted on such an uncertain pursuit—and what is more uncertain
than whether a particular boy will eventually make something of
himself, physically or mentally? Good men, of course, are willing to
make a law like this for themselves, but those other lovers, the vulgar
ones, need external restraint. For just this reason we have placed every
possible legal obstacle to their seducing our own wives and daughters.
These vulgar lovers are the people who have given love such a bad
reputation that some have gone so far as to claim that taking *any* man
as a lover is in itself disgraceful. Would anyone make this claim if he
weren't thinking of how hasty vulgar lovers are, and therefore how
unfair to their loved ones? For nothing done properly and in accordance with our customs would ever have provoked such righteous
disapproval.
    I should point out, however, that, although the customs regarding
Love in most cities are simple and easy to understand, here in Athens
(and in Sparta[50] as well) they are remarkably complex. In places where
the people are inarticulate, like Elis[51] or Boeotia,[52] tradition straight-
forwardly approves taking a lover in every case. No one there, young
or old, would ever consider it shameful. The reason, I suspect, is that,
being poor speakers, they want to save themselves the trouble of having to offer reasons and arguments in support of their suits.
    By contrast, in places like Ionia[53] and almost every other part of the

---

[49] Such lifelong relationships were unusual. But see below, 192a7–b5, and *Phaedrus* 255e4–256e2.

[50] Major city of the Peloponnese. Athens' rival in the fifth and fourth centuries.
Sparta was a militaristic and somewhat "closed" society, always prepared and
preparing for war. Its citizens, male and female, lived in military camps and ate
communally. Plato's thought, especially in the *Republic*, reflects Spartan influence.
Spartan sexual customs are discussed in Xenophon, *Constitution of Sparta* 2.12–4.

[51] City in the northwest Peloponnese.

[52] Area in northern Greece.

[53] Area on the central northwest coast of Asia Minor, where many great settle-
ments were located.

Persian empire, taking a lover is always considered disgraceful.[54] The Persian empire is absolute; that is why it condemns love as well as philosophy and sport.[55] It is no good for rulers if the people they rule 182c cherish ambitions for themselves or form strong bonds of friendship with one another. That these are precisely the effects of philosophy, sport, and especially of Love is a lesson the tyrants of Athens learned directly from their own experience: Didn't their reign come to a dismal 5 end because of the bonds uniting Harmodius and Aristogiton in love and affection?[56]

So you can see that plain condemnation of Love reveals lust for power in the rulers and cowardice in the ruled, while indiscriminate 182d approval testifies to general dullness and stupidity.

Our own customs, which, as I have already said, are much more difficult to understand, are also far superior. Recall, for example, that 5 we consider it more honorable to declare your love rather than to keep it a secret, especially if you are in love with a youth of good family and accomplishment, even if he isn't all that beautiful. Recall also that a lover is encouraged in every possible way; this means that what he does is not considered shameful. On the contrary, conquest is deemed noble, and failure shameful. And as for *attempts* at conquest, 182e our custom is to praise lovers for totally extraordinary acts—so extraordinary, in fact, that if they performed them for any other purpose whatever, they would reap the most profound contempt. 183a Suppose, for example, that in order to secure money, or a public post, or any other practical benefit from another person, a man were willing to do what lovers do for the ones they love. Imagine that, in press- 5 ing his suit, he went to his knees in public view and begged in the most humiliating way; that he swore all sorts of vows; that he spent the night at the other man's doorstep; that he were anxious to provide services even a slave would have refused—well, you can be sure that everyone, his enemies no less than his friends, would stand in his way.

---

[54] An apparent anachronism. At the dramatic date of the *Symposium* (416 BCE), Ionia was actually under Athenian influence.

[55] *Philogumnastia*: Gymnasia were meeting places where conversations on all manner of potentially seditious topics went on and friendships formed.

[56] Harmodius and Aristogiton attempted to overthrow the tyrant Hippias in 514 BC. Although their attempt failed, the tyranny fell three years later, and the lovers were celebrated as tyrannicides.

183b   His enemies would jeer at his fawning servility, while his friends, ashamed on his behalf, would try everything to bring him back to his senses. But let a lover act in any of these ways, and everyone will immediately say what a charming man he is! No blame attaches to his behavior: custom treats it as noble through and through. And what is
5   even more remarkable is that, at least according to popular wisdom, the gods will forgive a lover even for breaking his vows—a lover's vow, our people say, is no vow at all. The freedom given to the lover
183c   by both gods and men according to our custom is immense.

         In view of all this, you might well conclude that in our city we consider the lover's desire and the willingness to satisfy it as the noblest things in the world. When, on the other hand, you recall that fathers hire attendants[57] for their sons as soon as they're old enough to be at-
5   tractive, and that an attendant's main task is to prevent any contact between his charge and his suitors; when you recall how mercilessly a boy's own friends tease him if they catch him at it, and how strongly
183d   their elders approve and even encourage such mocking—when you take all this into account, you're bound to come to the conclusion that we Athenians consider such behavior the most shameful thing in the world.

         In my opinion, however, the fact of the matter is this. As I said earlier, love is, like everything else, complex: considered simply in itself,
5   it is neither honorable nor a disgrace—its character depends entirely on the behavior it gives rise to. To give oneself to a vile man in a vile way is truly disgraceful behavior; by contrast, it is perfectly honorable to give oneself honorably to the right man. Now, you may want to know who counts as vile in this context. I'll tell you: it is the com-
183e   mon, vulgar lover, who loves the body rather than the soul; the man whose love is bound to be inconstant, since what he loves is itself mutable and unstable. The moment the body is no longer in bloom, "he flies off and away,"[58] his promises and vows in tatters behind him. How different from this is a man who loves the right sort of charac-
5   ter, and who remains its lover for life, attached as he is to something that is permanent.

         We can now see the point of our customs: they are designed to sep-
184a   arate the wheat from the chaff, the proper love from the vile. That's

---

[57] *Paidagôgos*; also "tutors."

[58] *Iliad* 2.71.

why we do everything we can to make it as easy as possible for lovers to press their suits and as difficult as possible for young men to comply; it is like a competition, a kind of test to determine to which sort each belongs. This explains two further facts: First, why we consider 5 it shameful to yield too quickly: the passage of time in itself provides a good test in these matters. Second, why we also consider it shameful for a man to be seduced by money or political power, either because he cringes at ill treatment and will not endure it or because, 184b once he has tasted the benefits of wealth and power, he will not rise above them. None of these benefits is stable or permanent, apart from the fact that no genuine affection can possibly be based upon them.

Our customs, then, provide for only one honorable way of taking a 5 man as a lover. In addition to recognizing that the lover's total and willing subjugation to his beloved's wishes is neither servile nor reprehensible, we allow that there is one—and only one—further reason 184c for willingly subjecting oneself to another which is equally above reproach: that is subjection for the sake of virtue. If someone decides to put himself at another's disposal because he thinks that this will make him better in wisdom or in any other part of virtue, we approve of his 5 voluntary subjection: we consider it neither shameful nor servile. Both these principles—that is, both the principle governing the proper attitude toward the lover of young men and the principle governing the love of wisdom and of virtue in general—must be com- 184d bined if a young man is to accept a lover in an honorable way. When an older lover and a young man come together and each obeys the principle appropriate to him—when the lover realizes that he is justified in doing anything for a loved one who grants him favors, and 5 when the young man understands that he is justified in performing any service for a lover who can make him wise and virtuous—and when the lover *is* able to help the young man become wiser and better, and the young man *is* eager to be taught and improved by his 184e lover—then, and only then, when these two principles coincide absolutely, is it ever honorable for a young man to accept a lover.

Only in this case, we should notice, is it never shameful to be deceived; in every other case it is shameful, both for the deceiver and the 5 person he deceives. Suppose, for example, that someone thinks his lover is rich and accepts him for his money; his action won't be any 185a less shameful if it turns out that he was deceived and his lover was a poor man after all. For the young man has already shown himself to be the sort of person who will do anything for money—and that is far

5   from honorable. By the same token, suppose that someone takes a lover in the mistaken belief that this lover is a good man and likely to make him better himself, while in reality the man is horrible, totally lacking in virtue; even so, it is noble for him to have been deceived.

185b   For he too has demonstrated something about himself: that he is the sort of person who will do anything for the sake of virtue—and what could be more honorable than that? It follows, therefore, that giving in to your lover for virtue's sake is honorable, whatever the outcome.

5   And this, of course, is the Heavenly Love of the heavenly goddess. Love's value to the city as a whole and to the citizens is immeasurable, for he compels the lover and his loved one alike to make virtue their

185c   central concern. All other forms of love belong to the vulgar goddess.

Phaedrus, I'm afraid this hasty improvisation will have to do as my contribution on the subject of Love.

When Pausanias finally came to a pause (I've learned this sort of fine figure from our clever rhetoricians), it was Aristophanes' turn, ac-

5   cording to Aristodemus. But he had such a bad case of the hiccups— he'd probably stuffed himself again, though, of course, it could have been anything—that making a speech was totally out of the question.

185d   So he turned to the doctor, Eryximachus, who was next in line, and said to him:

"Eryximachus, it's up to you—as well it should be. Cure me or take my turn."

"As a matter of fact," Eryximachus replied, "I shall do both.[59] I shall take your turn—you can speak in my place as soon as you feel

5   better—and I shall also cure you. While I am giving my speech, you should hold your breath for as long as you possibly can. This may well eliminate your hiccups. If it fails, the best remedy is a thorough gargle.

185e   And if even this has no effect, then tickle your nose with a feather. A sneeze or two will cure even the most persistent case."

"The sooner you start speaking, the better," Aristophanes said. "I'll

5   follow your instructions to the letter."

This, then, was the speech of Eryximachus:

---

[59] Eryximachus' name is a pun on "belch-fighter," making it particularly appropriate that he should have a cure for hiccups.

Pausanias introduced a crucial consideration in his speech, though in my opinion he did not develop it sufficiently. Let me therefore try to carry his argument to its logical conclusion. His distinction be- **186a** tween the two species of Love seems to me very useful indeed. But if I have learned a single lesson from my own field, the science of medicine, it is that Love does not occur only in the human soul; it is not simply the attraction we feel toward human beauty: it is a significantly broader phenomenon. It certainly occurs within the animal kingdom, 5 and even in the world of plants. In fact, it occurs everywhere in the universe. Love is a deity of the greatest importance: he directs every- **186b** thing that occurs, not only in the human domain, but also in that of the gods.

Let me begin with some remarks concerning medicine—I hope you will forgive my giving pride of place to my own profession. The point is that our very bodies manifest the two species of Love. Consider for a moment the marked difference, the radical dissimilarity, 5 between healthy and diseased constitutions and the fact that dissimilar subjects desire and love objects that are themselves dissimilar. Therefore, the love manifested in health is fundamentally distinct from the love manifested in disease. And now recall that, as Pausanias claimed, it is as honorable to yield to a good man as it is shameful to consort with the debauched. Well, my point is that the case of the human body is strictly parallel. Everything sound and healthy in the body **186c** must be encouraged and gratified; that is precisely the object of medicine. Conversely, whatever is unhealthy and unsound must be frustrated and rebuffed: that's what it is to be an expert in medicine.

In short, medicine is simply the science of the effects of Love on 5 repletion and depletion of the body,[60] and the hallmark of the accomplished physician is his ability to distinguish the Love that is noble from the Love that is ugly and disgraceful. A good practitioner knows **186d** how to affect the body and how to transform its desires; he can implant the proper species of Love when it is absent and eliminate the other sort whenever it occurs. The physician's task is to effect a reconciliation and establish mutual love between the most basic bodily ele- 5 ments. Which are those elements? They are, of course, those that are most opposed to one another, as hot is to cold, bitter to sweet, wet to

---

[60] See Hippocrates, *Regimen in Health* 1; *On Humors* 1.

186e   dry, cases like those. In fact, our ancestor Asclepius[61] first established
medicine as a profession when he learned how to produce concord
and love between such opposites—that is what those poet fellows say,
and—this time—I concur with them.

Medicine, therefore, is guided everywhere by the god of Love, and
187a   so are physical education and farming as well. Further, a moment's reflection suffices to show that the case of poetry and music, too, is precisely the same. Indeed, this may have been just what Heraclitus had
in mind, though his mode of expression certainly leaves much to be
desired. The one, he says, "being at variance with itself is in agree-
5   ment with itself" "like the attunement of a bow or a lyre."[62] Naturally, it is patently absurd to claim that an attunement or a harmony is
in itself discordant or that its elements are still in discord with one another. Heraclitus probably meant that an expert musician creates a
187b   harmony by resolving the prior discord between high and low notes.
For surely there can be no harmony so long as high and low are still
discordant; harmony, after all, is consonance, and consonance is a
species of agreement. Discordant elements, as long as they are still in
5   discord, cannot come to an agreement, and they therefore cannot
produce a harmony. Rhythm, for example, is produced only when fast
and slow, though earlier discordant, are brought into agreement with
187c   each other. Music, like medicine, creates agreement by producing
concord and love between these various opposites. Music is therefore
5   simply the science of the effects of Love on rhythm and harmony.

These effects are easily discernible if you consider the constitution
of rhythm and harmony in themselves; Love does not occur in both
his forms in this domain. But the moment you consider, in their turn,
the effects of rhythm and harmony on their audience—either through
187d   composition, which creates new verses and melodies, or through musical education, which teaches the correct performance of existing
compositions—complications arise directly, and they require the
treatment of a good practitioner. Ultimately, the identical argument
applies once again: the love felt by good people or by those whom
5   such love might improve in this regard must be encouraged and

---

[61] A mythical figure regarded as the first doctor.

[62] Heraclitus of Ephesus, a philosopher of the early fifth century, was known for
his enigmatic sayings. This one is quoted elsewhere in a slightly different form,
fragment B51 (Diels-Kranz).

protected. This is the honorable, heavenly species of Love, produced by the melodies of Urania, the Heavenly Muse.[63] The other, produced by Polyhymnia, the muse of many songs, is common and vulgar.[64] Extreme caution is indicated here: we must be careful to enjoy his pleasures without slipping into debauchery—this case, I might add, is strictly parallel to a serious issue in my own field, namely, the problem of regulating the appetite so as to be able to enjoy a fine meal without unhealthy aftereffects.

In music, therefore, as well as in medicine and in all the other domains, in matters divine as well as in human affairs, we must attend with the greatest possible care to these two species of Love, which are, indeed, to be found everywhere. Even the seasons of the year exhibit their influence. When the elements to which I have already referred—hot and cold, wet and dry—are animated by the proper species of Love, they are in harmony with one another: their mixture is temperate, and so is the climate. Harvests are plentiful; men and all other living things are in good health; no harm can come to them. But when the sort of Love that is crude and impulsive controls the seasons, he brings death and destruction. He spreads the plague and many other diseases among plants and animals; he causes frost and hail and blights. All these are the effects of the immodest and disordered species of Love on the movements of the stars and the seasons of the year, that is, on the objects studied by the science called astronomy.

Consider further the rites of sacrifice and the whole area with which the art of divination is concerned, that is, the interaction between men and gods. Here, too, Love is the central concern: our object is to try to maintain the proper kind of Love and to attempt to cure the kind that is diseased. For what is the origin of all impiety? Our refusal to gratify the orderly kind of Love, and our deference to the other sort, when we should have been guided by the former sort of Love in every action in connection with our parents, living or dead, and with the gods. The task of divination is to keep watch over these two species of Love and to doctor them as necessary. Divination, therefore, is the practice that produces loving affection between gods and men; it is simply the science of the effects of Love on justice and piety.

187e

5

188a

5

188b

5

188c

5

188d

---

[63] See *Phaedrus* 259b3 note.

[64] Urania and Polyhymnia appear as Muses in Hesiod, *Theogony* 75–9. Eryximachus has made them correspond to Pausanias' Urania and Pandemos.

Such is the power of Love—so varied and great that in all cases it might be called absolute. Yet even so it is far greater when Love is directed, in temperance and justice, toward the good, whether in heaven or on earth: happiness and good fortune, the bonds of human society, concord with the gods above—all these are among his gifts. Perhaps I, too, have omitted a great deal in this discourse on Love. If so, I assure you, it was quite inadvertent. And if in fact I have overlooked certain points, it is now your task, Aristophanes, to complete the argument—unless, of course, you are planning on a different approach. In any case, proceed; your hiccups seem cured.

Then Aristophanes took over (so Aristodemus said): "The hiccups have stopped all right—but not before I applied the Sneeze Treatment to them. Makes me wonder whether the 'orderly sort of Love' in the body calls for the sounds and itchings that constitute a sneeze, because the hiccups stopped immediately when I applied the Sneeze Treatment."

"You're good, Aristophanes," Eryximachus answered. "But watch what you're doing. You are making jokes before your speech, and you're forcing me to prepare for you to say something funny, and to put up my guard against you, when otherwise you might speak at peace."

Then Aristophanes laughed. "Good point, Eryximachus. So let me 'unsay what I have said.' But don't put up your guard. I'm not worried about saying something funny in my coming oration. That would be pure profit, and it comes with the territory of my Muse. What I'm worried about is that I might say something ridiculous."

"Aristophanes, do you really think you can take a shot at me, and then escape? Use your head! Remember, as you speak, that you will be called upon to give an account. Though perhaps, if I decide to, I'll let you off."

"Eryximachus," Aristophanes said, "indeed I do have in mind a different approach to speaking than the one the two of you used, you and Pausanias. You see, I think people have entirely missed the power of Love, because, if they had grasped it, they'd have built the greatest temples and altars to him and made the greatest sacrifices. But as it is, none of this is done for him, though it should be, more than anything else! For he loves the human race more than any other god, he stands by us in our troubles, and he cures those ills we humans are most happy to have mended. I shall, therefore, try to explain his power to you; and you, please pass my teaching on to everyone else."

First you must learn what Human Nature was in the beginning and
what has happened to it since, because long ago our nature was not
what it is now, but very different. There were three kinds of human
beings, that's my first point—not two as there are now, male and female. In addition to these, there was a third, a combination of those
two; its name survives, though the kind itself has vanished. At that
time, you see, the word "androgynous" really meant something: a
form made up of male and female elements, though now there's
nothing but the word, and that's used as an insult. My second point is
that the shape of each human being was completely round, with back
and sides in a circle; they had four hands each, as many legs as hands,
and two faces, exactly alike, on a rounded neck. Between the two faces,
which were on opposite sides, was one head with four ears. There
were two sets of sexual organs, and everything else was the way you'd
imagine it from what I've told you. They walked upright, as we do
now, in whatever direction they wanted. And whenever they set out
to run fast, they thrust out all their eight limbs, the ones they had
then, and spun rapidly, the way gymnasts do cartwheels, by bringing
their legs around straight.

Now here is why there were three kinds, and why they were as I
described them: The male kind was originally an offspring of the sun,
the female of the earth, and the one that combined both genders was
an offspring of the moon, because the moon shares in both. They
were spherical, and so was their motion, because they were like their
parents in the sky.

In strength and power, therefore, they were terrible, and they had
great ambitions. They made an attempt on the gods, and Homer's
story about Ephialtes and Otus was originally about them: how they
tried to make an ascent to heaven so as to attack the gods.[65] Then
Zeus and the other gods met in council to discuss what to do, and
they were sore perplexed. They couldn't wipe out the human race
with thunderbolts and kill them all off, as they had the giants, because
that would wipe out the worship they receive, along with the sacrifices we humans give them. On the other hand, they couldn't let them
run riot. At last, after great effort, Zeus had an idea.

"I think I have a plan," he said, "that would allow human beings to
exist and stop their misbehaving: they will give up being wicked

---

[65] Giant people, who planned to pile one mountain on top of another to make
their assault (*Odyssey* 11.305–20).

190d   when they lose their strength. So I shall now cut each of them in two.
At one stroke they will lose their strength and also become more prof-
itable to us, owing to the increase in their number. They shall walk
upright on two legs. But if I find that they still run riot and do not
5   keep the peace," he said, "I will cut them in two again, and they'll
have to make their way on one leg, hopping."

So saying, he cut those human beings in two, the way people cut
190e   sorb-apples before they dry them or the way they cut eggs with hairs.
As he cut each one, he commanded Apollo[66] to turn its face and half
its neck toward the wound, so that each person would see that he'd
been cut and keep better order. Then Zeus commanded Apollo to
5   heal the rest of the wound, and Apollo did turn the face around, and
he drew skin from all sides over what is now called the stomach, and
there he made one mouth, as in a pouch with a drawstring, and fas-
tened it at the center of the stomach. This is now called the navel.
Then he smoothed out the other wrinkles, of which there were
191a   many, and he shaped the breasts, using some such tool as shoemakers
have for smoothing wrinkles out of leather on the form. But he left a
few wrinkles around the stomach and the navel, to be a reminder of
what happened long ago.

5   Now, since their natural form had been cut in two, each one
longed for its own other half, and so they would throw their arms
about each other, weaving themselves together, wanting to grow together. In that condition they would die from hunger and general
191b   idleness, because they would not do anything apart from each other.
Whenever one of the halves died and one was left, the one that was
left still sought another and wove itself together with that. Sometimes
the half he met came from a woman, as we'd call her now, sometimes
it came from a man; either way, they kept on dying.

5   Then, however, Zeus took pity on them, and came up with another plan: he moved their genitals around to the front! Before then,
you see, they used to have their genitals outside, like their faces, and
they cast seed and made children, not in one another, but in the
191c   ground, like cicadas. So Zeus brought about this relocation of genitals, and in doing so he invented interior reproduction, *by* the man *in*
the woman. The purpose of this was so that, when a man embraced a

---

[66] God of music, medicine, prophecy, and so on. It was he who destroyed
Ephialtes and Otus.

woman, he would cast his seed and they would have children; but   5
when male embraced male, they would at least have the satisfaction of
intercourse, after which they could stop embracing, return to their
jobs, and look after their other needs in life. This, then, is the source
of our desire to love each other. Love is born into every human being;   191d
it calls back the halves of our original nature together; it tries to make
one out of two and heal the wound of human nature.

Each of us, then, is a "matching half" of a human whole, because
each was sliced like a flatfish, two out of one, and each of us is always
seeking the half that matches him. That's why a man who is split from   5
the double sort (which used to be called "androgynous") runs after
women. Many lecherous men have come from this class, and so do
the lecherous women who run after men. Women who are split from   191e
a woman, however, pay no attention at all to men; they are oriented
more toward women, and lesbians come from this class. People who   5
are split from a male are male-oriented. While they are boys, because
they are chips off the male block, they love men and enjoy lying with
men and being embraced by men; those are the best of boys and lads,   **192a**
because they are the most manly in their nature. Of course, some say
such boys are shameless, but they're lying. It's not because they have
no shame that such boys do this, you see, but because they are bold
and brave and masculine, and they tend to cherish what is like themselves. Do you want me to prove it? Look, these are the only kind of   5
boys who grow up to be real men in politics. When they're grown
men, they are lovers of young men, and they naturally pay no attention to marriage or to making babies, except insofar as they are re-   192b
quired by local custom. They, however, are quite satisfied to live their
lives with one another unmarried. In every way, then, this sort of
man grows up as a lover of young men and a lover of Love, always re-
joicing in his own kind.

And so, when a person meets the half that is his very own, what-   5
ever his orientation, whether it's to young men or not, then something wonderful happens: the two are struck from their senses by love,
by a sense of belonging to one another, and by desire, and they don't
want to be separated from one another, not even for a moment.   192c

These are the people who finish out their lives together and still
cannot say what it is they want from one another. No one would
think it is the intimacy of sex—that mere sex is the reason each lover   5
takes so great and deep a joy in being with the other. It's obvious that
the soul of every lover longs for something else; his soul cannot say

192d   what it is, but like an oracle it has a sense of what it wants, and like an oracle it hides behind a riddle. Suppose two lovers are lying together, and Hephaestus[67] stands over them with his mending tools, asking, "What is it you human beings really want from each other?" And
5   suppose they're perplexed, and he asks them again: "Is this your heart's desire, then—for the two of you to become parts of the same whole, as near as can be, and never to separate, day or night? Because if that's your desire, I'd like to weld you together and join you into something that is naturally whole, so that the two of you are made
192e   into one. Then the two of you would share one life, as long as you lived, because you would be one being, and by the same token, when you died, you would be one and not two in Hades, having died a single death. Look at your love, and see if this is what you desire: wouldn't this be all the good fortune you could want?"
5   Surely you can see that no one who received such an offer would turn it down; no one would find anything else that he wanted. Instead, everyone would think he'd found out at last what he had always wanted: to come together and melt together with the one he loves, so that one person emerged from two. Why should this be so? It's because, as I said, we used to be complete wholes in our original nature,
10   and now "Love" is the name for our pursuit of wholeness, for our desire to be complete.
193a   Long ago we were united, as I said; but now the god has divided us as punishment for the wrong we did him, just as the Spartans divided the Arcadians.[68] So there's a danger that if we don't keep order before the gods, we'll be split in two again, and then we'll be walking around
5   in the condition of people carved on gravestones in bas-relief, sawn apart between the nostrils, like half dice. We should encourage all men, therefore, to treat the gods with all due reverence, so that we
193b   may escape this fate and find wholeness instead. And we will, if Love is our guide and our commander. Let no one work against him. Whoever opposes Love is hateful to the gods, but if we become friends of the god and cease to quarrel with him, then we shall find

---

[67] Divine armorer of the gods. Cf. *Odyssey* 8.266–366.

[68] Arcadia included the city of Mantinea, which opposed Sparta, and was punished by having its population divided and dispersed in 385 BC. Aristophanes seems to be referring anachronistically to those events; such anachronisms are not uncommon in Plato.

the young men that are meant for us and win their love, as very few   5
men do nowadays.

Now don't get ideas, Eryximachus, and turn this speech into a
comedy. Don't think I'm pointing this at Pausanias and Agathon.
Probably they both do belong to the group that are entirely masculine   193c
in nature. But I am speaking about everyone, men and women alike,
and I say there's just one way for the human race to flourish: we must
bring love to its perfect conclusion, and each of us must win the favors of his very own young man, so that he can recover his original
nature. If that is the ideal, then, of course, the nearest approach to it   5
is best in present circumstances, and that is to win the favor of young
men who are naturally sympathetic to us.

If we are to give due praise to the god who can give us this blessing, then, we must praise Love. Love does the best that can be done   193d
for the time being: he draws us toward what belongs to us. But for the
future, Love promises the greatest hope of all: if we treat the gods
with due reverence, he will restore to us our original nature, and by
healing us, he will make us blessed and happy.   5

"That," he said, "is my speech about Love, Eryximachus. It is
rather different from yours. As I begged you earlier, don't make a
comedy of it. I'd prefer to hear what all the others will say—or,
rather, what each of them will say, since Agathon and Socrates are the
only ones left."   193e

"I found your speech delightful," said Eryximachus, "so I'll do as
you say. Really, we've had such a rich feast of speeches on Love, that
if I couldn't vouch for the fact that Socrates and Agathon are masters
of the art of love, I'd be afraid that they'd have nothing left to say. But   5
as it is, I have no fears on this score."

Then Socrates said, "That's because *you* did beautifully in the con-
test, Eryximachus. But if you ever get in my position, or rather the   **194a**
position I'll be in after Agathon's spoken so well, then you'll really be
afraid. You'll be at your wit's end, as I am now."

"You're trying to bewitch me, Socrates," said Agathon, "by making   5
me think the audience expects great things of my speech, so I'll get
flustered."

"Agathon!" said Socrates, "How forgetful do you think I am? I saw
how brave and dignified you were when you walked right up to the   194b
theater platform along with the actors and looked straight out at that
enormous audience. You were about to put your own writing on

display, and you weren't the least bit panicked. After seeing that, how
5   could I expect you to be flustered by us, when we are so few?"

"Why, Socrates," said Agathon. "You must think I have nothing
but theater audiences on my mind! So you suppose I don't realize that,
if you're intelligent, you find a few sensible men much more fright-
ening than a senseless crowd?"

"No," he said, "It wouldn't be very handsome of me to think you
194c   crude in any way, Agathon. I'm sure that if you ever run into people
you consider wise, you'll pay more attention to them than to ordinary
people. But you can't suppose we're in that class; we were at the theater too, you know, part of the ordinary crowd. Still, if you did run
5   into any wise men, other than yourself, you'd certainly be ashamed at
the thought of doing anything ugly in front of them. Is that what you
mean?"

'That's true," he said.

"On the other hand, you wouldn't be ashamed to do something
10   ugly in front of ordinary people. Is that it?".

194d   At that point Phaedrus interrupted: "Agathon, my friend, if you
answer Socrates, he'll no longer care whether we get anywhere with
what we're doing here, so long as he has a partner for discussion. Especially if he's handsome. Now, like you, I enjoy listening to Socrates
5   in discussion, but it is my duty to see to the praising of Love and to
exact a speech from every one of this group. When each of you two
has made his offering to the god, then you can have your discussion."

194e   "You're doing a beautiful job, Phaedrus," said Agathon. "There's
nothing to keep me from giving my speech. Socrates will have many
opportunities for discussion later."

I wish first to speak of how I ought to speak, and only then to
5   speak. In my opinion, you see, all those who have spoken before me
did not so much celebrate the god as congratulate human beings on
the good things that come to them from the god. But who it is who
gave these gifts, what he is like—no one has spoken about that. Now,
195a   only one method is correct for every praise, no matter whose: you
must explain what qualities in the subject of your speech enable him
to give the benefits for which we praise him. So now, in the case of
Love, it is right for us to praise him first for what he is and afterwards
for his gifts.

5   I maintain, then, that while all the gods are happy, Love—if I may
say so without giving offense—is the happiest of them all, for he is the

most beautiful and the best. His great beauty lies in this: First, Phaedrus, he is the youngest of the gods.[69] He proves my point himself by
fleeing old age in headlong flight, fast-moving though it is (that's ob-   195b
vious—it comes after us faster than it should). Love was born to hate
old age and will come nowhere near it. Love always lives with young
people and is one of them: the old story holds good that like is always
drawn to like. And though on many other points I agree with Phae-   5
drus, I do not agree with this: that Love is more ancient than Cronus
and Iapetus.[70] No, I say that he is the youngest of the gods and stays
young forever.

Those old stories Hesiod and Parmenides tell about the gods—   195c
those things happened under Necessity, not Love, if what they say is
true. For not one of all those violent deeds would have been done—
no castrations, no imprisonments—if Love had been present among
them. There would have been peace and brotherhood instead, as
there has been now as long as Love has been king of the gods.   5

So he is young. And besides being young, he is delicate. It takes a
poet as good as Homer to show how delicate the god is. For Homer   195d
says that Mischief is a god and that she is delicate—well, that her feet
are delicate, anyway! He says:

> . . . *hers are delicate feet: not on the ground*
> *Does she draw nigh; she walks instead upon the heads of men.*[71]   5

A lovely proof, I think, to show how delicate she is: she doesn't
walk on anything hard; she walks only on what is soft. We shall use
the same proof about Love, then, to show that he is delicate. For he   195e
walks not on earth, not even on people's skulls, which are not really
soft at all; but in the softest of all the things that are, there he walks,
there he has his home. For he makes his home in the characters, in
the souls, of gods and men—and not even in every soul that comes
along: when he encounters a soul with a harsh character, he turns   5
away; but when he finds a soft and gentle character, he settles down in
it. Always, then, he is touching with his feet and with the whole of

---

[69] Contrast 178b.

[70] Cronus was the father of Zeus, who castrated, deposed, and imprisoned him.
Iatpetus was his brother.

[71] *Iliad* 19.92–3. "Mischief" translates to *Atê*.

himself what is softest in the softest places. He must therefore be most
delicate.

196a He is youngest, then, and most delicate; in addition he has a fluid,
supple shape. For if he were hard, he would not be able to enfold a
soul completely or escape notice when he first entered it or with-
drew. Besides, his graceful good looks prove that he is balanced and
5 fluid in his nature. Everyone knows that Love has extraordinary good
looks, and between ugliness and Love there is unceasing war.

And the exquisite coloring of his skin! The way the god consorts
with flowers shows that. For he never settles in anything, be it a body
196b or a soul, that cannot flower or has lost its bloom. His place is wherever it is flowery and fragrant; there he settles, there he stays.

Enough for now about the beauty of the god, though much remains still to be said. After this, we should speak of Love's moral char-
5 acter.[72] The main point is that Love is neither the cause nor the victim
of any injustice; he does no wrong to gods or men, nor they to him.
If anything has an effect on him, it is never by violence, for violence
196c never touches Love. And the effects he has on others are not forced,
for every service we give to love we give willingly. And whatever one
person agrees on with another, when both are willing, that is right
and just; so say "the laws that are kings of society."[73]

And besides justice, he has the biggest share of moderation.[74] For
moderation, by common agreement, is power over pleasures and pas-
5 sions, and no pleasure is more powerful than Love! But if they are
weaker, they are under the power of Love, and *he* has the power; and
because he has power over pleasures and passions, Love is exception-
ally moderate.

And as for manly bravery: "Not even Ares can stand up to" Love![75]
196d For Ares has no hold on Love, but Love does on Ares—love of

---

[72] *Aretê:* virtue.

[73] A proverbial expression attributed by Aristotle (*Rhetoric* 1406a17–23) to the
fourth-century liberal thinker and rhetorician Alcidamas.

[74] *Sôphrosunê.* The word can be translated also as "temperance" and, most literally, "sound-mindedness." (Plato and Aristotle generally contrast *sôphrosunê*, as a
virtue, with self-control: the person with *sôphrosunê* is naturally well tempered in
every way, and so does not need to control himself or hold himself back.)

[75] From Sophocles, fragment 234b (Dindorf): "Even Ares cannot withstand Necessity." Ares is the god of war.

Aphrodite, so runs the tale.[76] But he who has hold is more powerful than he who is held; and so, because Love has power over the bravest of the others, he is bravest of them all.

Now I have spoken about the god's justice, moderation, and bravery; his wisdom remains.[77] I must try not to leave out anything that can be said on this. In the first place—to honor *our* profession as Eryximachus did his[78]—the god is so skilled a poet that he can make others into poets: once Love touches him, *anyone* becomes a poet,

at the touch of Love everyone becomes a poet

. . . howe'er uncultured he had been before.[79]

This, we may fittingly observe, testifies that Love is a good poet, good, in sum, at every kind of artistic production. For you can't give to another what you don't have yourself, and you can't teach what you don't know.

And as to the production of animals—who will deny that they are all born and begotten through Love's skill?

And as for artisans and professionals—don't we know that whoever has this god for a teacher ends up in the light of fame, while a man untouched by Love ends in obscurity? Apollo, for one, invented archery, medicine, and prophecy when desire and love showed the way. Even he, therefore, would be a pupil of Love, and so would the Muses in music, Hephaestus in bronze work, Athena in weaving, and Zeus in "the governance of gods and men."

That too is how the gods' quarrels were settled, once Love came to be among them—love of beauty, obviously, because love is not drawn to ugliness. Before that, as I said in the beginning, and as the poets say, many dreadful things happened among the gods, because Necessity was king. But once this god was born, all goods came to gods and men alike through love of beauty.

This is how I think of Love, Phaedrus: first, he is himself the most beautiful and the best; after that, if anyone else is at all like that, Love

---

[76] See *Odyssey* 8.266–366. Aphrodite's husband Hephaestus made a snare that caught Ares in bed with Aphrodite.

[77] Agathon treats "wisdom" (*sophia*) and "skill" or "craft" (*technē*) as more or less equivalent.

[78] See 186b.

[79] Euripides, fragment 666 (Nauck).

is responsible. I am suddenly struck by a need to say something in poetic meter,[80] that it is he who—

5   *Gives peace to men and stillness to the sea,*
           Lays winds to rest, and careworn men to sleep.

Love fills us with togetherness and drains all of our divisiveness
197d away. Love calls gatherings like these together. In feasts, in dances, and
in ceremonies, he gives the lead. Love moves us to mildness, removes
from us wildness. He is giver of kindness, never of meanness. Gra-
5   cious, kindly[81]—let wise men see and gods admire! Treasure to lovers,
envy to others, father of elegance, luxury, delicacy, grace, yearning,
desire. Love cares well for good men, cares not for bad ones. In pain,
in fear, in desire or speech, Love is our best guide and guard; he is our
197e comrade and our savior. Ornament of all gods and men, most beautiful leader and the best! Every man should follow Love, sing beautifully
his hymns, and join with him in the song he sings that charms the
5   mind of god or man.

This, Phaedrus, is the speech I have to offer. Let it be dedicated to
the god, part of it in fun, part of it moderately serious, as best I could
manage.

198a When Agathon finished, Aristodemus said, everyone there burst
into applause, so becoming to himself and to the god did they think
the young man's speech.

Then Socrates glanced at Eryximachus and said, "Now, son of
Acumenus, do you think I was foolish to feel the fear I felt before?
5   Didn't I speak like a prophet a while ago when I said that Agathon
would give an amazing speech and I would be tongue-tied?"

"You were prophetic about one thing, I think," said Eryximachus,
"that Agathon would speak well. But you, tongue-tied? No, I don't
10   believe that."

"Bless you," said Socrates. "How am I not going to be tongue-
198b tied, I or anyone else, after a speech delivered with such beauty
and variety? The other parts may not have been so wonderful, but

---

[80] After these two lines of poetry, Agathon continues with an extremely poetical
prose peroration.

[81] Accepting the emendation *aganos* at d5.

that at the end! Who would not be struck dumb on hearing the beauty of the words and phrases? Anyway, I was worried that I'd not be able to say anything that came close to them in beauty, and so I would almost have run away and escaped, if there had been a place to go. And, you see, the speech reminded me of Gorgias,[82] so that I actually experienced what Homer describes: I was afraid that Agathon would end by sending the Gorgian head,[83] awesome at speaking in a speech, against my speech, and this would turn me to stone by striking me dumb. Then I realized how ridiculous I'd been to agree to join with you in praising Love and to say that I was a master of the art of love, when I knew nothing whatever of this business, of how anything whatever ought to be praised. In my foolishness, I thought you should tell the truth about whatever you praise, that this should be your basis, and that from this a speaker should select the most beautiful truths and arrange them most suitably. I was quite vain, thinking that I would talk well and that I knew the truth about praising anything whatever. But now it appears that this is not what it is to praise anything whatever; rather, it is to apply to the object the grandest and the most beautiful qualities, whether he actually has them or not. And if they are false, that is no objection; for the proposal, apparently, was that everyone here make the rest of us think he is praising Love—and not that he actually praise him. I think that is why you stir up every word and apply it to Love; your description of him and his gifts is designed to make him look better and more beautiful than anything else—to ignorant listeners, plainly, for of course he wouldn't look that way to those who knew. And your praise did seem beautiful and respectful. But I didn't even know the method for giving praise; and it was in ignorance that I agreed to take part in this. So "the tongue" promised, and "the mind" did not.[84] Goodbye to that! I'm not giving another eulogy using that method, not at all—I wouldn't be able to do it!—but, if you wish, I'd like to tell the truth my way. I want to avoid any comparison with your speeches, so as not to give you a reason to laugh at me. So look, Phaedrus, would a speech like this satisfy your

---

[82] Gorgias of Leontini (c. 485–380 BCE) was an important sophist and orator, noted for his distinctive style.

[83] "Gorgian head" is a pun on "Gorgon's head." In his peroration, Agathon had spoken in the style of Gorgias, and this style was considered to be irresistibly powerful. The sight of a Gorgon's head would turn a man to stone.

[84] The allusion is to Euripides, *Hippolytus* 612.

requirement? You will hear the truth about Love, and the words and
5   phrasing will take care of themselves."

Then Aristodemus said that Phaedrus and the others urged him to
speak in the way he thought was required, whatever it was.

"Well then, Phaedrus," said Socrates, "allow me to ask Agathon a
few little questions, so that, once I have his agreement, I may speak on
10   that basis."

"You have my permission," said Phaedrus. "Ask away."

199c   After that, said Aristodemus, Socrates began: "Indeed, Agathon,
my friend, I thought you led the way beautifully into your speech
when you said that one should first show the qualities of Love himself,
5   and only then those of his deeds. I must admire that beginning.
Come, then, since you have beautifully and magnificently expounded
his qualities in other ways, tell me this, too, about Love. Is Love such
199d   as to be a love of something or of nothing? I'm not asking if he is
born *of* some mother or father (for the question whether Love is love
of mother or of father would really be ridiculous), but it's as if I'm
asking this about a father—whether a father is the father *of* something
5   or not. You'd tell me, of course, if you wanted to give me a good answer, that it's *of* a son or a daughter that a father is the father. Would-
n't you?"

"Certainly," said Agathon.

"Then does the same go for the mother?"

He agreed to that also.

199e   "Well, then," said Socrates, "answer a little more fully, and you will
understand better what I want. If I should ask, 'What about this: a
brother, just insofar as he *is* a brother, is he the brother of something
or not?'"

He said that he was.

"And he's of a brother or a sister, isn't he?"

5   He agreed.

"Now try to tell me about love," he said. "Is Love the love of nothing or of something?"

"Of something, surely!"

200a   "Then keep this object of love in mind, and remember what it is.[85]
But tell me this much: does Love desire that of which it is the love, or
not?"

---

[85] Cf. 197b.

"Certainly," he said.

"At the time he desires and loves something, does he actually have what he desires and loves at that time, or doesn't he?"

"He doesn't. At least, that wouldn't be likely," he said.

"Instead of what's *likely,*" said Socrates, "ask yourself whether it's *necessary* that this be so: a thing that desires, desires something of which it is in need; otherwise, if it were not in need, it would not desire it. I can't tell you, Agathon, how strongly it strikes me that this is necessary. But how about you?"

"I think so, too."

"Good. Now then, would someone who is tall want to be tall? Or someone who is strong want to be strong?"

"Impossible, on the basis of what we've agreed."

"Presumably because no one is in need of those things he already has."

"True."

"But maybe a strong man could want to be strong," said Socrates, "or a fast one fast, or a healthy one healthy: in cases like these, you might think people really do want to be things they already are and do want to have qualities they already have—I bring them up so they won't deceive us. But in these cases, Agathon, if you stop to think about them, you will see that these people are what they are at the present time, whether they want to be or not, by a logical necessity. And who, may I ask, would ever bother to desire what's necessary in any event? But when someone says 'I am healthy, but that's just what I want to be,' or 'I am rich, but that's just what I want to be,' or 'I desire the very things that I have,' let us say to him: 'You already have riches and health and strength in your possession, my man; what you want is to possess these things in time to come, since in the present, whether you want to or not, you have them. Whenever you say, *I desire what I already have,* ask yourself whether you don't mean this: *I want the things I have now to be mine in the future as well.*' Wouldn't he agree?"

According to Aristodemus, Agathon said that he would.

So Socrates said, "Then this is what it is to love something which is not at hand, which the lover does not have: it is to desire the preservation of what he now has in time to come, so that he will have it then."

"Quite so," he said.

"So such a man or anyone else who has a desire, desires what is not at hand and not present, what he does not have, and what he is not,

margin references: 5, 200b, 5, 10, 200c, 5, 200d, 5, 10, 200e

and that of which he is in need; for such are the objects of desire
5   and love."

"Certainly," he said.

"Come, then," said Socrates. "Let us review the points on which
we've agreed. Aren't they, first, that Love is the love of something,
and, second, that he loves things of which he has a present need?"

201a   "Yes," he said.

"Now, remember, in addition to these points, what you said in
your speech about what it is that Love loves. If you like, I'll remind
you. I think you said something like this: that the gods' quarrels were
settled by love of beautiful things, for there is no love of ugly ones.[86]
5   Didn't you say something like that?"

"I did," said Agathon.

"And that's a suitable thing to say, my friend," said Socrates. "But if
this is so, wouldn't Love have to be a desire for beauty, and never for
10   ugliness?"

He agreed.

"And we also agreed that he loves just what he needs and does not
201b   have."

"Yes," he said.

"So Love needs beauty, then, and does not have it."

5   "Necessarily," he said.

"So! If something needs beauty and has got no beauty at all, would
you still say that it is beautiful?"

"Certainly not."

10   "Then do you still agree that Love is beautiful, if those things are so?"

Then Agathon said, "It turns out, Socrates, I didn't know what I
was talking about in that speech."

"It was a beautiful speech, anyway, Agathon," said Socrates. "Now
201c   take it a little further. Don't you think that good things are always
beautiful as well?"

"I do."

"Then if Love needs beautiful things, and if all good things are
5   beautiful, he will need good things too."

"As for me, Socrates," he said, "I am unable to contradict you. Let
it be as you say."

"Then it's the truth, my beloved Agathon, that you are unable to
contradict," he said. "It is not hard at all to contradict Socrates."

---

[86] Cf. 197b3–5.

Now I'll let you go. I shall try to go through for you the speech about Love I once heard from a woman of Mantinea, Diotima—a 201d woman who was wise about many things besides this: once she even put off the plague for ten years by telling the Athenians what sacrifices to make. She is the one who taught me the art of love, and I shall go 5 through her speech as best I can on my own, using what Agathon and I have agreed to as a basis.

Following your lead, Agathon, one should first describe who Love is and what he is like, and afterward describe his works—I think it will 201e be easiest for me to proceed the way Diotima did and tell you how she questioned me.

You see, I had told her almost the same things Agathon told me just now: that Love is a great god and that he belongs to beautiful things.[87] And she used the very same arguments against me that I used 5 against Agathon; she showed how, according to my very own speech, Love is neither beautiful nor good.

So I said, "What do you mean, Diotima? Is Love ugly, then, and bad?"

But she said, "Watch your tongue! Do you really think that, if a thing is not beautiful, it has to be ugly?" 10

"I certainly do." **202a**

"And if a thing's not wise, it's ignorant? Or haven't you found out yet that there's something in between wisdom and ignorance?"

"What's that?"

"It's judging things correctly without being able to give a reason. 5 Surely you see that this is not the same as knowing—for how could knowledge be unreasoning? And it's not ignorance either—for how could what hits the truth be ignorance? Correct judgment, of course, has this character: it is *in between* understanding and ignorance."

"True," said I, "as you say." 10

"Then don't force whatever is not beautiful to be ugly, nor what- 202b ever is not good to be bad. It's the same with Love: when you agree he is neither good nor beautiful, you need not think he is ugly and bad; he could be something in between," she said. 5

"Yet everyone agrees he's a great god," I said.

---

[87] The Greek is ambiguous between "Love loves beautiful things" and "Love is one of the beautiful things." Agathon had asserted the former (197b5, 201a5), and this will be a premise in Diotima's argument; but he asserted the latter as well (195a7), and this is what Diotima proceeds to refute.

"Only those who don't know?" she said. "Is that how you mean 'everyone'? Or do you include those who do know?"

"Oh, everyone together."

And she laughed. "Socrates, how could those who say that he's not a god at all agree that he's a great god?"

"Who says that?" I asked.

"You, for one," she said, "and I for another."

"How can you say this!" I exclaimed.

"That's easy," said she. "Tell me, wouldn't you say that all gods are beautiful and happy? Surely you'd never say a god is not beautiful or happy?"

"Zeus! Not I," I said.

"Well, by calling anyone 'happy,' don't you mean they possess good and beautiful things?"

"Certainly."

"What about Love? You agreed he needs good and beautiful things, and that's why he desires them—because he needs them."

"I certainly did."

"Then how could he be a god if he has no share in good and beautiful things?"

"There's no way he could, apparently."

"Now do you see? You don't believe Love is a god either!"

"Then, what could Love be?" I asked. "A mortal?"

"Certainly not."

"Then, what is he?"

"He's like what we mentioned before," she said. "He is in between mortal and immortal."

"What do you mean, Diotima?"

"He's a great spirit,[88] Socrates. Everything spiritual, you see, is in between god and mortal."

"What is their function?" I asked.

"They are messengers who shuttle back and forth between the two, conveying prayer and sacrifice from men to gods, while to men they bring commands from the gods, and gifts in return for sacrifices. Being in the middle of the two, they round out the whole and bind fast the all to all. Through them all divination passes, through them

---

[88] *Daimōn*: Like Socrates' well-known *daimōn* or familiar spirit, which speaks to him only to veto or prevent some action he's contemplating. See *Apology* 31c7–d4.

the art of priests in sacrifice and ritual, in enchantment, prophecy, and sorcery. Gods do not mix with men; they mingle and converse   203a
with us through spirits instead, whether we are awake or asleep. He who is wise in any of these ways is a man of the spirit, but he who is wise in any other way, in a profession or any manual work, is merely a   5
mechanic. These spirits are many and various, then, and one of them is Love."

"Who are his father and mother?" I asked.

"That's rather a long story," she said. "I'll tell it to you, all the same."   203b

"When Aphrodite was born, the gods held a celebration. Poros, the son of Metis, was there among them.[89] When they had feasted, Penia came begging, as poverty does when there's a party, and stayed by the gates. Now Poros got drunk on nectar (there was no wine yet,   5
you see) and, feeling drowsy, went into the garden of Zeus, where he fell asleep. Then Penia schemed up a plan to relieve her lack of resources: she would get a child from Poros. So she lay beside him and got pregnant with Love. That is why Love was born to follow   203c
Aphrodite and serve her: because he was conceived on the day of her birth. And that's why he is also by nature a lover of beauty, because Aphrodite herself is especially beautiful.

"As the son of Poros and Penia, his lot in life is set to be like theirs.   5
In the first place, he is always poor, and he's far from being delicate and beautiful (as ordinary people think he is); instead, he is tough and shriveled and shoeless and homeless, always lying on the dirt without   203d
a bed, sleeping at people's doorsteps and in roadsides under the sky, having his mother's nature, always living with Need. But on his father's side he is a schemer after the beautiful and the good; he is brave, impetuous, and intense, an awesome hunter, always weaving snares,   5
resourceful in his pursuit of intelligence, a lover of wisdom[90] through all his life; a genius with enchantments, potions, and clever pleadings.

"He is by nature neither immortal nor mortal. But now he springs   203e
to life when he gets his way; now he dies—all in the very same day. Because he is his father's son, however, he keeps coming back to life, but then the resources he acquires always slip away, and for this reason Love is never completely without resources, nor is he ever rich.

---

[89] *Poros* means "way," "resource." "*Aporia*," which is what being examined by Socrates induces, means "puzzle" or "problem." *Mêtis* means "cunning," *Penia* "poverty."

[90] I.e., a philosopher.

5   "He is in between wisdom and ignorance as well. In fact, you see,
204a none of the gods loves wisdom or wants to become wise—for they
are wise—and no one else who is wise already loves wisdom; on the
other hand, no one who is ignorant will love wisdom either or want
to become wise. For what's especially difficult about being ignorant is
that you are content with yourself, even though you're neither beauti-
5   ful and good nor intelligent. If you don't think you need anything, of
course you won't want what you don't think you need."

"In that case, Diotima, who *are* the people who love wisdom, if
they are neither wise nor ignorant?"

"That's obvious," she said. "A child could tell you. Those who love
204b wisdom fall in between those two extremes. And Love is one of them,
because he is in love with what is beautiful, and wisdom is extremely
beautiful. It follows that Love *must* be a lover of wisdom and, as such,
5   is in between being wise and being ignorant. This, too, comes to him
from his parentage, from a father who is wise and resourceful and a
mother who is not wise and lacks resource.

"My dear Socrates, that, then, is the nature of the Spirit called
Love. Considering what you thought about Love, it's no surprise that
you were led into thinking of Love as you did. On the basis of what
204c you say, I conclude that you thought Love was *being loved,* rather than
being a lover. I think that's why Love struck you as beautiful in every
way: because it is what is really beautiful and graceful that deserves to
5   be loved, and this is perfect and highly blessed; but being a lover takes
a different form, which I have just described."

So I said, "All right then, Diotima. What you say about Love is
beautiful, but if you're right, what use is Love to human beings?"

204d "I'll try to teach you that, Socrates, after I finish this. So far I've been
explaining the character and the parentage of Love. Now, according
to you, he is love for beautiful things. But suppose someone asks us,
'Socrates and Diotima, what is the point of loving beautiful things?'"

5   "It's clearer this way: 'The lover of beautiful things has a desire;
what does he desire?'"

"That they become his own," I said.

"But that answer calls for still another question, that is, 'What will this
man have when the beautiful things he wants have become his own?'"

10   I said there was no way I could give a ready answer to that question.

Then she said, "Suppose someone changes the question, putting
204e 'good' in place of 'beautiful,' and asks you this: 'Tell me, Socrates, a
lover of good things has a desire; what does he desire?'"

"That they become his own," I said.

"And what will he have, when the good things he wants have become his own?" 5

"This time it's easier to come up with the answer," I said. "He'll have happiness."[91]

"That's what makes happy people happy, isn't it—possessing good things. There's no need to ask further, 'What's the point of wanting 205a happiness?' The answer you gave seems to be final."

"True," I said.

"Now this desire for happiness, this kind of love—do you think it 5 is common to all human beings and that everyone wants to have good things forever and ever? What would you say?"

"Just that," I said. "It is common to all."

"Then, Socrates, why don't we say that everyone is in love," she asked, "since everyone always loves the same things? Instead, we say some people are in love and others not; why is that?" 205b

"I wonder about that myself," I said.

"It's nothing to wonder about," she said. "It's because we divide out a special kind of love, and we refer to it by the word that means the whole—'love'; and for the other kinds of love we use other words." 5

"What do you mean?" I asked.

"Well, you know, for example, that 'poetry' has a very wide range.[92] After all, everything that is responsible for creating something out of nothing is a kind of poetry; and so all the creations of every craft and profession are themselves a kind of poetry, and everyone 205c who practices a craft is a poet."

"True."

"Nevertheless," she said, "as you also know, these craftsmen are not called poets. We have other words for them, and out of the whole of poetry we have marked off one part, the part the Muses give us with 5 melody and rhythm, and we refer to this by the word that means the whole. For this alone is called 'poetry,' and those who practice this part of poetry are called poets."

"True." 10

---

[91] *Eudaimonia*: no English word catches the full range of this term, which is used for the whole of well-being and the good, flourishing life.

[92] "Poetry" translates as *poiêsis*, literally "making," which can be used for any kind of production or creation. However, the word *poiêtês*, literally "maker," was used mainly for poets—writers of metrical verses set to music.

205d   "That's also how it is with love. The main point is this: every desire for good things or for happiness is 'the supreme and treacherous love' in everyone.[93] But those who pursue this along any of its many other ways—through making money, or through the love of sports, or

5   through philosophy—we don't say that *these* people are in love, and we don't call them lovers. It's only when people are devoted exclusively to one special kind of love that we use these words that really belong to the whole of it: 'love' and 'in love' and 'lovers.'"

          "I am beginning to see your point," I said.

10   "Now there is a certain story," she said, "according to which lovers are those people who seek their other halves. But according to my

205e   story, a lover does not seek the half or the whole, unless, my friend, it turns out to be good as well. I say this because people are even willing to cut off their own arms and legs if they think they are diseased. I

5   don't think an individual takes joy in what belongs to him personally unless by 'belonging to me' he means 'good' and by 'belonging to another' he means 'bad.' That's because what everyone loves is really

206a   nothing other than the good. Do you disagree?"[94]

          "Zeus! Not I," I said.

          "Now, then," she said. "Can we simply say that people love the good?"

5   "Yes," I said.

          "But shouldn't we add that, in loving it, they want the good to be theirs?"

          "We should."

          "And not only that," she said. "They want the good to be theirs forever, don't they?"

10   "We should add that too."

          "In a word, then, love is wanting to possess the good forever."

          "That's very true," I said.

206b   "This, then, is the object of love,"[95] she said. "Now, how do lovers pursue it? We'd rightly say that when they are in love they do something with eagerness and zeal. But what is it precisely that they do? Can you say?"

          "If I could, Diotima," I said, "I wouldn't be your student, filled with

5   admiration for your wisdom, and trying to learn these very things."

---

[93] The source of this apparent quotation is unknown.

[94] See *Lysis* 219c–220e.

[95] Accepting the emendation *toutou* in b1.

"Well, I'll tell you," she said. "It is giving birth in beauty,[96] whether in body or in soul."

"It would take divination to figure out what you mean. I can't."   10

"Well, I'll tell you more clearly," she said. "All of us are pregnant, Socrates, both in body and in soul, and, as soon as we come to a certain age, we naturally desire to give birth. Now no one can possibly   206c give birth in anything ugly; only in something beautiful. That's because when a man and a woman come together in order to give birth,   5 this is a godly affair. Pregnancy, reproduction—this is an immortal thing for a mortal animal to do, and it cannot occur in anything that is out of harmony, but ugliness is out of harmony with all that is godly. Beauty, however, is in harmony with the divine. Therefore the   206d goddess who presides at childbirth—she's called Moira or Eilithuia— is really Beauty.[97] That's why, whenever pregnant animals or persons draw near to beauty, they become gentle and joyfully disposed and give birth and reproduce; but near ugliness they frown and draw back   5 in pain; they turn away and shrink back and do not reproduce, and because they hold on to what they carry inside them, the labor is painful. This is the source of the great excitement about beauty that comes to anyone who is pregnant and already teeming with life: beauty releases them from their great pain. You see, Socrates," she   206e said, "what Love wants is not beauty, as you think it is."

"Well, what is it, then?"

"Reproduction and birth in beauty."   5

"Maybe," I said.

"Certainly," she said. "Now, why reproduction? It's because reproduction goes on forever; it is what mortals have in place of immortality. A lover must desire immortality along with the good, if what we   207a agreed earlier was right, that Love wants to possess the good forever. It follows from our argument that Love must desire immortality."

All this she taught me, on those occasions when she spoke on the art of love. And once she asked, "What do you think causes love and   5

---

[96] The preposition is ambiguous between "within" and "in the presence of." Diotima may mean that the lover causes the newborn (which may be an idea) to come to be within a beautiful person; or she may mean that he is stimulated to give birth to it in the presence of a beautiful person.

[97] Moira is known mainly as a Fate, but she was also a birth goddess (*Iliad* 24.209), and was identified with the birth goddess Eilithuia (Pindar, *Olympian Odes* 6.42; *Nemean Odes* 7.1).

desire, Socrates? Don't you see what an awful state a wild animal is in when it wants to reproduce? Footed and winged animals alike, all are plagued by the disease of Love. First they are sick for intercourse with each other, then for nurturing their young—for their sake the weakest animals stand ready to do battle against the strongest and even to die for them, and they may be racked with famine in order to feed their young. They would do anything for their sake. Human beings, you'd think, would do this because they understand the reason for it; but what causes wild animals to be in such a state of love? Can you say?"

And I said again that I didn't know.

So she said, "How do you think you'll ever master the art of love, if you don't know that?"

"But that's why I came to you, Diotima, as I just said. I knew I needed a teacher. So tell me what causes this, and everything else that belongs to the art of love."

"If you really believe that Love by its nature aims at what we have often agreed it does, then don't be surprised at the answer," she said. "For among animals the principle is the same as with us, and mortal nature seeks so far as possible to live forever and be immortal. And this is possible in one way only: by reproduction, because it always leaves behind a new young one in place of the old. Even while each living thing is said to be alive and to be the same—as a person is said to be the same from childhood till he turns into an old man—even then he never consists of the same things, though he is called the same, but he is always being renewed and in other respects passing away, in his hair and flesh and bones and blood and his entire body. And it's not just in his body, but in his soul, too, for none of his manners, customs, opinions, desires, pleasures, pains, or fears ever remains the same, but some are coming to be in him while others are passing away. And what is still far stranger than that is that not only does one branch of knowledge come to be in us while another passes away and that we are never the same even in respect of our knowledge, but that each single piece of knowledge has the same fate. For what we call *studying* exists because knowledge is leaving us, because forgetting is the departure of knowledge, while studying puts back a fresh memory in place of what went away, thereby preserving a piece of knowledge, so that it seems to be the same. And in that way everything mortal is preserved, not, like the divine, by always being the same in every way, but because what is departing and aging leaves behind something new, something such as it had been. By this device, Socrates," she said, "what is mortal shares in immortality, whether it is a body or anything else, while the immortal has another way. So don't be surprised if everything naturally values its own offspring, because it is for the sake of immortality that everything shows this zeal, which is Love."

Yet when I heard her speech I was amazed, and spoke: "Well," said I, "Most wise Diotima, is this really the way it is?"

And in the manner of a perfect sophist[98] she said, "Be sure of it, Socrates. Look, if you will, at how human beings seek honor. You'd be amazed at their irrationality, if you didn't have in mind what I spoke about and if you hadn't pondered the awful state of love they're in, wanting to become famous and 'to lay up glory immortal forever,'[99] and how they're ready to brave any danger for the sake of this, much more than they are for their children; and they are prepared to spend money, suffer through all sorts of ordeals, and even die for the sake of glory. Do you really think that Alcestis would have died for Admetus," she asked, "or that Achilles would have died after Patroclus, or that your Codrus would have died so as to preserve the throne for his sons,[100] if they hadn't expected the memory of their virtue—which we still hold in honor—to be immortal? Far from it," she said. "I believe that anyone will do anything for the sake of immortal virtue and the glorious fame that follows; and the better the people, the more they will do, for they are all in love with immortality.

"Now, some people are pregnant in body, and for this reason turn more to women and pursue love in that way, providing themselves through childbirth with immortality and remembrance and happiness, as they think, for all time to come; while others are pregnant in soul—because there surely *are* those who are even more pregnant in their souls than in their bodies, and these are pregnant with what is fitting for a soul to bear and bring to birth. And what is fitting? Wisdom and the rest of virtue, which all poets beget, as well as all the craftsmen who are said to be creative. But by far the greatest and most beautiful part of wisdom deals with the proper ordering of cities and households, and that is called moderation and justice. When someone

---

[98] See 177b2 note.

[99] Otherwise unknown.

[100] Codrus was the legendary last king of Athens. He gave his life to satisfy a prophecy that promised victory to Athens and salvation from the invading Dorians if their king was killed by the enemy.

has been pregnant with these in his soul from early youth, while he is still a virgin, and, having arrived at the proper age, desires to beget and give birth, he too will certainly go about seeking the beauty in which he would beget; for he will never beget in anything ugly. Since he is pregnant, then, he is much more drawn to bodies that are beautiful than to those that are ugly; and if he also has the luck to find a soul that is beautiful and noble and well-formed, he is even more drawn to this combination; such a man makes him instantly teem with speeches about virtue—about the qualities a virtuous man should have and the customary activities in which he should engage; and so he tries to educate him. In my view, you see, when he makes contact with someone beautiful and keeps company with him, he conceives and gives birth to what he has been carrying inside him for ages. And whether they are together or apart, he remembers that beauty. And in common with him, he nurtures the newborn; such people, therefore, have much more to share than do the parents of human children, and have a firmer bond of friendship, because the children in whom they have a share are more beautiful and more immortal. Everyone would rather have such children than human ones, and would look up to Homer, Hesiod, and the other good poets with envy and admiration for the offspring they have left behind—offspring, which, because they are immortal themselves, provide their parents with immortal glory and remembrance. "For example," she said, "those are the sort of children Lycurgus[101] left behind in Sparta as the saviors of Sparta and virtually all of Greece. Among you the honor goes to Solon for his creation of your laws.[102] Other men in other places everywhere, Greek or barbarian, have brought a host of beautiful deeds into the light and begotten every kind of virtue. Already many shrines have sprung up to honor them for their immortal children, which hasn't happened yet to anyone for human offspring.

"Even you, Socrates, could probably come to be initiated into these rites of love. But as for the purpose of these rites when they are done correctly—that is the final and highest mystery, and I don't know if you are capable of it. I myself will tell you," she said, "and I won't stint any effort. And you must try to follow if you can."

---

[101] Lycurgus was supposed to have been the founder of the oligarchic laws and stern customs of Sparta.

[102] Approximately 640–560 BCE: Athenian statesman, poet, and founder of the Athenian constitution.

"A lover who goes about this matter correctly must begin in his youth to devote himself to beautiful bodies. First, if the leader[103] leads aright, he should love one body and beget beautiful speeches there; then he should realize that the beauty of any one body is brother to the beauty of any other and that if he is to pursue beauty of form he'd be very foolish not to think that the beauty of all bodies is one and the same. When he grasps this, he must become a lover of all beautiful bodies, and he must think that this wild gaping after just one body is a small thing and despise it.

"After this he must think that the beauty of people's souls is more valuable than the beauty of their bodies, so that if someone is decent in his soul, even though he is scarcely blooming in his body, our lover must be content to love and care for him and to seek to give birth to such ideas as will make young men better. The result is that our lover will be forced to gaze at the beauty of activities and laws and to see that all this is akin to itself, with the result that he will think that the beauty of bodies is a thing of small importance. After customs he must move on to various kinds of knowledge. The result is that he will see the beauty of knowledge and be looking mainly not at beauty in a single example—as a servant would who favored the beauty of a little boy or a man or a single custom (being a slave, of course, he's low and small-minded)—but the lover is turned to the great sea of beauty, and, gazing upon this, he gives birth to many gloriously beautiful speeches, in unstinting love of wisdom,[104] until, having grown and been strengthened there, he catches sight of such knowledge, and it is the knowledge of such beauty. . . .

"Try to pay attention to me," she said, "as best you can. You see, the man who has been thus far guided in matters of Love, who has beheld beautiful things in the right order and correctly, is coming now to the goal of Loving: all of a sudden he will catch sight of something wonderfully beautiful in its nature; that, Socrates, is the reason for all his earlier labors:

"First, it always *is* and neither comes to be nor passes away, neither waxes nor wanes. Second, it is not beautiful this way and ugly that way, nor beautiful at one time and ugly at another, nor beautiful in relation to one thing and ugly in relation to another; nor is it beautiful here

---

[103] The leader: Love.

[104] I.e., philosophy.

but ugly there, as it would be if it were beautiful for some people and
5   ugly for others. Nor will the beautiful appear to him in the guise of a
face or hands or anything else that belongs to the body. It will not appear to him as a speech or a kind of knowledge does. It is not anywhere in another thing, as in an animal, or in earth, or in heaven, or
211b in anything else, but itself by itself with itself, it is always one in form;
and all the other beautiful things share in that, in such a way that
when those others come to be or pass away, this does not become the
least bit smaller or greater nor suffer any change. So when someone
5   rises by these stages, through loving boys correctly, and begins to see
this beauty, he has almost grasped his goal. This is what it is to go
aright, or be led by another, into the art of Love: one goes always up-
211c wards for the sake of this Beauty, starting out from beautiful things
and using them like rising stairs: from one body to two and from two
to all beautiful bodies, then from beautiful bodies to beautiful cus-
5   toms, and from customs to learning beautiful things, and from these
lessons he arrives[105] in the end at this lesson, which is learning of this
very Beauty, so that in the end he comes to know just what it is to be
beautiful.

211d   "And there in life, Socrates, my friend," said the woman from
Mantinea, "there if anywhere should a person live his life, beholding
that Beauty. If you once see that, it won't occur to you to measure
beauty by gold or clothing or beautiful boys and youths—who, if you
5   see them now, strike you out of your senses, and make you, you and
many others, eager to be with the boys you love and look at them forever, if there were any way to do that, forgetting food and drink,
everything but looking at them and being with them. But how would
it be, in our view," she said, "if someone got to see the Beautiful it-
211e self, absolute, pure, unmixed, not polluted by human flesh or colors
or any other great nonsense of mortality, but if he could see the divine Beauty itself in its one form? Do you think it would be a poor
212a life for a human being to look there and to behold it by that which he
ought, and to be with it? Or haven't you remembered," she said, "that
in that life alone, when he looks at Beauty in the only way that Beauty
can be seen—only then will it become possible for him to give birth
not to images of virtue (because he's in touch with no images), but to
true virtue (because he is in touch with the true Beauty). The love of

---

[105] Reading *teleutêsêi* at c7.

the gods belongs to anyone who has given birth to true virtue and   5
nourished it, and if any human being could become immortal, it
would be he."

This, Phaedrus and the rest of you, was what Diotima told me. I   212b
was persuaded. And once persuaded, I try to persuade others too that
human nature can find no better workmate for acquiring this than
Love. That's why I say that every man must honor Love, why I honor   5
the rites of Love myself and practice them with special diligence, and
why I commend them to others. Now and always I praise the power
and courage of Love so far as I am able. Consider this speech, then,
Phaedrus, if you wish, a speech in praise of Love. Or if not, call it   212c
whatever and however you please to call it.

Socrates' speech finished to loud applause. Meanwhile, Aristophanes was trying to make himself heard over their cheers in order to
make a response to something Socrates had said about his own   5
speech.[106] Then, all of a sudden, there was even more noise. A large
drunken party had arrived at the courtyard door and they were rat-
tling it loudly, accompanied by the shrieks of some flute-girl they had
brought along. Agathon at that point called to his slaves:
    "Go see who it is. If it's people we know, invite them in. If not, tell   212d
them the party's over, and we're about to turn in."
    A moment later they heard Alcibiades[107] shouting in the courtyard,
very drunk and very loud. He wanted to know where Agathon was,
he demanded to see Agathon at once. Actually, he was half carried   5
into the house by the flute-girl and by some other companions of his,

---

[106] Cf. 205d–e.

[107] Controversial Athenian statesman (452–404 BCE). He was 36 in 416 (the dramatic date of Agathon's party). In 415, during the Peloponnesian War with
Sparta, he was appointed joint leader of a daring, perhaps foolhardy, military expedition against Sicily—an expedition he advocated and encouraged before the
Athenian Assembly. Alleged to have mutilated statues of the god Hermes and formally charged with having parodied the secret initiation rites of the Eleusynian
Mysteries, he was recalled to Athens on religious charges. Rather than face these
accusations, he went over to the Spartans and helped them fight against the Athenians. In 407, he rejoined the Athenians. He was assassinated in 404 by agents of
Persia, with whom the Spartans had allied themselves. See Thucydides 5.43–6,
52–6, 6.8–32, 60–1, 88–93; 7.18; 8.45–89, 97; Plutarch, *Life of Alcibiades*.

but, at the door, he managed to stand by himself, crowned with a
beautiful wreath of violets and ivy and ribbons in his hair.

"Good evening, gentlemen. I'm plastered," he announced. "May I
join your party? Or should I crown Agathon with this wreath—
which is all I came to do, anyway—and make myself scarce? I really
couldn't make it yesterday," he continued, "but nothing could stop
me tonight! See, I'm wearing the garland myself. I want this crown to
come directly from my head to the head that belongs, I don't mind
saying, to the cleverest and best looking man in town. Ah, you laugh;
you think I'm drunk! Fine, go ahead—I know I'm right anyway.
Well, what do you say? May I join you on these terms? Will you have
a drink with me or not?"

Naturally they all made a big fuss. They implored him to join
them, they begged him to take a seat, and Agathon called him to his
side. So Alcibiades, again with the help of his friends, approached
Agathon. At the same time, he kept trying to take his ribbons off so
that he could crown Agathon with them, but all he succeeded in
doing was to push them further down his head until they finally
slipped over his eyes. What with the ivy and all, he didn't see Socrates,
who had made room for him on the couch as soon as he saw him. So
Alcibiades sat down between Socrates and Agathon and, as soon as he
did so, he put his arms around Agathon, kissed him, and placed the ribbons on his head.

Agathon asked his slaves to take Alcibiades' sandals off. "We can all
three fit on my couch," he said.

"What a good idea!" Alcibiades replied. "But wait a moment!
Who's the third?"

As he said this, he turned around, and it was only then that he saw
Socrates. No sooner had he seen him than he leaped up and cried:

"Good lord, what's going on here? It's Socrates! You've trapped me
again! You always do this to me—all of a sudden you'll turn up out of
nowhere where I least expect you! Well, what do you want now?
Why did you choose this particular couch? Why aren't you with
Aristophanes or anyone else we could tease you about? But no, you
figured out a way to find a place next to the most handsome man in
the room!"

"I beg you, Agathon," Socrates said, "protect me from this man!
You can't imagine what it's like to be in love with him: from the very
first moment he realized how I felt about him, he hasn't allowed me to
say two words to anybody else—what am I saying, I can't so much as

look at an attractive man but he flies into a fit of jealous rage. He 213d
yells; he threatens; he can hardly keep from slapping me around!
Please, try to keep him under control. Could you perhaps make him
forgive me? And if you can't, if he gets violent, will you defend me? 5
The fierceness of his passion terrifies me!"

"I shall never forgive you!" Alcibiades cried. "I promise you, you'll
pay for this! But for the moment," he said, turning to Agathon, "give
me some of these ribbons. I'd better make a wreath for him as well— 213e
look at that magnificent head! Otherwise, I know, he'll make a scene.
He'll be grumbling that, though I crowned you for your first victory,
I didn't honor him even though he has never lost an argument in his
life."

So Alcibiades took the ribbons, arranged them on Socrates' head, 5
and lay back on the couch. Immediately, however, he started up again:

"Friends, you look sober to me; we can't have that! Let's have a
drink! Remember our agreement? We need a master of ceremonies;
who should it be? . . . Well, at least till you are all too drunk to care,
I elect . . . myself! Who else? Agathon, I want the largest cup around 10
. . . . No! Wait! You! Bring me that cooling jar over there!"

He'd seen the cooling jar, and he realized it could hold more than
two quarts of wine. He had the slaves fill it to the brim, drained it, 214a
and ordered them to fill it up again for Socrates.

"Not that the trick will have any effect on *him*," he told the group.
"Socrates will drink whatever you put in front of him, but no one yet
has seen him drunk." 5

The slave filled the jar and, while Socrates was drinking, Eryximachus said to Alcibiades:

"This is certainly most improper. We cannot simply pour the wine
down our throats in silence: we must have some conversation, or at
least a song. What we are doing now is hardly civilized." 214b

What Alcibiades said to him was this:

"O Eryximachus, best possible son to the best possible, the most
temperate father: Hi!"

"Greetings to you, too," Eryximachus replied. "Now what do you
suggest we do?"

"Whatever you say. Ours to obey you, 'For a medical mind is 5
worth a million others'.[108] Please prescribe what you think fit."

---

[108] *Iliad* 11.514.

"Listen to me," Eryximachus said. "Earlier this evening we decided
to use this occasion to offer a series of encomia of Love. We all took
our turn—in good order, from left to right—and gave our speeches,
each according to his ability. You are the only one not to have spoken
yet, though, if I may say so, you have certainly drunk your share. It's
only proper, therefore, that you take your turn now. After you have
spoken, you can decide on a topic for Socrates on your right; he can
then do the same for the man to his right, and we can go around the
table once again."

"Well said, O Eryximachus," Alcibiades replied. "But do you really
think it's fair to put my drunken ramblings next to your sober orations?
And anyway, my dear fellow, I hope you didn't believe a single word
Socrates said: the truth is just the opposite! He's the one who will
most surely beat me up if I dare praise anyone else in his presence—
even a god!"

"Hold your tongue!" Socrates said.

"By god,[109] don't you dare deny it!" Alcibiades shouted. "I would
never—never—praise anyone else with you around."

"Well, why not just do that, if you want?" Eryximachus suggested.
"Why don't you offer an encomium to Socrates?"

"What do you mean?" asked Alcibiades. "Do you really think so,
Eryximachus? Should I unleash myself upon him? Should I give him
his punishment in front of all of you?"

"Now, wait a minute," Socrates said. "What do you have in mind?
Are you going to praise me only in order to mock me? Is that it?"

"I'll only tell the truth—please, let me!"

"I would certainly like to hear the truth from you. By all means, go
ahead," Socrates replied.

"Nothing can stop me now," said Alcibiades. "But here's what you
can do: if I say anything that's not true, you can just interrupt, if you
want, and correct me; at worst, there'll be mistakes in my speech, not
lies. But you can't hold it against me if I don't get everything in the
right order—I'll say things as they come to mind. It is no easy task for
one in my condition to give a smooth and orderly account of your
bizarreness!"

I'll try to praise Socrates, my friends, but I'll have to use an image.
And though he may think I'm trying to make fun of him, I assure you

---

[109] *Ma ton Poseidô*: "By Poseidon!" God of the sea.

my image is no joke: it aims at the truth. Look at him! Isn't he just like   5
a statue of Silenus?[110] You know the kind of statue I mean; you'll find
them in any shop in town. It's a Silenus sitting, his flute or his pipes in   215b
his hands, and it's hollow. It's split right down the middle, and inside
it's full of tiny statues of the gods. Now look at him again! Isn't he also
just like the satyr Marsyas?[111]

Nobody, not even you, Socrates, can deny that you *look* like them.   5
But the resemblance goes beyond appearance, as you're about to hear.

You are impudent, contemptuous, and vile! No? If you won't
admit it, I'll bring witnesses. And you're quite a fluteplayer, aren't
you? In fact, you're much more marvelous than Marsyas, who needed
instruments to cast his spells on people. And so does anyone who plays   215c
his tunes today—for even the tunes Olympus[112] played are Marsyas'
work, since Olympus learned everything from him. Whether they are
played by the greatest flautist or the meanest flute-girl, his melodies
have in themselves the power to possess and so reveal those people
who are ready for the god and his mysteries. That's because his   5
melodies are themselves divine. The only difference between you and
Marsyas is that you need no instruments; you do exactly what he
does, but with words alone. You know, people hardly ever take a   215d
speaker seriously, even if he's the greatest orator; but let anyone—
man, woman, or child—listen to you or even to a poor account of
what you say—and we are all transported, completely possessed.   5

If I were to describe for you what an extraordinary effect his words
have always had on me (I can feel it this moment even as I'm speaking), you might actually suspect that I'm drunk! Still, I swear to you,
the moment he starts to speak, I am beside myself: my heart starts
leaping in my chest, the tears come streaming down my face, even the
frenzied Corybantes[113] seem sane compared to me—and, let me tell   215e

---

[110] A satyr who taught or was taught by Dionysus, characterized by ignorance,
drunkenness, and lust.

[111] Satyrs had the sexual appetites and manners of wild beasts and were usually
portrayed with large erections. Sometimes they had horses' tails or ears, sometimes the traits of goats. Marsyas, in myth, dared to compete in music with
Apollo and was skinned alive for his impudence.

[112] Olympus was a legendary musician who was said to be loved by Marsyas
(*Minos* 318b5), and to have made music that moved its listeners out of their
senses.

[113] Legendary worshippers of Cybele, who brought about their own derangement
through music and dance.

you, I am not alone. I have heard Pericles[114] and many other great orators, and I have admired their speeches. But nothing like this ever happened to me: they never upset me so deeply that my very own soul started protesting that my life—*my* life!—was no better than the most miserable slave's. And yet that is exactly how this Marsyas here at my side makes me feel all the time: he makes it seem that my life isn't worth living! You can't say that isn't true, Socrates. I know very well that you could make me feel that way this very moment if I gave you half a chance. He always traps me, you see, and he makes me admit that my political career is a waste of time, while all that matters is just what I most neglect: my personal shortcomings, which cry out for the closest attention. So I refuse to listen to him; I stop my ears and tear myself away from him, for, like the Sirens,[115] he could make me stay by his side till I die.

Socrates is the only man in the world who has made me feel shame—ah, you didn't think I had it in me, did you? Yes, he makes me feel ashamed: I know perfectly well that I can't prove he's wrong when he tells me what I should do; yet, the moment I leave his side, I go back to my old ways: I cave in to my desire to please the crowd. My whole life has become one constant effort to escape from him and keep away, but when I see him, I feel deeply ashamed, because I'm doing nothing about my way of life, though I have already agreed with him that I should. Sometimes, believe me, I think I would be happier if he were dead. And yet I know that if he dies I'll be even more miserable. I can't live with him, and I can't live without him! What *can* I do about him?

That's the effect of this satyr's music—on me and many others. But that's the least of it. He's like these creatures in all sorts of other ways; his powers are really extraordinary. Let me tell you about them, because, you can be sure of it, none of you really understands him. But, now I've started, I'm going to show you what he really is.

To begin with, he's crazy about beautiful boys; he constantly follows them around in a perpetual daze. Also, he likes to say he's ignorant and knows nothing. Isn't this just like Silenus? Of course it is!

[114] Approximately 495–429 BCE. Athenian statesman, orator, and democratic leader. Alcibiades was his ward.

[115] Mythical women whose singing led sailors to their death. See Homer, *Odyssey* xii.

And all this is just on the surface, like the outsides of those statues of
Silenus. I wonder, my fellow drinkers, if you have any idea what a
sober and temperate man he proves to be once you have looked inside. Believe me, it couldn't matter less to him whether a boy is beautiful. You can't imagine how little he cares whether a person is
beautiful, or rich, or famous in any other way that most people ad-   216e
mire. He considers all these possessions beneath contempt, and that's
exactly how he considers all of us as well. In public, I tell you, his
whole life is one big game—a game of irony. I don't know if any of   5
you have seen him when he's really serious. But I once caught him
when he was open like Silenus' statues, and I had a glimpse of the figures he keeps hidden within: they were so godlike—so bright and
beautiful, so utterly amazing—that I no longer had a choice—I just   **217a**
had to do whatever he told me.

What I thought at the time was that what he really wanted was *me*,
and that seemed to me the luckiest coincidence: all I had to do was to
let him have his way with me, and he would teach me everything he
knew—believe me, I had a lot of confidence in my looks. Naturally,   5
up to that time we'd never been alone together; one of my attendants
had always been present. But with this in mind, I sent the attendant
away, and met Socrates alone. (You see, in this company I must tell
the whole truth: so pay attention. And, Socrates, if I say anything un-   217b
true, I want you to correct me.)

So there I was, my friends, alone with him at last. My idea, naturally, was that he'd take advantage of the opportunity to tell me whatever it is that lovers say when they find themselves alone; I relished the
moment. But no such luck! Nothing of the sort occurred. Socrates   5
had his usual sort of conversation with me, and at the end of the day
he went off.

My next idea was to invite him to the gymnasium with me. We   217c
took exercise together, and I was sure that this would lead to something. He took exercise and wrestled with me many times when no
one else was present. What can I tell you? I got nowhere. When I realized that my ploy had failed, I decided on a frontal attack. I refused
to retreat from a battle I myself had begun, and I needed to know just   5
where matters stood. So what I did was to invite him to dinner, as if *I*
were his lover and he my young prey! To tell the truth, it took him
quite a while to accept my invitation, but one day he finally arrived.   217d
That first time, he left right after dinner: I was too shy to try to stop
him. But on my next attempt, I started some discussion just as we

were finishing our meal and kept him talking late into the night. When he said he should be going, I used the lateness of the hour as an excuse and managed to persuade him to spend the night at my house. He had had his meal on the couch next to mine, so he just made himself comfortable and lay down on it. No one else was there.

Now you must admit that my story so far has been perfectly decent; I could have told it in any company. But you'd never have heard me tell the rest of it, as you're about to do, if it weren't that, as the saying goes, 'there's truth in wine when the slaves have left'[116]—and when they're present, too. Also, would it be fair to Socrates for me to praise him and yet to fail to reveal one of his proudest accomplishments? And, furthermore, you know what people say about snakebite—that you'll only talk about it with your fellow victims: only they will understand the pain and forgive you for all the things it made you do. Well, something much more painful than a snake has bitten me in my most sensitive part—I mean my heart, or my soul, or whatever you want to call it, which has been struck and bitten by philosophy, whose grip on young and eager souls is much more vicious than a viper's and makes them do the most amazing things. Now, all you people here, Phaedrus, Agathon, Eryximachus, Pausanias, Aristodemus, Aristophanes—I need not mention Socrates himself—and all the rest, have all shared in the madness, the Bacchic frenzy of philosophy. And that's why you will hear the rest of my story; you will understand and forgive both what I did then and what I say now. As for the house slaves and for anyone else who is not an initiate, my story's not for you: block your ears!

To get back to the story. The lights were out; the slaves had left; the time was right, I thought, to come to the point and tell him freely what I had in mind. So I shook him and whispered:

"Socrates, are you asleep?"

"No, no, not at all," he replied.

"You know what I've been thinking?"

"Well, no, not really."

"I think," I said, "you're the only worthy lover I have ever had—and yet, look how shy you are with me! Well, here's how I look at it. It would be really stupid not to give you anything you want: you can have me, my belongings, anything my friends might have. Nothing is

---

[116] Source unknown.

more important to me than becoming the best man I can be, and no   218d
one can help me more than you to reach that aim. With a man like
you, in fact, I'd be much more ashamed of what wise people would
say if I did *not* take you as my lover, than I would of what all the others, in their foolishness, would say if I did."   5

He heard me out, and then he said in that absolutely inimitable
ironic manner of his:

"Dear Alcibiades, if you are right in what you say about me, you
are already more accomplished than you think. If I really have in me
the power to make you a better man, then you can see in me a beauty   218e
that is really beyond description and makes your own remarkable
good looks pale in comparison. But, then, is this a fair exchange that
you propose? You seem to me to want more than your proper share: 5
you offer me the merest appearance of beauty, and in return you
want the thing itself, 'gold in exchange for bronze.'[117]

"Still, my dear boy, you should think twice, because you could be   **219a**
wrong, and I may be of no use to you. The mind's sight becomes
sharp only when the body's eyes go past their prime—and you are still
a good long time away from that."

When I heard this I replied:

"I really have nothing more to say. I've told you exactly what I think.   5
Now it's your turn to consider what you think best for you and me."

"You're right about that," he answered. "In the future, let's consider things together. We'll always do what seems the best to the two   219b
of us."

His words made me think that my own had finally hit their mark,
that he was smitten by my arrows. I didn't give him a chance to say
another word. I stood up immediately and placed my mantle over the   5
light cloak which, though it was the middle of winter, was his only
clothing. I slipped underneath the cloak and put my arms around this
man—this utterly unnatural, this truly extraordinary man—and spent
the whole night next to him. Socrates, you can't deny a word of it.   219c
But in spite of all my efforts, this hopelessly arrogant, this unbeliev-
ably insolent man—he turned me down! He spurned my beauty, of
which I was so proud, members of the jury—for this is really what   5
you are: you're here to sit in judgment of Socrates' amazing arrogance

---

[117] The *Iliad* (6.232–36) tells the famous story of the exchange by Glaucus of
golden armor for bronze.

and pride. Be sure of it, I swear to you by all the gods and goddesses together, my night with Socrates went no further than if I had spent it with my own father or older brother!

219d

How do you think I felt after that? Of course, I was deeply humiliated, but also I couldn't help admiring his natural character, his moderation, his fortitude—here was a man whose strength of character[118] and wisdom went beyond my wildest dreams! How could I bring myself to hate him? I couldn't bear to lose his friendship. But how could I possibly win him over? I knew very well that money meant much less to him than enemy weapons ever meant to Ajax,[119] and the only trap by means of which I had thought I might capture him had already proved a dismal failure. I had no idea what to do, no purpose in life; ah, no one else has ever known the real meaning of slavery!

5

219e

5

All this had already occurred when Athens invaded Potidaea,[120] where we served together and shared the same mess. Now, first, he took the hardships of the campaign much better than I ever did— much better, in fact, than anyone in the whole army. When we were cut off from our supplies, as often happens in the field, no one else stood up to hunger as well as he did. And yet he was the one man who could really enjoy a feast; and though he didn't much want to drink, when he had to, he could drink the best of us under the table. Still, and most amazingly, no one ever saw him drunk (as we'll straightaway put to the test).

220a

5

Add to this his amazing resistance to the cold—and, let me tell you, the winter there is something awful. Once, I remember, it was frightfully cold; no one so much as stuck his nose outside. If we absolutely had to leave our tent, we wrapped ourselves in anything we could lay our hands on and tied extra pieces of felt or sheepskin over our boots. Well, Socrates went out in that weather wearing nothing but this same old light cloak, and even in bare feet he made better progress on the ice than the other soldiers did in their boots. You should have seen the looks they gave him; they thought he was only doing it to spite them!

220b

5

---

[118] *Karteria*: "fortitude," "endurance," capacity to stand up to hardship.

[119] Ajax, a hero of the Greek army at Troy, carried an enormous shield and so was virtually invulnerable to enemy weapons.

[120] Potidaea, a city in Thrace allied to Athens, was induced by Corinth to revolt in 432 BCE. The city was besieged by the Athenians and eventually defeated in a bloody local war (432–430).

So much for that! But you should hear what else he did during that   220c
same campaign,

> *The exploit our strong-hearted hero dared to do.*[121]

One day, at dawn, he started thinking about some problem or
other; he just stood outside, trying to figure it out. He couldn't re-
solve it, but he wouldn't give up. He simply stood there, glued to the
same spot. By midday, many soldiers had seen him, and, quite mysti-   5
fied, they told everyone that Socrates had been standing there all day,
thinking about something. He was still there when evening came, and
after dinner some Ionians moved their bedding outside, where it was
cooler and more comfortable (all this took place in the summer),   220d
mainly in order to watch if Socrates was going to stay out there all
night. And so he did; he stood on the very same spot until dawn! He
only left next morning, when the sun came out, and he made his
prayers to the new day.

And if you would like to know what he was like in battle—this is a   5
tribute he really deserves. You know that I was decorated for bravery
during that campaign: well, during that very battle, Socrates single-
handedly saved my life! He absolutely did! He just refused to leave me
behind when I was wounded, and he rescued not only me but my   220e
armor as well. For my part, Socrates, I told them right then that the
decoration really belonged to you, and you can blame me neither for
doing so then nor for saying so now. But the generals, who seemed
much more concerned with my social position, insisted on giving the
decoration to me, and, I must say, you were more eager than the gen-   5
erals themselves for me to have it.

You should also have seen him at our horrible retreat from
Delium.[122] I was there with the cavalry, while Socrates was a foot sol-   221a
dier. The army had already dispersed in all directions, and Socrates
was retreating together with Laches.[123] I happened to see them just by
chance, and the moment I did I started shouting encouragements to

---

[121] *Odyssey* 4.242, 271.

[122] At Delium, a town on the Boeotian coastline just north of Attica, a major
Athenian expeditionary force was routed by a Boeotian army in 424 BCE. For another description of Socrates' action during the retreat, see *Laches* 181b.

[123] Well-known Athenian general, who died at the battle of Mantinea (418 BCE).
He appears in the eponymous *Laches*, which discusses courage.

them, telling them I was never going to leave their side, and so on.
5   That day I had a better opportunity to watch Socrates than I ever had
at Potidaea, for, being on horseback, I wasn't in very great danger.
Well, it was easy to see that he was remarkably more collected than
221b Laches. But when I looked again I couldn't get your words, Aristophanes, out of my mind: in the midst of battle he was making his way
exactly as he does around town,

. . . *with swagg'ring gait and roving eye.*[124]

He was observing everything quite calmly, looking out for friendly
troops and keeping an eye on the enemy. Even from a great distance
5   it was obvious that this was a very brave man, who would put up a
terrific fight if anyone approached him. This is what saved both of
them. For, as a rule, you try to put as much distance as you can between yourself and such men in battle; you go after the others, those
221c who run away helter-skelter.

You could say many other marvelous things in praise of Socrates.
Perhaps he shares some of his specific accomplishments with others.
But, as a whole, he is unique; he is like no one else in the past and no
5   one in the present—this is by far the most amazing thing about him.
For we might be able to form an idea of what Achilles was like by
comparing him to Brasidas or some other great warrior, or we might
compare Pericles with Nestor or Antenor or one of the other great
221d orators.[125] There is a parallel for everyone—everyone else, that is. But
this man here is so bizarre, his ways and his arguments are so unusual,
that, search as you might, you'll never find anyone else, alive or dead,
who's even remotely like him. The best you can do is not to compare
him to anything human, but to liken him, as I do, to Silenus and the
5   satyrs, and the same goes for his arguments.

Come to think of it, I should have mentioned this much earlier:
even his arguments are just like those hollow statues of Silenus. If you
221e were to listen to his arguments, at first they'd strike you as totally
ridiculous; they're clothed in words as coarse as the hides worn by the

---

[124] Cf. Aristophanes, *Clouds* 362.

[125] Brasidas, among the most effective Spartan generals during the Peloponnesian
War, was mortally wounded while defeating the Athenians at Amphipolis in 422
BCE. Antenor (for the Trojans) and Nestor (for the Greeks) were legendary, wise
counselors during the Trojan War. On Pericles, see 215e4 note.

most vulgar satyrs. He's always going on about pack asses, or black-smiths, or cobblers, or tanners; he's always making the same tired old points in the same tired old words. If you are foolish, or simply unfa-miliar with him, you'd find it impossible not to laugh at his argu-ments. But if you see them when they open up like the statues, if you go behind their surface, you'll realize that no other arguments make any sense. They're truly worthy of a god, bursting with figures of virtue inside. They're of great—no, of the greatest—importance for anyone who wants to become a truly good man.

Well, gentlemen, this is my praise of Socrates, though I haven't spared him my reproach, either; I told you how horribly he treated me—and not only me but also Charmides, Euthydemus,[126] and many others. He has deceived us all: he presents himself as your lover, and, before you know it, you're in love with him yourself! I warn you, Agathon, don't let him fool you! Remember our torments; be on your guard: don't wait, like the fool in the proverb, to learn your lesson from your own misfortune.[127]

Alcibiades' frankness provoked a lot of laughter, especially since it was obvious that he was still in love with Socrates, who immediately said to him:

"You're perfectly sober after all, Alcibiades. Otherwise you could never have concealed your motive so gracefully: how casually you let it drop, almost like an afterthought, at the very end of your speech! As if the real point of all this has not been simply to make trouble be-tween Agathon and me! You think that I should be in love with you and no one else, while you, and no one else, should be in love with Agathon—well, we were *not* deceived; we've seen through your little satyr play. Agathon, my friend, don't let him get away with it: let no one come between us!"

Agathon said to Socrates:

"I'm beginning to think you're right; isn't it proof of that that he literally came between us here on the couch? Why would he do this

---

[126] Charmides was Plato's uncle, a member of Socrates' circle, and a supporter of the oligarchic Thirty Tyrants, who briefly controlled Athens in 404 BCE. He was killed in 303 fighting the counterrevolutionary democrats. Euthydemus (not to be confused with the sophist of the same name) is unknown outside the various Platonic dialogues (including the *Republic*) in which he is mentioned.

[127] Cf. *Iliad* 17.32.

if he weren't set on separating us? But he won't get away with it; I'm coming right over to lie down next to you."

5 "Wonderful," Socrates said. "Come here, on my other side."

"My god!" cried Alcibiades. "How I suffer in his hands! He kicks me when I'm down; he never lets me go. Come, don't be selfish, Socrates; at least, let's compromise: let Agathon lie down between us."

10 "Why, that's impossible," Socrates said. "You have already delivered your praise of me, and now it's my turn to praise whoever's on my right. But if Agathon were next to you, he'd have to praise me all over again instead of having me speak in his honor, as I very much

223a want to do in any case. Don't be jealous; let me praise the boy."

"Oh, marvelous," Agathon cried. "Alcibiades, nothing can make me stay next to you now. I'm moving no matter what. I simply *must*

5 hear what Socrates has to say about me."

"There we go again," said Alcibiades. "It's the same old story: when Socrates is around, nobody else can get close to a good-looking man. Look how smoothly and plausibly he found a reason for Agathon to lie down next to him!"

222b And then, all of a sudden, while Agathon was changing places, a large drunken group, finding the gates open because someone was just leaving, walked into the room and joined the party. There was noise

5 everywhere, and everyone was made to start drinking again in no particular order.

At that point, Aristodemus said, Eryximachus, Phaedrus, and some others among the original guests made their excuses and left. He himself fell asleep and slept for a long time (it was winter, and the nights

223c were quite long). He woke up just as dawn was about to break; the roosters were crowing already. He saw that the others had either left or were asleep on their couches, and that only Agathon, Aristophanes, and Socrates were still awake, drinking out of a large cup which they

5 were passing around from left to right. Socrates was talking to them. Aristodemus couldn't remember exactly what they were saying—he'd

223d missed the first part of their discussion, and he was half asleep anyway—but the main point was that Socrates was trying to prove to them that authors should be able to write both comedy and tragedy:

5 the skillful tragic dramatist should also be a comic poet. He was about to clinch his argument, though, to tell the truth, sleepy as they were, they were hardly able to follow his reasoning. In fact, Aristophanes fell asleep in the middle of the discussion, and very soon thereafter, as day

5 was breaking, Agathon also drifted off.

But after getting them off to sleep, Socrates got up and left, and Aristodemus followed him, as always. He said that Socrates went directly to the Lyceum,[128] washed up, spent the rest of the day just as he always did, and only then, as evening was falling, went home to rest.

10

---

[128] See *Lysis* 203a note.

PHAEDRUS

227a

SOCRATES: Phaedrus,[1] my friend! Where have you been? And where are you going?

PHAEDRUS: I was with Lysias, the son of Cephalus,[2] Socrates, and I am going for a walk outside the city walls because I was with him for a long time, sitting there the whole morning. You see, I'm keeping in mind the advice of our mutual friend Acumenus,[3] who says it's more refreshing to walk along country roads than city streets.

5

277b

SOCRATES: He is quite right, too, my friend. So Lysias, I take it, is in the city?

PHAEDRUS: Yes, at the house of Epicrates,[4] which used to belong to Morychus,[5] near the temple of the Olympian Zeus.

5

SOCRATES: What were you doing there? Oh, I know: Lysias must have been entertaining you with a feast of eloquence.

PHAEDRUS: You'll hear about it, if you are free to come along and listen.

SOCRATES: What? Don't you think I would consider it "more important than the most pressing engagement," as Pindar says, to hear how you and Lysias spent your time?[6]

10

227c

PHAEDRUS: Lead the way, then.

Translated by Alexander Nehamas and Paul Woodruff

[1] See *Symposium* 176c2 note.

[2] Lysias of Thurii and Athens (459–c. 380 BCE), a well-known orator and writer of legal speeches. His brother, Polemarchus, and father, Cephalus, appear in the *Republic*.

[3] A relative of the doctor Eryximachus, who speaks in the *Symposium*, and a doctor himself (*Protagoras* 315c).

[4] Epicrates of Cephisia (born in the 440s and active through 390 BCE), rhetorician and politician.

[5] Mentioned several times by Aristophanes (see *Symposium* 176b2 note) for his luxurious way of life.

[6] Pindar of Cynoscephalae (518–438 BCE) was a lyric poet from Boeotia, most famous for his poems celebrating the victors in the Olympian and other games. Plato is adapting his *Isthmian* 1.2.

SOCRATES: If only you will tell me.

PHAEDRUS: In fact, Socrates, you're just the right person to hear the speech that occupied us, since, in a roundabout way, it was about love. It is aimed at seducing a beautiful boy, but the speaker is not in love with him—this is actually what is so clever and elegant about it: Lysias argues that it is better to give your favors to someone who does not love you than to someone who does.

SOCRATES: What a wonderful man! I wish he would write that you should give your favors to a poor rather than to a rich man, to an older rather than to a younger one—that is, to someone like me and most other people: then his speeches would be really sophisticated, and they'd contribute to the public good besides! In any case, I am so eager to hear it that I would follow you even if you were walking all the way to Megara, as Herodicus[7] recommends, to touch the wall and come back again.

PHAEDRUS: What on earth do you mean, Socrates? Do you think that a mere dilettante like me could recite from memory in a manner worthy of him a speech that Lysias, the best of our writers, took such time and trouble to compose? Far from it—though actually I would rather be able to do that than come into a large fortune!

SOCRATES: Oh, Phaedrus, if I don't know my Phaedrus I must be forgetting who I am myself—and neither is the case. I know very well that he did not hear Lysias' speech only once: he asked him to repeat it over and over again, and Lysias was eager to oblige. But not even that was enough for him. In the end, he took the book himself and pored over the parts he liked best. He sat reading all morning long, and when he got tired, he went for a walk, having learned—I am quite sure—the whole speech by heart, unless it was extraordinarily long. So he started for the country, where he could practice reciting it. And running into a man who is sick with passion for hearing speeches, seeing him—just seeing him—he was filled with delight: he had found a partner for his frenzied dance, and he urged him to lead the way. But when that lover of speeches asked him to recite it, he played coy and pretended that he did not want to. In the end, of course, he was going to recite it even if he had to force an unwilling

---

[7] A medical expert. Socrates criticizes him at *Republic* 406a–b.

audience to listen. So, please, Phaedrus, beg him to do it right now.
5   He'll do it soon enough anyway.

PHAEDRUS: Well, I'd better try to recite it as best I can: you'll obviously not leave me in peace until I do so one way or another.

SOCRATES: You are absolutely right.

228d   PHAEDRUS: That's what I'll do, then. But, Socrates, it really is true that I did not memorize the speech word for word; instead, I will give a careful summary of its general sense, listing all the ways he said the
5   lover differs from the non-lover, in the proper order.

SOCRATES: Only if you first show me what you are holding in your left hand under your cloak, my friend. I strongly suspect you have the speech itself. And if I'm right, you can be sure that, though
228e   I love you dearly, I'll never, as long as Lysias himself is present, allow you to practice your own speechmaking on me. Come on, then, show me.

PHAEDRUS: Enough, enough. You've dashed my hopes of using you as my training partner, Socrates. All right, where do you want to
5   sit while we read?

229a   SOCRATES: Let's leave the path here and walk along the Ilisus; then we can sit quietly wherever we find the right spot.

PHAEDRUS: How lucky, then, that I am barefoot today—you, of course, are always so. The easiest thing to do is to walk right in the stream; this way, we'll also get our feet wet, which is very pleasant, es-
5   pecially at this hour and season.

SOCRATES: Lead the way, then, and find us a place to sit.

PHAEDRUS: Do you see that very tall plane tree?[8]

SOCRATES: Of course.

229b   PHAEDRUS: It's shady, with a light breeze; we can sit or, if we prefer, lie down on the grass there.

SOCRATES: Lead on, then.

---

[8] *Platanos*: A European sycamore or buttonwood tree. Perhaps a pun on "Plato" (*Platôn*).

PHAEDRUS: Tell me, Socrates, isn't it from somewhere near this stretch of the Ilisus that people say Boreas carried Oreithuia away?[9]

SOCRATES: So they say.

PHAEDRUS: Couldn't this be the very spot? The stream is lovely, pure and clear: just right for girls to be playing nearby.

SOCRATES: No, it is two or three hundred yards farther downstream, where one crosses to get to the district of Agra.[10] I think there is even an altar to Boreas there.

PHAEDRUS: I hadn't noticed it. But tell me, Socrates, in the name of Zeus, do you really believe that that legend is true?

SOCRATES: Actually, it would not be out of place for me to reject it, as our intellectuals do. I could then tell a clever story: I could claim that a gust of the North Wind blew her over the rocks where she was playing with Pharmaceia; and once she was killed that way people said she had been carried off by Boreas—or was it, perhaps, from the Areopagus?[11] The story is also told that she was carried away from there instead. Now, Phaedrus, such explanations are amusing enough, but they are a job for a man I cannot envy at all. He'd have to be far too ingenious and work too hard—mainly because after that he will have to go on and give a rational account of the form of the Hippocentaurs, and then of the Chimera; and a whole flood of Gorgons and Pegasuses and other monsters, in large numbers and absurd forms, will overwhelm him.[12] Anyone who does not believe in them, who wants to explain them away and make them plausible by means of some sort of rough ingenuity, will need a great deal of time.

But I have no time for such things; and the reason, my friend, is this. I am still unable, as the Delphic inscription orders, to know myself;[13]

---

[9] According to the legend, Oreithuia, daughter of the Athenian king Erechtheus, was abducted by Boreas (personification of the north wind) while she was playing along the banks of the Ilisis with her friend Pharmaceia.

[10] One of the demes of classical Athens.

[11] "The Hill of Ares (god of war)," located northwest of the Acropolis in Athens; it was, from very ancient times, the seat of a civic council, also called the Areopagus.

[12] A Hippocentaur was half man, half horse; the Chimera had a lion's head, a goat's body, and a serpent's tail; a Gorgon was a woman with snakes for hair; Pegasus was a winged horse.

[13] *Gnôthi sauton*: inscribed in the temple of Apollo at Delphi. See *Alcibiades* 124a8–9.

and it really seems to me ridiculous to look into other things before I
230a have understood that. This is why I do not concern myself with them.
I accept what is generally believed, and, as I was just saying, I look not
into them but into my own self:[14] Am I a beast more complicated and
savage than Typhon,[15] or am I a tamer, simpler animal with a share in
5 a divine and gentle nature? But look, my friend—while we were talking, haven't we reached the tree you were taking us to?

230b PHAEDRUS: That's the one.

SOCRATES: By Hera,[16] it really is a beautiful resting place. The plane
tree is tall and very broad; the chaste-tree,[17] high as it is, is wonderfully shady, and since it is in full bloom, the whole place is filled with
5 its fragrance. From under the plane tree the loveliest spring runs with
very cool water—our feet can testify to that. The place appears to be
dedicated to Achelous and some of the Nymphs, if we can judge
from the statues and votive offerings.[18] Feel the freshness of the air;
230c how pretty and pleasant it is; how it echoes with the summery, sweet
song of the cicadas' chorus! The most exquisite thing of all, of
course, is the grassy slope: it rises so gently that you can rest your
head perfectly when you lie down on it. You've really been the most
5 marvelous guide, my dear Phaedrus.

PHAEDRUS: And you, my remarkable friend, appear to be totally
out of place. Really, just as you say, you seem to need a guide, not to
230d be one of the locals. Not only do you never travel abroad—as far as I
can tell, you never even set foot beyond the city walls.

SOCRATES: Forgive me, my friend. I am devoted to learning;
landscapes and trees have nothing to teach me—only the people in
5 the city can do that. But you, I think, have found a potion[19] to charm
me into leaving. For just as people lead hungry animals forward by

---

[14] See *Apology* 38a.

[15] A fabulous, multiform beast with a hundred heads resembling many different
animal species. See Hesiod, *Theogony* 820ff; Plato, *Republic* 588c ff.

[16] Wife of Zeus, queen of the Greek pantheon, guardian of marriage.

[17] *Agnos*: A tall tree rather like a willow. It is associated with chastity because *hag-
nos* means "chaste."

[18] Achelous was a river god. Nymphs were benevolent, female deities particularly
associated with streams, woods, and mountains.

[19] *Pharmakon*: A medicinal drug, a poison, or a magical potion. Cf. 274e6, 275a5.

shaking branches of fruit before them, you can lead me all over Attica or anywhere else you like simply by waving in front of me the leaves of a book containing a speech. But now, having gotten as far as this place this time around, I intend to lie down; so choose whatever position you think will be most comfortable for you, and read on. 230e

PHAEDRUS: Listen, then:[20] 5

"You understand my situation. I've told you how good it would be for us, in my opinion, if this worked out. In any case, I don't think I should lose the chance to get what I am asking for, merely because I don't happen to be in love with you. **231a**

"A man in love will wish he had not done you any favors once his desire dies down, but the time will never come for a man who's not in love to change his mind. That is because the favors he does for you are not forced but voluntary; and he does the best that he possibly can for you, just as he would for his own business. 5

"Besides, a lover keeps his eye on the balance sheet—where his interests have suffered from love, and where he has done well; and when he adds up all the trouble he has taken, he thinks he's long since given the boy he loved a fair return. A non-lover, on the other hand, can't 231b complain about love's making him neglect his own business; he can't keep a tab on the trouble he's been through, or blame you for the quarrels he's had with his relatives. Take away all those headaches and 5 there's nothing left for him to do but put his heart into whatever he thinks will give pleasure.

"Besides, suppose a lover does deserve to be honored because, as 231c they say, he is the best friend his loved one will ever have, and he stands ready to please his boy with all those words and deeds that are so annoying to everyone else. It's easy to see (if he is telling the truth) that the next time he falls in love he will care more for his new love than for the old one, and it's clear he'll treat the old one shabbily 5 whenever that will please the new one.

"And anyway, what sense does it make to throw away something like that on a person who has fallen into such a miserable condition 231d that those who have suffered it don't even try to defend themselves against it? A lover will admit that he's more sick than sound in the head. He's well aware that he is not thinking straight; but he'll say he

---

[20] Scholars are divided on the question of whether this a genuine speech by Lysias or a Platonic parody.

can't get himself under control. So when he does start thinking straight, why would he stand by decisions he had made when he was sick?

"Another point: if you were to choose the best of those who are in love with you, you'd have a pretty small group to pick from; but you'll have a large group if you don't care whether he loves you or not and just pick the one who suits you best; and in that larger pool you'll have a much better hope of finding someone who deserves your friendship.

"Now suppose you're afraid of conventional standards and the stigma that will come to you if people find out about this. Well, it stands to reason that a lover—thinking that everyone else will admire him for his success as much as he admires himself—will fly into words and proudly declare to all and sundry that his labors were not in vain. Someone who does not love you, on the other hand, can control himself and will choose to do what is best, rather than seek the glory that comes from popular reputation.

"Besides, it's inevitable that a lover will be found out: many people will see that he devotes his life to following the boy he loves. The result is that whenever people see you talking with him they'll think you are spending time together just before or just after giving way to desire. But they won't even begin to find fault with people for spending time together if they are not lovers; they know one has to talk to someone, either out of friendship or to obtain some other pleasure.

"Another point: have you been alarmed by the thought that it is hard for friendships to last? Or that when people break up, it's ordinarily just as awful for one side as it is for the other, but when you've given up what is most important to you already, then your loss is greater than his? If so, it would make more sense for you to be afraid of lovers. For a lover is easily annoyed, and whatever happens, he'll think it was designed to hurt him. That is why a lover prevents the boy he loves from spending time with other people. He's afraid that wealthy men will outshine him with their money, while men of education will turn out to have the advantage of greater intelligence. And he watches like a hawk everyone who may have any other advantage over him! Once he's persuaded you to turn those people away, he'll have you completely isolated from friends; and if you show more sense than he does in looking after your own interests, you'll come to quarrel with him.

"But if a man really does not love you, if it is only because of his excellence that he got what he asked for, then he won't be jealous of

the people who spend time with you. Quite the contrary! He'll hate
anyone who does not want to be with you; he'll think they look down
on him while those who spend time with you do him good; so you
should expect friendship, rather than enmity, to result from this affair.

"Another point: lovers generally start to desire your body before
they know your character or have any experience of your other traits,
with the result that even they can't tell whether they'll still want to be
friends with you after their desire has passed. Non-lovers, on the
other hand, are friends with you even before they achieve their goal,
and you've no reason to expect that benefits received will ever detract
from their friendship for you. No, those things will stand as reminders
of more to come.

"Another point: you can expect to become a better person if you
are won over by me, rather than by a lover. A lover will praise what
you say and what you do far beyond what is best, partly because he is
afraid of being disliked, and partly because desire has impaired his
judgment. Here is how love draws conclusions: When a lover suffers a
reverse that would cause no pain to anyone else, love makes him think
he's accursed! And when he has a stroke of luck that's not worth a
moment's pleasure, love compels him to sing its praises. The result is,
you should feel sorry for lovers, not admire them.

"If my argument wins you over, I will, first of all, give you my
time with no thought of immediate pleasure; I will plan instead for
the benefits that are to come, since I am master of myself and have not
been overwhelmed by love. Small problems will not make me very
hostile, and big ones will make me only gradually, and only a little,
angry. I will forgive you for unintentional errors and do my best to
keep you from going wrong intentionally. All this, you see, is the
proof of a friendship that will last a long time.

"Have you been thinking that there can be no strong friendship in
the absence of erotic love? Then you ought to remember that we
would not care so much about our children if that were so, nor about
our fathers and mothers. And we wouldn't have had any trustworthy
friends, since those relationships did not come from such a desire but
from doing quite different things.

"Besides, if it were true that we ought to give the biggest favor to
those who need it most, then we should all be helping out the very
poorest people, not the best ones, because people we've saved from the
worst troubles will give us the most thanks. For instance, the right
people to invite to a dinner party would be beggars and people who

232e

233a

233b

233c

233d

233e

need to sate their hunger, because they're the ones who'll be fond of us,
follow us, knock on our doors, take the most pleasure with the deepest
5   gratitude, and pray for our success. No, it's proper, I suppose, to grant
your favors to those who are best able to return them, not to those in
the direst need—that is, not to those who merely desire the thing, but
234a   to those who really deserve it—not to people who will take pleasure in
the bloom of your youth, but to those who will share their goods with
you when you are older; not to people who achieve their goal and then
boast about it in public, but to those who will keep a modest silence
5   with everyone; not to people whose devotion is short-lived, but to
those who will be steady friends their whole lives; not to the people
who look for an excuse to quarrel as soon as their desire has passed, but
to those who will prove their worth when the bloom of your youth has
234b   faded. Now, remember what I said and keep this in mind: friends often
criticize a lover for bad behavior; but no one close to a non-lover ever
5   thinks that desire has led him into bad judgment about his interests.

"And now I suppose you'll ask me whether I'm urging you to give
your favors to everyone who is not in love with you. No. As I see it,
a lover would not ask you to give in to all your lovers either. You
234c   would not, in that case, earn as much gratitude from each recipient,
and you would not be able to keep one affair secret from the others in
the same way. But this sort of thing is not supposed to cause any
harm, and really should work to the benefit of both sides.

"Well, I think this speech is long enough. If you are still longing for
5   more, if you think I have passed over something, just ask."

How does the speech strike you, Socrates? Don't you think it's simply superb, especially in its choice of words?

234d   SOCRATES: It's a miracle, my friend; I'm in ecstasy. And it's all your
doing, Phaedrus: I was looking at you while you were reading and it
seemed to me the speech had made you radiant with delight; and
since I believe you understand these matters better than I do, I fol-
5   lowed your lead, and following you I shared your Bacchic frenzy.

PHAEDRUS: Come, Socrates, do you think you should joke about
this?

SOCRATES: Do you really think I am joking, that I am not
serious?

PHAEDRUS: You are not at all serious, Socrates. But now tell me
234e   the truth, in the name of Zeus, god of friendship: Do you think that

any other Greek could say anything more impressive or more complete on this same subject?

SOCRATES: What? Must we praise the speech even on the ground   5
that its author has said what the situation demanded, and not instead simply on the ground that he has spoken in a clear and concise manner, with a precise turn of phrase? If we must, I will have to go along for your sake, since—surely because I am so ignorant—that passed me by. I paid attention only to the speech's style. As to the other part, I   **235a**
wouldn't even think that Lysias himself could be satisfied with it. For it seemed to me, Phaedrus—unless, of course, you disagree—that he said the same things two or even three times, as if he really didn't have much to say about the subject, almost as if he just weren't very interested in it. In fact, he seemed to me to be showing off, trying to   5
demonstrate that he could say the same thing in two different ways, and say it just as well both times.

PHAEDRUS: You are absolutely wrong, Socrates. That is in fact the   **235b**
best thing about the speech: He has omitted nothing worth mentioning about the subject, so that no one will ever be able to add anything of value to complete what he has already said himself.   5

SOCRATES: You go too far: I can't agree with you about that. If, as a favor to you, I accept your view, I will stand refuted by all the wise men and women of old who have spoken or written about this subject.

PHAEDRUS: Who are these people? And where have you heard anything better than this?   **235c**

SOCRATES: I can't tell you offhand, but I'm sure I've heard better somewhere; perhaps it was the lovely Sappho or the wise Anacreon or even some writer of prose.[21] So, what's my evidence? The fact, my dear friend, that my breast is full and I feel I can make a different   5
speech, even better than Lysias'. Now I am well aware that none of

---

[21] Sappho was a lyric poet, born on the island of Lesbos in the second half of the seventh century BCE and known for her poetry about love. Anacreon, also a lyric poet, flourished in Teos the middle of the sixth century BCE. Neither praises the nonlover directly. Socrates' point may be that they do so indirectly by characterizing love in such a way that no sane person would have anything to do with someone suffering from it.

these ideas can have come from me—I know my own ignorance.[22]

235d The only other possibility, I think, is that I was filled, like an empty jar, by the words of other people streaming in through my ears, though I'm so stupid that I've even forgotten where and from whom I heard them.

PHAEDRUS: But, my dear friend, you couldn't have said a better thing! Don't bother telling me when and from whom you've heard

5 this, even if I ask you—instead, do exactly what you said: You've just promised to make another speech making more points, and better ones, without repeating a word from my book. And I promise you that, like the Nine Archons, I shall set up in return a life-sized, golden

235e statue at Delphi, not only of myself, but also of you.[23]

SOCRATES: You're a real friend, Phaedrus, good as gold, to think I'm claiming that Lysias failed in absolutely every respect and that I can make a speech that is different on every point from his. I am sure that that couldn't happen even to the worst possible author. In our

5 own case, for example, do you think that anyone could argue that one should favor the non-lover rather than the lover without praising the former for keeping his wits about him or condemning the latter for

236a losing his—points that are essential to make—and still have something left to say? I believe we must allow these points, and concede them to the speaker. In their case, we cannot praise their novelty but only their skillful arrangement; but we can praise both the arrangement

5 and the novelty of the nonessential points that are harder to think up.

PHAEDRUS: I agree with you; I think that's reasonable. This, then, is what I shall do. I will allow you to presuppose that the lover is less

236b sane than the non-lover—and if you are able to add anything of value to complete what we already have in hand, you will stand in hammered gold beside the offering of the Cypselids in Olympia.[24]

---

[22] Cf. *Apology* 24b4–5.

[23] The Archons were Athenian magistrates chosen by lot. On taking office, they swore an oath to set up a golden statue at the temple of Apollo at Delphi if they violated the laws. See Aristotle, *Constitution of Athens* 7.1.

[24] The Cypselids were rulers of Corinth during a period of great prosperity in the seventh century BCE. We do not know what offering Phaedrus has in mind; but an ornate chest in which Cypselus was said to have hidden as an infant was on display at Olympus.

SOCRATES: Oh, Phaedrus, I was only criticizing your beloved in   5
order to tease you—did you take me seriously? Do you think I'd
really try to match the product of his wisdom with a fancier speech?

PHAEDRUS: Well, as far as that goes, my friend, you've fallen into
your own trap. You have no choice but to give your speech as best   236c
you can: otherwise you will force us into trading vulgar jibes the way
they do in comedy. Don't make me say what you said: "Socrates, if I
don't know my Socrates, I must be forgetting who I am myself," or   5
"He wanted to speak, but he was being coy." Get it into your head
that we shall not leave here until you recite what you claimed to have
"in your breast." We are alone, in a deserted place, and I am younger
and stronger. From all this, "take my meaning"[25] and don't make me   236d
force you to speak when you can do so willingly.

SOCRATES: But, my dear Phaedrus, I'll be ridiculous—a mere dilettante, improvising on the same topics as a seasoned professional!   5

PHAEDRUS: Do you understand the situation? Stop playing hard to
get! I know what I can say to make you give your speech.

SOCRATES: Then please don't say it!

PHAEDRUS: Oh, yes, I will. And what I say will be an oath. I
swear to you—by which god, I wonder? How about this very plane   10
tree?—I swear in all truth that, if you don't make your speech right   236e
next to this tree here, I shall never, never again recite another speech
for you—I shall never utter another word about speeches to you!

SOCRATES: My oh my, what a horrible man you are! You've really
found the way to force a lover of speeches to do just as you say!   5

PHAEDRUS: So why are you still twisting and turning like that?

SOCRATES: I'll stop—now that you've taken this oath. How could
I possibly give up such treats?

PHAEDRUS: Speak, then.   237a

SOCRATES: Do you know what I'll do?

PHAEDRUS: What?

SOCRATES: I'll cover my head while I'm speaking. In that way, as
I'm going through the speech as fast as I can, I won't get embarrassed
by having to look at you and lose the thread of my argument.   5

---

[25] Plato attributes this phrase to Pindar (227b9 note) at *Meno* 76d.

PHAEDRUS: Just give your speech! You can do anything else you like.

SOCRATES: Come to me, O you clear-voiced Muses, whether you are called so because of the quality of your song or from the musical people of Liguria,[26] "come, take up my burden"[27] in telling the tale that this fine fellow forces upon me so that his companion may now seem to him even more clever than he did before:

There once was a boy, a youth rather, and he was very beautiful, and had very many lovers. One of them was wily and had persuaded him that he was not in love, though he loved the lad no less than the others. And once in pressing his suit to him, he tried to persuade him that he ought to give his favors to a man who did not love him rather than to one who did. And this is what he said:

"If you wish to reach a good decision on any topic, my boy, there is only one way to begin: You must know what the decision is about, or else you are bound to miss your target altogether. Ordinary people cannot see that they do not know the true nature of a particular subject, so they proceed as if they did; and because they do not work out an agreement at the start of the inquiry, they wind up as you would expect—in conflict with themselves and each other. Now you and I had better not let this happen to us, since we criticize it in others. Because you and I are about to discuss whether a boy should make friends with a man who loves him rather than with one who does not, we should agree on defining what love is and what effects it has. Then we can look back and refer to that as we try to find out whether to expect benefit or harm from love. Now, as everyone plainly knows, love is some kind of desire; but we also know that even men who are not in love have a desire for what is beautiful. So how shall we distinguish between a man who is in love and one who is not? We must realize that each of us is ruled by two principles which we follow wherever they lead: one is our inborn desire for pleasures, the other is our acquired judgment that pursues what is best. Sometimes these two are in agreement; but there are times when they quarrel inside us, and then sometimes one of them gains control, sometimes the other. Now when judgment is in control and leads us by reasoning toward what is best, that sort of self-control is called 'being in your right

---

[26] Liguria is what is now known as the French Riviera.

[27] Apparently a quotation from an unknown source.

mind';[28] but when desire takes command in us and drags us without
reasoning toward pleasure, then its command is known as 'outra-   **238a**
geousness'.[29] Now outrageousness has as many names as the forms it
can take, and these are quite diverse.[30] Whichever form stands out in
a particular case gives its name to the person who has it—and that is
not a pretty name to be called, not worth earning at all. If it is desire   5
for food that overpowers a person's reasoning about what is best and
suppresses his other desires, it is called gluttony and it gives him the   **238b**
name of a glutton, while if it is desire for drink that plays the tyrant
and leads the man in that direction, we all know what name we'll call
him then! And now it should be clear how to describe someone appropriately in the other cases: call the man by that name—sister to
these others—that derives from the sister of these desires that controls
him at the time. As for the desire that has led us to say all this, it should   5
be obvious already, but I suppose things said are always better understood than things unsaid: The unreasoning desire that overpowers a
person's considered impulse to do right and is driven to take pleasure
in beauty, its force reinforced by its kindred desires for beauty in   **238c**
human bodies—this desire, all-conquering in its forceful drive, takes
its name from the word for force (*rhômê*) and is called love (*erôs*)."

     There, Phaedrus my friend, don't you think, as I do, that I'm in the   5
grip of something divine?

     PHAEDRUS: This is certainly an unusual flow of words for you,
Socrates.

     SOCRATES: Then be quiet and listen. There's something really di-
vine about this place, so don't be surprised if I'm quite taken by the   **238d**
Nymphs' madness as I go on with the speech. I'm on the edge of
speaking in dithyrambs[31] as it is.

     PHAEDRUS: Very true!

     SOCRATES: Yes, and you're the cause of it. But hear me out; the at-   5
tack may yet be prevented. That, however, is up to the god; what we
must do is face the boy again in the speech:

---

[28] *Sôphrosunê;* also "temperance," "moderation."

[29] *Hubris.*

[30] Reading *polumeles kai polueides* with most editors.

[31] A dithyramb was a choral poem originally connected with the worship of
Dionysus (see *Symposium* 175e9 note).

"All right then, my brave friend, now we have a definition for the subject of our decision; now we have said what it really is; so let us keep that in view as we complete our discussion. What benefit or

238e   harm is likely to come from the lover or the non-lover to the boy who gives him favors? It is surely necessary that a man who is ruled by

 desire and is a slave to pleasure will turn his boy into whatever is most pleasing to himself. Now a sick man takes pleasure in anything that does not resist him, but sees anyone who is equal or superior to him

5   as an enemy. That is why a lover will not willingly put up with a

239a   boyfriend who is his equal or superior, but is always working to

 make the boy he loves weaker and inferior to himself. Now, the ignorant man is inferior to the wise one, the coward to the brave, the ineffective speaker to the trained orator, the slow-witted to the quick. By necessity, a lover will be delighted to find all these mental

5   defects and more, whether acquired or innate in his boy; and if he does not, he will have to supply them or else lose the pleasure of the moment. The necessary consequence is that he will be jealous and

239b   keep the boy away from the good company of anyone who would

 make a better man of him; and that will cause him a great deal of harm, especially if he keeps him away from what would most improve his mind—and that is, in fact, divine philosophy, from which it is necessary for a lover to keep his boy a great distance away, out of

5   fear the boy will eventually come to look down on him. He will have to invent other ways, too, of keeping the boy in total ignorance and so in total dependence on himself. That way the boy will give his lover the most pleasure, though the harm to himself will be severe. So it will not be of any use to your intellectual development to

239c   have as your mentor and companion a man who is in love.

"Now let's turn to your physical development. If a man is bound by necessity to chase pleasure at the expense of the good, what sort of shape will he want you to be in? How will he train you, if he is in

5   charge? You will see that what he wants is someone who is soft, not muscular, and not trained in full sunlight but in dappled shade— someone who has never worked out like a man, never touched hard, sweaty exercise. Instead, he goes for a boy who has known only a soft unmanly style of life, who makes himself pretty with cosmetics be-

239d   cause he has no natural color at all. There is no point in going on with this description: it is perfectly obvious what other sorts of behavior follow from this. We can take up our next topic after drawing all this to a head: the sort of body a lover wants in his boy is one that

will give confidence to the enemy in a war or other great crisis while   5
causing alarm to friends and even to his lovers. Enough of that; the
point is obvious.

"Our next topic is the benefit or harm to your possessions that will
come from a lover's care and company. Everyone knows the answer,   239e
especially a lover: His first wish will be for a boy who has lost his dearest, kindliest and godliest possessions—his mother and father and   5
other close relatives. He would be happy to see the boy deprived of
them, since he would expect them either to block him from the sweet
pleasure of the boy's company or to criticize him severely for taking   240a
it. What is more, a lover would think any money or other wealth the
boy owns would only make him harder to snare and, once snared,
harder to handle. It follows by absolute necessity that wealth in a
boyfriend will cause his lover to envy him, while his poverty will be a
delight. Furthermore, he will wish for the boy to stay wifeless, child-   5
less, and homeless for as long as possible, since that's how long he desires to go on plucking his sweet fruit.

"There are other troubles in life, of course, but some divinity has
mixed most of them with a dash of immediate pleasure. A flatterer,
for example, may be an awful beast and a dreadful nuisance, but na-   240b
ture makes flattery rather pleasant by mixing in a little culture with its
words. So it is with a mistress—for all the harm we accuse her of
causing—and with many other creatures of that character, and their
callings: at least they are delightful company for a day. But besides   5
being harmful to his boyfriend, a lover is simply disgusting to spend
the day with. 'Youth delights youth,' as the old proverb runs—   240c
because, I suppose, friendship grows from similarity, as boys of the same
age go after the same pleasures. But you can even have too much of
people your own age. Besides, as they say, it is miserable for anyone to
be forced into anything by necessity—and this (to say nothing of the
age difference) is most true for a boy with his lover. The older man   5
clings to the younger day and night, never willing to leave him, driven
by necessity and goaded on by the sting that gives him pleasure every   240d
time he sees, hears, touches, or perceives his boy in any way at all, so
that he follows him around like a servant, with pleasure.

"As for the boy, however, what comfort or pleasure will the lover
give to him during all the time they spend together? Won't it be dis-   5
gusting in the extreme to see the face of that older man who's lost his
looks? And everything that goes with that face—why, it is a misery
even to hear them mentioned, let alone actually handle them, as you

240e would constantly be forced to do! To be watched and guarded suspiciously all the time, with everyone! To hear praise of yourself that is out of place and excessive! And then to be falsely accused—which is unbearable when the man is sober and not only unbearable but posi-

5 tively shameful when he is drunk and lays into you with a pack of wild barefaced insults!

"While he is still in love he is harmful and disgusting, but after his love fades he breaks his trust with you for the future, in spite of all the promises he has made with all those oaths and entreaties which just

10 barely kept you in a relationship that was troublesome at the time, in

241a hope of future benefits. So, then, by the time he should pay up, he has made a change and installed a new ruling government in himself: right-minded reason in place of the madness of love. The boy does not even realize that his lover is a different man. He insists on his re-

5 ward for past favors and reminds him of what they had done and said before—as if he were still talking to the same man! The lover, however, is so ashamed that he does not dare tell the boy how much he has changed or that there is no way, now that he is in his right mind

241b and under control again, that he can stand by the promises he had sworn to uphold when he was under that old mindless regime. He is afraid that if he acted as he had before he would turn out the same and revert to his old self. So now he is a refugee, fleeing from those old promises on which he must default by necessity; he, the former lover, has to switch roles and flee, since the coin has fallen the other

5 way,[32] while the boy must chase after him, angry and cursing. All along he has been completely unaware that he should never have given his favors to a man who was in love—and who therefore had by necessity lost his mind. He should much rather have done it for a man who was

241c not in love and had his wits about him. Otherwise it follows necessarily that he'd be giving himself to a man who is deceitful, irritable, jealous, disgusting, harmful to his property, harmful to his physical fitness, and absolutely devastating to the cultivation of his soul, which

5 truly is, and will always be, the most valuable thing to gods and men.

"These are the points you should bear in mind, my boy. You should know that the friendship of a lover arises without any good

---

[32] In a game like tag, Plato's contemporaries tossed a shell, which could land bright side or dark side up, to decide who should chase whom.

will at all. No, like food, its purpose is to sate hunger. 'Do wolves love lambs? That's how lovers befriend a boy!' "[33]

That's it, Phaedrus. You won't hear another word from me, and you'll have to accept this as the end of the speech.

PHAEDRUS: But I thought you were right in the middle—I thought you were about to speak at the same length about the non-lover, to list his good points and argue that it's better to give one's favors to him. So why are you stopping now, Socrates?

SOCRATES: Didn't you notice, my friend, that even though I am criticizing the lover, I have passed beyond lyric into epic poetry?[34] What do you suppose will happen to me if I begin to praise his opposite? Don't you realize that the Nymphs to whom you so cleverly exposed me will take complete possession of me? So I say instead, in a word, that every shortcoming for which we blamed the lover has its contrary advantage, and the non-lover possesses it. Why make a long speech of it? That's enough about them both. This way my story will meet the end it deserves, and I will cross the river and leave before you make me do something even worse.

PHAEDRUS: Not yet, Socrates, not until this heat is over. Don't you see that it is almost exactly noon, "straight-up" as they say? Let's wait and discuss the speeches, and go as soon as it turns cooler.

SOCRATES: You're really superhuman when it comes to speeches, Phaedrus; you're truly amazing. I'm sure you've brought into being more of the speeches that have been given during your lifetime than anyone else, whether you composed them yourself or in one way or another forced others to make them; with the single exception of Simmias the Theban, you are far ahead of the rest.[35] Even as we speak, I think, you're managing to cause me to produce yet another one.

PHAEDRUS: Oh, how wonderful! But what do you mean? What speech?

SOCRATES: My friend, just as I was about to cross the river, the familiar divine sign came to me which, whenever it occurs, holds me

241d

5

241e

5

242a

5

242b

5

---

[33] Perhaps an allusion to Homer, *Iliad* 22.262–3.

[34] Epic poetry glorified its hero (previous note); lyric poets, such as Sappho and Anacreon, complained about the effects of love.

[35] Simmias is one of Socrates' two questioners in the *Phaedo*.

242c   back from something I am about to do.[36] I thought I heard a voice
coming from this very spot, forbidding me to leave until I made
atonement for some offense against the gods. In effect, you see, I am a
seer, and though I am not particularly good at it, still—like people
who are just barely able to read and write—I am good enough for my
5   own purposes. I recognize my offense clearly now. In fact, the soul
too, my friend, is itself a sort of seer; that's why, almost from the beginning of my speech, I was disturbed by a very uneasy feeling, as
242d   Ibycus puts it, that "for offending the gods I am honored by men."[37]
But now I understand exactly what my offense has been.

PHAEDRUS: Tell me, what is it?

SOCRATES: Phaedrus, that speech you carried with you here—it was
5   horrible, as horrible as the speech you made me give.

PHAEDRUS: How could that be?

SOCRATES: It was foolish, and close to being impious. What could
be more horrible than that?

PHAEDRUS: Nothing—if, of course, what you say is right.

SOCRATES: Well, then? Don't you believe that Love is the son of
Aphrodite?[38] Isn't he one of the gods?

10   PHAEDRUS: This is certainly what people say.

SOCRATES: Well, Lysias certainly doesn't and neither does your
speech, which you charmed me through your potion into delivering
242e   myself. But if Love is a god or something divine—which he is—he
can't be bad in any way;[39] and yet our speeches just now spoke of him
as if he were. That is their offense against Love. And they've com-
5   pounded it with their utter foolishness in parading their dangerous
falsehoods and preening themselves over perhaps deceiving a few silly
243a   people and coming to be admired by them.
        And so, my friend, I must purify myself. Now for those whose of-
fense lies in telling false stories about matters divine, there is an ancient rite of purification—Homer did not know it, but Stesichorus
5   did. When he lost his sight for speaking ill of Helen, he did not, like

---

[36] See *Apology* 31c–d.

[37] Sixth-century lyric poet from Regium in Southern Italy.

[38] See *Symposium* 177e note.

[39] Cf. *Symposium* 202a–204a.

Homer, remain in the dark about the reason why. On the contrary, true follower of the Muses that he was, he understood it and immediately composed these lines:

> *There's no truth to that story:*
> *You never sailed that lovely ship,*
> *You never reached the tower of Troy.*[40]

243b

And as soon as he completed the poem we call the Palinode, he immediately regained his sight. Now I will prove to be wiser than Homer and Stesichorus to this small extent: I will try to offer my Palinode to Love before I am punished for speaking ill of him—with my head bare, no longer covered in shame.

PHAEDRUS: No words could be sweeter to my ears, Socrates.

SOCRATES: You see, my dear Phaedrus, you understand how shameless the speeches were, my own as well as the one in your book. Suppose a noble and gentle man, who was (or had once been) in love with a boy of similar character, were to hear us say that lovers start serious quarrels for trivial reasons and that, jealous of their beloved, they do him harm—don't you think that man would think we had been brought up among the most vulgar of sailors, totally ignorant of love among the freeborn? Wouldn't he most certainly refuse to acknowledge the flaws we attributed to Love?

PHAEDRUS: Most probably, Socrates.

SOCRATES: Well, that man makes me feel ashamed, and as I'm also afraid of Love himself, I want to wash out the bitterness of what we've heard with a more tasteful speech. And my advice to Lysias, too, is to write as soon as possible a speech urging one to give similar favors to a lover rather than to a non-lover.

PHAEDRUS: You can be sure he will. For once you have spoken in praise of the lover, I will most definitely make Lysias write a speech on the same topic.

SOCRATES: I do believe you will, so long as you are who you are.

---

[40] Stesichorus was a lyric and dithyrambic poet of the early sixth century. In his famous Palinode, or "taking-it-back" poem, he explained away the evidence for Helen's (willing) abduction by Paris—the alleged precipitating cause of the Trojan War.

PHAEDRUS: Speak on, then, in full confidence.

SOCRATES: Where, then, is the boy to whom I was speaking? Let him hear this speech, too. Otherwise he may be too quick to give his favors to the non-lover.

PHAEDRUS: He is here, always right by your side, whenever you want him.

SOCRATES: You'll have to understand, beautiful boy, that the previous speech was by Phaedrus, Pythocles' son, from Myrrhinus, while the one I am about to deliver is by Stesichorus, Euphemus' son, from Himera.[41] And here is how the speech should go:

"'There's no truth to that story"—that when a lover is available you should give your favors to a man who doesn't love you instead, because he is in control of himself while the lover has lost his head. That would have been fine to say if madness were bad, pure and simple; but in fact the best things we have come from madness, when it is given as a gift of the god.

"The prophetess of Delphi and the priestesses at Dodona[42] are out of their minds when they perform that fine work of theirs for all of Greece, either for an individual person or for a whole city, but they accomplish little or nothing when they are in control of themselves. We will not mention the Sibyl[43] or the others who foretell many things by means of god-inspired prophetic trances and give sound guidance to many people—that would take too much time for a point that's obvious to everyone. But here's some evidence worth adding to our case: The people who designed our language in the old days never thought of madness as something to be ashamed of or worthy of blame; otherwise they would not have used the word 'manic' for the finest experts of all—the ones who tell the future—thereby weaving insanity into prophecy. They thought it was wonderful when it came as a gift of the god, and that's why they gave its name to prophecy; but nowadays people don't know the fine points, so they stick in a 't' and call it 'mantic.' Similarly, the clear-headed study of the future, which

---

[41] Etymologically: "Stesichorus, son of Good Speaker, from the Land of Desire." Myrrhinous was on of the demes of ancient Athens.

[42] The priestesses at the temple of Apollo at Delphi and of Zeus at Dodona in Epirus were thought to deliver their oracular utterance while in a divinely inspired trance.

[43] Originally the name of a single prophetess, then a generic term.

uses birds and other signs, was originally called *oionoïstic,* since it uses reasoning to bring intelligence (*nous*) and learning (*historia*) into human thought; but now modern speakers call it *oiônistic,* putting on airs with their long '*ô*'. To the extent, then, that prophecy, *mantic,* is   244d more perfect and more admirable than sign-based prediction, *oiônistic,* in both name and achievement, madness (*mania*) from a god is finer than self-control of human origin, according to the testimony of the ancient language givers.

"Next, madness can provide relief from the greatest plagues of trouble that beset certain families because of their guilt for ancient   5 crimes: it turns up among those who need a way out; it gives prophecies and takes refuge in prayers to the gods and in worship, discover-   244e ing mystic rites and purifications that bring the man it touches[44] through to safety for this and all time to come. So it is that the right sort of madness finds relief from present hardships for a man it has possessed.   245a

"Third comes the kind of madness that is possession by the Muses, which takes a tender virgin soul and awakens it to a Bacchic frenzy of songs and poetry that glorifies the achievements of the past and teaches them to future generations. If anyone comes to the gates of   5 poetry and expects to become an adequate poet by acquiring expert knowledge of the subject without the Muses' madness, he will fail, and his self-controlled verses will be eclipsed by the poetry of men who have been driven out of their minds.

"There you have some of the fine achievements—and I could tell you even more—that are due to god-sent madness. We must not have   245b any fear on this particular point, then, and we must not let anyone disturb us or frighten us with the claim that you should prefer a friend who is in control of himself to one who is disturbed. Besides proving that point, if he is to win his case, our opponent must show that love   5 is not sent by the gods as a benefit to a lover and his boy. And we, for our part, must prove the opposite, that this sort of madness is given us by the gods to ensure our greatest good fortune. It will be a proof that   245c convinces the wise if not the clever.

"Now we must first understand the truth about the nature of the soul, divine or human, by examining what it does and what is done to it. Here begins the proof: 5

---

[44] That is, a person who is mad. Reading *heautês* with the manuscripts.

"Every soul[45] is immortal. That is because whatever is always in motion is immortal, while what moves, and is moved by, something else stops living when it stops moving. So it is only what moves itself that never desists from motion, since it does not leave off being itself. In fact, this self-mover is also the source[46] and spring of motion in everything else that moves; and a source has no beginning. That is because anything that has a beginning comes from some source, but there is no source for this, since a source that got its start from something else would no longer be the source. And since it cannot have a beginning, then necessarily it cannot be destroyed. That is because if a source were destroyed it could never get started again from anything else and nothing else could get started from it—that is, if everything gets started from a source. This then is why a self-mover is a source of motion. And *that* is incapable of being destroyed or starting up; otherwise all heaven and everything that has been started up[47] would collapse, come to a stop, and never have cause to start moving again. But since we have found that a self-mover is immortal, we should have no qualms about declaring that this is the very essence and principle of a soul, for every bodily object that is moved from outside has no soul, while a body whose motion comes from within, from itself, does have a soul, that being the nature of a soul; and if this is so—that whatever moves itself is essentially a soul—then it follows necessarily that soul should have neither birth nor death.

"That, then, is enough about the soul's immortality. Now here is what we must say about its structure. To describe what the soul actually is would require a very long account, altogether a task for a god in every way; but to say what it is like is humanly possible and takes less time. So let us do the second in our speech. Let us then liken the soul to the natural union of a team of winged horses and their charioteer. The gods have horses and charioteers that are themselves all good and come from good stock besides, while everyone else has a mixture. To begin with, our driver is in charge of a pair of horses; second, one of his horses is beautiful and good and from stock of the same sort, while the other is the opposite and has the opposite sort of bloodline. This means that chariot-driving in our case is inevitably a painfully difficult business.

---

[45] Or "all soul."

[46] *Archê*: often translated by the technical expression "first principle."

[47] Reading *genesin* with Rowe and de Vries.

"And now I should try to tell you why living things are said to include both mortal and immortal beings. All soul looks after all that lacks a soul, and patrols all of heaven, taking different shapes at different times. So long as its wings are in perfect condition it flies high, and the entire universe is its dominion; but a soul that sheds its wings wanders until it lights on something solid, where it settles and takes on an earthly body, which then, owing to the power of this soul, seems to move itself. The whole combination of soul and body is called a living thing, or animal, and has the designation 'mortal' as well. Such a combination cannot be immortal, not on any reasonable account. In fact it is pure fiction, based neither on observation nor on adequate reasoning, that a god is an immortal living thing which has a body and a soul, and that these are bound together by nature for all time—but of course we must let this be as it may please the gods, and speak accordingly.

"Let us turn to what causes the shedding of the wings, what makes them fall away from a soul. It is something of this sort: By their nature wings have the power to lift up heavy things and raise them aloft where the gods all dwell, and so, more than anything that pertains to the body, they are akin to the divine, which has beauty, wisdom, goodness, and everything of that sort. These nourish the soul's wings, which grow best in their presence; but foulness and ugliness make the wings shrink and disappear.

"Now Zeus, the great commander in heaven, drives his winged chariot first in the procession, looking after everything and putting all things in order. Following him is an army of gods and spirits arranged in eleven sections.[48] Hestia[49] is the only one who remains at the home of the gods; all the rest of the twelve are lined up in formation, each god in command of the unit to which he is assigned. Inside heaven are many wonderful places from which to look and many aisles which the blessed gods take up and back, each seeing to his own work, while anyone who is able and wishes to do so follows along, since jealousy has no place in the gods' chorus. When they go to feast at the banquet

5

246c

5

246d

5

246e

5

247a

5

---

[48] The 12 principal gods were central to civic religion in classical Greece; an alter to them, placed in the marketplace in Athens (Thucydides 6.5), was considered the center of the city for the purposes of measurement (Herodotus 2.7). Plato's pupil, Eudoxus, was probably the first to assign these gods to the signs of the zodiac.

[49] Goddess of hearth and home.

247b they have a steep climb to the high tier at the rim of heaven; on this slope the gods' chariots move easily, since they are balanced and well under control, but the other chariots barely make it. The heaviness of the bad horse drags its charioteer toward the earth and weighs him down if he has failed to train it well, and this causes the most extreme

5 toil and struggle that a soul will face. But when the souls we call immortals reach the top, they move outward and take their stand on the high ridge of heaven, where its circular motion carries them around

247c as they stand while they gaze upon what is outside heaven.

"The place beyond heaven—none of our earthly poets has ever sung or ever will sing its praises enough! Still, this is the way it is— risky as it may be, you see, I must attempt to speak the truth, espe-

5 cially since the truth is my subject. What is in this place is without color and without shape and without solidity, a being that really is what it is,[50] the subject of all true knowledge, visible only to intelligence, the soul's steersman. Now a god's mind is nourished by in-

247d telligence and pure knowledge, as is the mind of any soul that is concerned to take in what is appropriate to it, and so it is delighted at last to be seeing what is real and watching what is true, feeding on all this and feeling wonderful, until the circular motion brings it around

5 to where it started. On the way around it has a view of Justice as it is; it has a view of Self-control; it has a view of Knowledge—not the knowledge that is close to change, that becomes different as it knows

247e the different things which we consider real down here. No, it is the knowledge of what really is what it is. And when the soul has seen all the things that are as they are and feasted on them, it sinks back inside heaven and goes home. On its arrival, the charioteer stables the horses

5 by the manger, throws in ambrosia, and gives them nectar to drink besides.

248a   "Now that is the life of the gods. As for the other souls, one that follows a god most closely, making itself most like that god, raises the head of its charioteer up to the place outside and is carried around in the circular motion with the others. Although distracted by the horses, this soul does have a view of Reality, just barely. Another soul

5 rises at one time and falls at another, and because its horses pull it violently in different directions, it sees some real things and misses

---

[50] *Ousia ontôs ousa*: a way of referring to Platonic, transcendent forms. See Introduction, pp. xiv–xvi.

others. The remaining souls are all eagerly straining to keep up, but are unable to rise; they are carried around below the surface, trampling and striking one another as each tries to get ahead of the others. The result is terribly noisy, very sweaty, and disorderly. Many souls are crippled by the incompetence of the drivers, and many wings break much of their plumage. After so much trouble, they all leave without having seen reality, uninitiated, and when they have gone they will depend on what they think is nourishment—their own opinions.

"The reason there is so much eagerness to see the plain where truth stands is that this pasture has the grass that is the right food for the best part of the soul, and it is the nature of the wings that lift up the soul to be nourished by it. Besides, the law of Destiny is this: If any soul becomes a companion to a god and catches sight of any true thing, it will be unharmed until the next circuit; and if it is able to do this every time, it will always be safe. If, on the other hand, it does not see anything true because it could not keep up, and by some accident takes on a burden of forgetfulness and wrongdoing, then it is weighed down, sheds its wings and falls to earth. At that point, according to the law, the soul is not born into a wild animal in its first incarnation; but a soul that has seen the most will be planted in the seed of a man who will become a lover of wisdom[51] or of beauty, or who will be cultivated in the arts and prone to erotic love. The second sort of soul will be put into someone who will be a lawful king or warlike commander; the third, a statesman, a manager of a household, or a financier; the fourth will be a trainer who loves exercise or a doctor who cures the body; the fifth will lead the life of a prophet or priest of the mysteries. To the sixth the life of a poet or some other representational artist is properly assigned; to the seventh the life of a manual laborer or farmer; to the eighth the career of a sophist or demagogue, and to the ninth a tyrant.

"Of all these, any who have led their lives with justice will change to a better fate, and any who have led theirs with injustice, to a worse one. In fact, no soul returns to the place from which it came for ten thousand years, since its wings will not grow before then, except for the soul of a man who practices philosophy without guile or who loves boys philosophically. If, after the third cycle of one thousand years, the last-mentioned souls have chosen such a life three times in a

248b

5

248c

5

248d

5

248e

5

249a

---

[51] That is, a philosopher.

row, they grow their wings back, and they depart in the three-
5 thousandth year. As for the rest, once their first life is over, they come
to judgment; and, once judged, some are condemned to go to places
of punishment beneath the earth and pay the full penalty for their injustice, while the others are lifted up by justice to a place in heaven
where they live in the manner the life they led in human form has
249b earned them. In the thousandth year both groups arrive at a choice
and allotment of second lives, and each soul chooses the life it wants.
From there, a human soul can enter a wild animal, and a soul that was
once human can move from an animal to a human being again. But a
5 soul that never saw the truth cannot take a human shape, since a
human being must understand speech in terms of general forms, proceeding to bring many perceptions together into a reasoned unity.[52]
249c That process is the recollection of the things our soul saw when it was
traveling with god, when it disregarded the things we now call real and
lifted up its head to what is truly real instead.

"For just this reason it is fair that only a philosopher's mind grows
wings, since its memory always keeps it as close as possible to those
5 realities by being close to which the gods are divine. A man who uses
reminders of these things correctly is always at the highest, most perfect level of initiation, and he is the only one who is perfect as perfect
can be. He stands outside human concerns and draws close to the di-
249d vine; ordinary people think he is disturbed and rebuke him for this,
unaware that he is possessed by god. Now this takes me to the whole
point of my discussion of the fourth kind of madness—that which
5 someone shows when he sees the beauty we have down here and is
reminded of true beauty; then he takes wing and flutters in his eagerness to rise up, but is unable to do so; and he gazes aloft, like a bird,
paying no attention to what is down below—and that is what brings
on him the charge that he has gone mad. This is the best and noblest
249e of all the forms that possession by god can take for anyone who has it
or is connected to it, and when someone who loves beautiful boys is
touched by this madness he is called a lover. As I said, nature requires
that the soul of every human being has seen reality; otherwise, no
5 soul could have entered this sort of living thing. But not every soul is
250a easily reminded of the reality there by what it finds here—not souls
that got only a brief glance at the reality there, not souls who had such

---

[52] Reading *iont'* with Badham.

bad luck when they fell down here that they were twisted by bad
company into lives of injustice so that they forgot the sacred objects
they had seen before. Only a few remain whose memory is good
enough; and they are startled when they see an image of what they   5
saw up there. Then they are beside themselves, and their experience is
beyond their comprehension because they cannot fully grasp what it
is that they are seeing.

"Justice and self-control do not shine out through their images   250b
down here, and neither do the other objects of the soul's admiration;
the senses are so murky that only a few people are able to make out,
with difficulty, the original of the likenesses they encounter here. But
beauty was radiant to see at that time when the souls, along with the   5
glorious chorus (we[53] were with Zeus, while others followed other
gods), saw that blessed and spectacular vision and were ushered into
the mystery that we may rightly call the most blessed of all. And we
who celebrated it were wholly perfect and free of all the troubles that   250c
awaited us in time to come, and we gazed in rapture at sacred revealed
objects that were perfect, and simple, and unshakeable and blissful.
That was the ultimate vision, and we saw it in pure light because we
were pure ourselves, not buried in this thing we are carrying around
now, which we call a body, locked in it like an oyster in its shell.   5

"Well, all that was for love of a memory that made me stretch out
my speech in longing for the past. Now beauty, as I said, was radiant
among the other objects; and now that we have come down here we   250d
grasp it sparkling through the clearest of our senses. Vision, of course,
is the sharpest of our bodily senses, although it does not see wisdom.
It would awaken a terribly powerful love if an image of wisdom came   5
through our sight as clearly as beauty does, and the same goes for the
other objects of inspired love. But now beauty alone has this privi-
lege, to be the most clearly visible and the most loved. Of course a
man who was initiated long ago or who has become defiled is not to   250e
be moved abruptly from here to a vision of Beauty itself when he sees
what we call beauty here; so instead of gazing at the latter reverently,
he surrenders to pleasure and sets out in the manner of a four-footed
beast, eager to make babies; and, wallowing in vice, he goes after un-   5
natural pleasure too, without a trace of fear or shame. A recent initi-   **251a**
ate, however, one who has seen much in heaven—when he sees a

---

[53] We philosophers.

godlike face or bodily form that has captured Beauty well, first he
shudders and a fear comes over him like those he felt at the earlier
time; then he gazes at him with the reverence due a god, and if he
5   weren't afraid people would think him completely mad, he'd even
sacrifice to his boy as if he were the image of a god. Once he has
looked at him, his chill gives way to sweating and a high fever, be-
251b   cause the stream of beauty that pours into him through his eyes
warms him up and waters the growth of his wings. Meanwhile, the
heat warms him and melts the places where the wings once grew,
places that were long ago closed off with hard scabs to keep the
5   sprouts from coming back; but as nourishment flows in, the feather
shafts swell and rush to grow from their roots beneath every part of
the soul (long ago, you see, the entire soul had wings). Now the
251c   whole soul seethes and throbs in this condition. Like a child whose
teeth are just starting to grow in, and its gums are all aching and itch-
ing—that is exactly how the soul feels when it begins to grow wings.
5   It swells up and aches and tingles as it grows them. But when it looks
upon the beauty of the boy and takes in the stream of particles flow-
ing into it from his beauty (that is why this is called "desire"[54]), when
it is watered and warmed by this, then all its pain subsides and is re-
placed by joy. When, however, it is separated from the boy and runs
251d   dry, then the openings of the passages in which the feathers grow are
dried shut and keep the wings from sprouting. Then the stump of
each feather is blocked in its desire and it throbs like a pulsing artery
while the feather pricks at its passageway, with the result that the
5   whole soul is stung all around, and the pain simply drives it wild—but
then, when it remembers the boy in his beauty, it recovers its joy.
From the outlandish mix of these two feelings—pain and joy—comes
anguish and helpless raving: in its madness the lover's soul cannot sleep
251e   at night or stay put by day; it rushes, yearning, wherever it expects to
see the person who has that beauty. When it does see him, it opens
the sluice-gates of desire and sets free the parts that were blocked up
before. And now that the pain and the goading have stopped, it can
5   catch its breath and once more suck in, for the moment, this sweetest
252a   of all pleasures. This it is not at all willing to give up, and no one is
more important to it than the beautiful boy. It forgets mother and

---

[54] *Himeros*: from *merê* ("particles"), *ienai* ("go"), and *rhein* ("flow"). A different
Platonic etymology is given at *Cratylus* 420a.

brothers and friends entirely and doesn't care at all if it loses its wealth through neglect. And as for proper and decorous behavior, in which it used to take pride, the soul despises the whole business. Why, it is even willing to sleep like a slave, anywhere, as near to the object of its longing as it is allowed to get! That is because in addition to its reverence for one who has such beauty, the soul has discovered that the boy is the only doctor for all that terrible pain.

"This is the experience we humans call love, you beautiful boy (I mean the one to whom I am making this speech[55]). You are so young that what the gods call it is likely to strike you as funny. Some of the successors of Homer, I believe, report two lines from the less well known poems, of which the second is quite indecent and does not scan very well. They praise love this way:

> *Yes, mortals call him powerful winged "Love";*
> *But because of his need to thrust out the wings,*
> *the gods call him "Shove."*[56]

You may believe this or not as you like. But, seriously, the cause of love is as I have said, and this is how lovers really feel.

"If the man who is taken by love used to be an attendant on Zeus, he will be able to bear the burden of this feathered force with dignity. But if it is one of Ares' troops who has fallen prisoner of love—if that is the god with whom he took the circuit—then if he has the slightest suspicion that the boy he loves has done him wrong, he turns murderous, and he is ready to make a sacrifice of himself as well as the boy.

"So it is with each of the gods: everyone spends his life honoring the god in whose chorus he danced, and emulates that god in every way he can, so long as he remains undefiled and in his first life down here. And that is how he behaves with everyone at every turn, not just with those he loves. Everyone chooses his love after his own fashion from among those who are beautiful, and then treats the boy like his very own god, building him up and adorning him as an image to honor and worship. Those who followed Zeus, for example, choose

---

[55] The boy being courted by the nonlover in the fictional example.

[56] The lines are probably Plato's invention, as the language is not consistently Homeric. The pun is on *erôs* and *pterôs* ("the winged one"). John Cooper helped with the English version presented here.

someone to love who is a Zeus himself in the nobility of his soul. So
they make sure he has a talent for phiiosophy and the guidance of
others, and once they have found him and are in love with him they
do everything to develop that talent. If any lovers have not yet em-
5   barked on this practice, then they start to learn, using any source they
can and also making progress on their own. They are well equipped
to track down their god's true nature with their own resources be-
253a   cause of their driving need to gaze at the god, and as they are in touch
with the god by memory they are inspired by him and adopt his customs and practices, so far as a human being can share a god's life. For
all of this they know they have the boy to thank, and so they love him
all the more; and if they draw their inspiration from Zeus, then, like
5   the Bacchants,[57] they pour it into the soul of the one they love in
order to help him take on as much of their own god's qualities as pos-
253b   sible. Hera's[58] followers look for a kingly character, and once they
have found him they do all the same things for him. And so it is for
followers of Apollo[59] or any other god: They take their god's path and
seek for their own a boy whose nature is like the god's; and when they
5   have got him they emulate the god, convincing the boy they love and
training him to follow their god's pattern and way of life, so far as is
possible in each case. They show no envy, no mean-spirited lack of
generosity, toward the boy, but make every possible effort to draw
253c   him into being totally like themselves and the god to whom they are
devoted. This, then, is any true lover's heart's desire: if he follows that
desire in the manner I described, this friend who has been driven mad
by love will secure a consummation[60] for the one he has befriended
5   that is as beautiful and blissful as I said—if, of course, he captures him.
Here, then, is how the captive is caught:
    "Remember how we divided each soul in three at the beginning of
our story—two parts in the form of horses and the third in that of a
253d   charioteer? Let us continue with that. One of the horses, we said, is
good, the other not; but we did not go into the details of the goodness of the good horse or the badness of the bad. Let us do that now.
The horse that is on the right, or nobler, side is upright in frame and
well jointed, with a high neck and a regal nose; his coat is white, his

---

[57] Worshippers of Dionysus, not Zeus.

[58] See 232b2 note above.

[59] See *Symposium* 190e2 note.

[60] Reading *teleutê* with Rowe. Most editors prefer *teletê* ("initiation").

eyes are black, and he is a lover of honor with modesty and self-   5
control; companion to true glory, he needs no whip, and is guided by
verbal commands alone. The other horse is a crooked great jumble of
limbs with a short bull-neck, a pug nose, black skin, and bloodshot   253e
white eyes; companion to wild boasts and indecency, he is shaggy
around the ears—deaf as a post—and just barely yields to horsewhip
and goad combined. Now when the charioteer looks love in the eye,   5
his entire soul is suffused with a sense of warmth and starts to fill with
tingles and the goading of desire. As for the horses, the one who is
obedient to the charioteer is still controlled, then as always, by its   254a
sense of shame, and so prevents itself from jumping on the boy. The
other one, however, no longer responds to the whip or the goad of
the charioteer; it leaps violently forward and does everything to ag-
gravate its yokemate and its charioteer, trying to make them go up to   5
the boy and suggest to him the pleasures of sex. At first the other two
resist, angry in their belief that they are being made to do things that
are dreadfully wrong. At last, however, when they see no end to their   254b
trouble, they are led forward, reluctantly agreeing to do as they have
been told. So they are close to him now, and they are struck by the
boy's face as if by a bolt of lightning. When the charioteer sees that
face, his memory is carried back to the real nature of Beauty, and he   5
sees it again where it stands on the sacred pedestal next to Self-
control. At the sight he is frightened, falls over backwards awestruck,
and at the same time has to pull the reins back so fiercely that both   254c
horses are set on their haunches, one falling back voluntarily with no
resistance, but the other insolent and quite unwilling. They pull back
a little further; and while one horse drenches the whole soul with
sweat out of shame and awe, the other—once it has recovered from
the pain caused by the bit and its fall—bursts into a torrent of insults   5
as soon as it has caught its breath, accusing its charioteer and yokemate of all sorts of cowardice and unmanliness for abandoning their
position and their agreement. Now once more it tries to make its unwilling partners advance, and gives in grudgingly only when they beg   254d
it to wait till later. Then, when the promised time arrives, and they
are pretending to have forgotten, it reminds them; it struggles, it
neighs, it pulls them forward and forces them to approach the boy
again with the same proposition; and as soon as they are near, it drops   5
its head, straightens its tail, bites the bit, and pulls without any shame
at all. The charioteer is now struck with the same feelings as before,
only worse, and he's falling back as he would from a starting gate; and   254e

he violently yanks the bit back out of the teeth of the insolent horse, only harder this time, so that he bloodies its foul-speaking tongue and jaws, sets its legs and haunches firmly on the ground, and 'gives it over
5   to pain.'[61] When the bad horse has suffered this same thing time after time, it stops being so insolent; now it is humble enough to follow the charioteer's warnings, and when it sees the beautiful boy it dies of fright, with the result that now at last the lover's soul follows its boy in reverence and awe.

255a   "And because he is served with all the attentions due a god by a lover who is not pretending otherwise but is truly in the throes of love, and because he is by nature disposed to be a friend of the man who is serving him (even if he has already been set against love by school friends or others who say that it is shameful to associate with a
5   lover, and initially rejects the lover in consequence), as time goes forward he is brought by his ripening age and a sense of what must be to a point where he lets the man spend time with him. It is a decree of
255b fate, you see, that bad is never friends with bad, while good cannot fail to be friends with good. Now that he allows his lover to talk and spend time with him, and the man's good will is close at hand, the boy is amazed by it as he realizes that all the friendship he has from his
5   other friends and relatives put together is nothing compared to that of this friend who is inspired by a god.

"After the lover has spent some time doing this, staying near the boy (and even touching him during sports and on other occasions),
255c then the spring that feeds the stream Zeus named 'Desire' when he was in love with Ganymede begins to flow mightily in the lover and is partly absorbed by him, and when he is filled it overflows and runs away outside him. Think how a breeze or an echo bounces back from
5   a smooth solid object to its source; that is how the stream of beauty goes back to the beautiful boy and sets him aflutter. It enters through his eyes, which are its natural route to the soul; there it waters the pas-
255d sages for the wings, starts the wings growing, and fills the soul of the loved one with love in return. Then the boy is in love, but has no idea what he loves. He does not understand, and cannot explain, what has happened to him. It is as if he had caught an eye disease from some-
5   one else, but could not identify the cause; he does not realize that he is seeing himself in the lover as in a mirror. So when the lover is near,

---

[61] Cf. *Iliad* 5.397 and *Odyssey* 17.567.

the boy's pain is relieved just as the lover's is, and when they are apart
he yearns as much as he is yearned for, because he has a mirror image
of love in him—'backlove'—though he neither speaks nor thinks of it
as love, but as friendship. Still, his desire is nearly the same as the   255e
lover's, though weaker: he wants to see, touch, kiss, and lie down with
him; and of course, as you might expect, he acts on these desires soon
after they occur.

"When they are in bed, the lover's undisciplined horse has a word   5
to say to the charioteer—that after all its sufferings it is entitled to a
little fun. Meanwhile, the boy's bad horse has nothing to say, but   256a
swelling with desire, confused, it hugs the lover and kisses him in delight at his great good will. And whenever they are lying together it is
completely unable, for its own part, to deny the lover any favor he
might beg to have. Its yokemate, however, along with its charioteer,   5
resists such requests with modesty and reason. Now if the victory
goes to the better elements in both their minds, which lead them to
follow the assigned regimen of philosophy, their life here below is one
of bliss and shared understanding. They are modest and fully in con-   256b
trol of themselves now that they have enslaved the part that brought
trouble into the soul and set free the part that gave it virtue. After
death, when they have grown wings and become weightless, they
have won the first of three rounds in these, the true Olympic Con-
tests. There is no greater good than this that either human self-control   5
or divine madness can offer a man. If, on the other hand, they adopt a
lower way of living, with ambition in place of philosophy, then pretty
soon when they are careless because they have been drinking or for   256c
some other reason, the pair's undisciplined horses will catch their souls
off guard and together bring them to commit that act which ordinary
people would take to be the happiest choice of all; and when they
have consummated it once, they go on doing this for the rest of their
lives, but sparingly, since they have not approved of what they are   5
doing with their whole minds. So these two also live in mutual
friendship (though weaker than that of the philosophical pair), both
while they are in love and after they have passed beyond it, because   256d
they realize they have exchanged such firm vows that it would be for-
bidden for them ever to break them and become enemies. In death
they are wingless when they leave the body, but their wings are bursting to sprout, so the prize they have won from the madness of love is
considerable, because those who have begun the sacred journey in   5
lower heaven may not by law be sent into darkness for the journey

256e under the earth; their lives are bright and happy as they travel to-gether, and thanks to their love they will grow wings together when the time comes.

"These are the rewards you will have from a lover's friendship, my boy, and they are as great as divine gifts should be. A non-lover's com-panionship, on the other hand, is diluted by human self-control; all it 5 pays are cheap, human dividends, and though the slavish attitude it engenders in a friend's soul is widely praised as virtue, it tosses the 257a soul around for nine thousand years on the earth and leads it, mind-less, beneath it.

"So now, dear Love, this is the best and most beautiful palinode[62] we could offer as payment for our debt, especially in view of the 5 rather poetical choice of words Phaedrus made me use.[63] Forgive us our earlier speeches in return for this one; be kind and gracious to-ward my expertise at love, which is your own gift to me: do not, out of anger, take it away or disable it; and grant that I may be held in higher esteem than ever by those who are beautiful. If Phaedrus and I 257b said anything that shocked you in our earlier speech, blame it on Lysias, who was its father, and put a stop to his making speeches of this sort; convert him to philosophy like his brother Polemarchus[64] so that his lover here may no longer play both sides as he does now, but 5 simply devote his life to Love through philosophical discussions."

PHAEDRUS: I join you in your prayer, Socrates. If this is really 257c best for us, may it come to pass. As to your speech, I admired it from the moment you began: You managed it much better than your first one. I'm afraid that Lysias' effort to match it is bound to fall flat, if of course he even dares to try to offer a speech of his own. In fact, my marvelous friend, a politician I know was only recently taking Lysias 5 to task for just that reason: All through his invective, he kept calling him a "speech writer." So perhaps his pride will keep him from writ-ing this speech for us.

SOCRATES: Ah, what a foolish thing to say, young man. How 257d wrong you are about your friend: he can't be intimidated so easily! But perhaps you thought the man who was taking him to task meant what he said as a reproach?

---

[62] See 243b1 note.

[63] Cf. 238c.

[64] See 227a2 note.

PHAEDRUS: He certainly seemed to, Socrates. In any case, you are surely aware yourself that the most powerful and renowned politicians are ashamed to compose speeches or leave any writings behind; they are afraid that in later times they may come to be known as "sophists."[65]

SOCRATES: Phaedrus, you don't understand the expression "Pleasant Bend" it originally referred to the long bend of the Nile.[66] And, besides the bend, you also don't understand that the most ambitious politicians love speechwriting and long for their writings to survive. In fact, when they write one of their speeches, they are so pleased when people praise it that they add at the beginning a list of its admirers everywhere.

PHAEDRUS: What do you mean? I don't understand.

SOCRATES: Don't you know that the first thing politicians put in their writings[67] is the names of their admirers?

PHAEDRUS: How so?

SOCRATES: "Resolved," the author often begins, "by the Council" or "by the People" or by both, and "So-and-so said"[68]—meaning himself, the writer, with great solemnity and self-importance. Only then does he go on with what he has to say, showing off his wisdom to his admirers, often composing a very long document. Do you think there's any difference between that and a written speech?

PHAEDRUS: No, I don't.

SOCRATES: Well, then, if it remains on the books, he is delighted and leaves the stage a poet. But if it is struck down, if he fails as a speech writer and isn't considered worthy of having his work written down, he goes into deep mourning, and his friends along with him.

---

[65] See *Symposium* 177b2 note.

[66] *Glukus agkôn:* Apparently, a familiar example of something that means the opposite of what it says—though called "pleasant," it was really a long, nasty bend. Some scholars, however, take it as a term of endearment for Phaedrus, rejecting the clause referring to the Nile as a gloss added by an ancient editor.

[67] Reading *suggramatos* with most editors.

[68] This is the standard form for decisions, including legislation, made by the Athenian Assembly, but not that for political speeches. With Phaedrus' agreement, Socrates is overlooking the difference between writing a speech and drafting legislation.

PHAEDRUS: He certainly does.

SOCRATES: Clearly, then, they don't feel contempt for speechwriting; on the contrary, they are in awe of it.

PHAEDRUS: Quite so.

SOCRATES: There's this too. What of an orator or a king who acquires enough power to match Lycurgus,[69] Solon,[70] or Darius[71] as a lawgiver and acquires immortal fame as a speech writer in his city? Doesn't he think that he is equal to the gods while he is still alive? And don't those who live in later times believe just the same about him when they behold his writings?

PHAEDRUS: Very much so.

SOCRATES: Do you really believe then that any one of these people, whoever he is and however much he hates Lysias, would reproach him for being a writer?

PHAEDRUS: It certainly isn't likely in view of what you said, for he would probably be reproaching his own ambition as well.

SOCRATES: This, then, is quite clear: Writing speeches is not in itself a shameful thing.

PHAEDRUS: How could it be?

SOCRATES: It's not speaking or writing well that's shameful; what's really shameful is to engage in either of them shamefully or badly.

PHAEDRUS: That is clear.

SOCRATES: So what distinguishes good from bad writing? Do we need to ask this question of Lysias or anyone else who ever did or will write anything—whether a public or a private document, poetic verse or plain prose?

PHAEDRUS: You ask if we need to? Why else should one live, I say, if not for pleasures of this sort? Certainly not for those you cannot feel unless you are first in pain, like most of the pleasures of the body, and which for this reason we call the pleasures of slaves.

---

[69] The legendary lawgiver of Sparta.

[70] See *Symposium* 209d7 note.

[71] See *Lysis* 209d6 note.

SOCRATES: It seems we clearly have the time. Besides, I think that the cicadas, who are singing and carrying on conversations with one another in the heat of the day above our heads, are also watching us. And if they saw the two of us avoiding conversation at midday like **259a** most people, diverted by their song and, sluggish of mind, nodding off, they would have every right to laugh at us, convinced that a pair of slaves had come to their resting place to sleep like sheep gathering 5 around the spring in the afternoon. But if they see us in conversation, steadfastly navigating around them as if they were the Sirens,[72] they will be very pleased and immediately give us the gift from the gods they are able to give to mortals. **259b**

PHAEDRUS: What is this gift? I don't think I have heard of it.

SOCRATES: Everyone who loves the Muses[73] should have heard of 5 this. The story goes that the cicadas used to be human beings who lived before the birth of the Muses. When the Muses were born and song was created for the first time, some of the people of that time were so overwhelmed with the pleasure of singing that they forgot to eat or drink; so they died without even realizing it. It is from them **259c** that the race of the cicadas came into being; and, as a gift from the Muses, they have no need of nourishment once they are born. Instead, they immediately burst into song, without food or drink, until it is time for them to die. After they die, they go to the Muses and tell 5 each one of them which mortals have honored her. To Terpsichore they report those who have honored her by their devotion to the dance and thus make them dearer to her. To Erato, they report those **259d** who honored her by dedicating themselves to the affairs of love, and so too with the other Muses, according to the activity that honors each. And to Calliope, the oldest among them, and Urania, the next after her, who preside over the heavens and all discourse, human and divine, and sing with the sweetest voice, they report those who honor their special kind of music by leading a philosophical life. 5

There are many reasons, then, why we should talk and not waste our afternoon in sleep.

---

[72] See *Symposium* 216a7 note.

[73] Although they were usually referred to collectively in this period, each of the Muses was assigned as a sort of patron saint to one of the arts—Terpsichore to dance, Erato to lyric poetry, Urania to astronomy, Calliope (eventually) to epic poetry.

PHAEDRUS: By all means, let's talk.

SOCRATES: Well, then, we ought to examine the topic we proposed just now: When is a speech well written and delivered, and when is it not?

PHAEDRUS: Plainly.

SOCRATES: Won't someone who is to speak well and nobly have to have in mind the truth about the subject he is going to discuss?

PHAEDRUS: What I have actually heard about this, Socrates, my friend, is that it is not necessary for the intending orator to learn what is really just, but only what will seem just to the crowd who will act as judges. Nor again what is really good or noble, but only what will seem so. For that is what persuasion proceeds from, not truth.

SOCRATES: Anything that wise men say, Phaedrus, "is not lightly to be cast aside";[74] we must consider whether it might be right. And what you just said, in particular, must not be dismissed.

PHAEDRUS: You're right.

SOCRATES: Let's look at it this way, then.

PHAEDRUS: How?

SOCRATES: Suppose I were trying to convince you that you should fight your enemies on horseback, and neither one of us knew what a horse is, but I happened to know this much about you, that Phaedrus believes a horse is the tame animal with the longest ears—

PHAEDRUS: But that would be ridiculous, Socrates.

SOCRATES: Not quite yet, actually. But if I were seriously trying to convince you, having composed a speech in praise of the donkey in which I called it a horse and claimed that having such an animal is of immense value both at home and in military service, that it is good for fighting and for carrying your baggage and that it is useful for much else besides—

PHAEDRUS: Well, that would be totally ridiculous.

SOCRATES: Well, which is better? To be ridiculous and a friend? Or clever and an enemy?

PHAEDRUS: The former.

---

[74] Homer, *Iliad* 2.361.

SOCRATES: And so, when a rhetorician who does not know good from bad addresses a city which knows no better and attempts to sway it, not praising a miserable donkey as if it were a horse, but bad as if it were good, and, having studied what the people believe, persuades them to do something bad instead of good—with that as its seed, what sort of crop do you think rhetoric can harvest?

10

260d

PHAEDRUS: A crop of really poor quality.

SOCRATES: But could it be, my friend, that we have mocked the art of speaking more rudely than it deserves? For it might perhaps reply, "What bizarre nonsense! Look, I am not forcing anyone to learn how to make speeches without knowing the truth; on the contrary, my advice, for what it is worth, is to take me up only after mastering the truth. But I do make this boast: even someone who knows the truth couldn't produce conviction on the basis of a systematic art without me."

5

PHAEDRUS: Well, is that a fair reply?

260e

SOCRATES: Yes, it is—if, that is, the arguments now advancing upon rhetoric testify that it is an art. For it seems to me as if I hear certain arguments approaching and protesting that that is a lie and that rhetoric is not an art but an artless practice.[75] As the Spartan said, there is no genuine art of speaking without a grasp of truth, and there never will be.

5

PHAEDRUS: We need to hear these arguments, Socrates. Come, produce them, and examine them: What is their point? How do they make it?

261a

SOCRATES: Come to us, then, noble creatures; convince Phaedrus, him of the beautiful offspring,[76] that unless he pursues philosophy properly he will never be able to make a proper speech on any subject either. And let Phaedrus be the one to answer.

5

PHAEDRUS: Let them put their questions.

SOCRATES: Well, then, isn't the rhetorical art, taken as a whole, a way of directing the soul by means of speech, not only in the law-courts and on other public occasions but also in private? Isn't it one

---

[75] *Atechnos tribê.* Cf. *Gorgias* 462b–c.

[76] Phaedrus' offspring are philosophical speeches or discussions. Cf. 242a–b and *Symposium* 209b–e.

and the same art whether its subject is great or small, and no more to be
261b   held in esteem—if it is followed correctly—when its questions are serious than when they are trivial? Or what have you heard about all this?

PHAEDRUS: Well, certainly not what *you* have! Artful speaking and
writing is found mainly in the lawcourts; also perhaps in the Assem-
5   bly.[77] That's all I've heard.

SOCRATES: Well, have you only heard of the rhetorical treatises of
Nestor and Odysseus—those they wrote in their spare time in Troy?
Haven't you also heard of the works of Palamedes?[78]

261c   PHAEDRUS: No, by Zeus, I haven't even heard of Nestor's—unless
by Nestor you mean Gorgias,[79] and by Odysseus, Thrasymachus[80] or
Theodorus.[81]

SOCRATES: Perhaps. But let's leave these people aside. Answer this
question yourself: What do adversaries do in the lawcourts? Don't
5   they speak on opposite sides? What else can we call what they do?

PHAEDRUS: That's it, exactly.

SOCRATES: About what is just and what is unjust?

PHAEDRUS: Yes.

---

[77] Public speaking was at the center of all Greek political life (see Homer, *Iliad*
2.118–277), but it was especially prominent in Athens. Athenians prided themselves on their democratic Assembly, which could be influenced by any citizen
who could speak well, regardless of his social rank. Athenian courts consisted of
large juries of ordinary people—too many to bribe, but also too many to persuade without expert techniques of speaking. For an accused person, the ability
to speak could make the difference between life and death, a point that sophists
used to their advantage (*Gorgias* 485e–6b).

[78] Nestor and Odysseus were Homeric heroes known for their speaking ability
(*Iliad* 1.249, 3.223). Palamedes, who does not figure in Homer, was proverbial for
his cunning.

[79] See *Symposium* 198c1 note.

[80] About Thrasymachus of Chalcedon (who flourished c. 430–400 BCE), a sophist
and rhetorician of note, we know little beyond what we can infer from his appearance in Book 1 of the *Republic*. Some fragments of his writing are translated
in Michael Gargarin and Paul Woodruff, *Early Greek Political Thought from Homer
to the Sophists* (Cambridge: Cambridge University Press, 1995), pp. 254–6.

[81] Theodorus of Byzantium, otherwise largely unknown (not to be confused with
the mathematician who appears in the *Theaetetus*). But see 266e and Aristotle,
Rhetoric 3.13.5.

SOCRATES: And won't whoever does this artfully make the same thing appear to the same people sometimes just and sometimes, when he prefers, unjust?

PHAEDRUS: Of course.

SOCRATES: And when he addresses the Assembly, he will make the city approve a policy at one time as a good one, and reject it—the very same policy—as just the opposite at another.

PHAEDRUS: Right.

SOCRATES: Now, don't we know that the Eleatic Palamedes is such an artful speaker that his listeners will perceive the same things to be both similar and dissimilar, both one and many, both at rest and also in motion?[82]

PHAEDRUS: Most certainly.

SOCRATES: We can therefore find the practice of speaking on opposite sides not only in the lawcourts and in the Assembly. Rather, it seems that one single art—if, of course, it is an art in the first place—governs all speaking. By means of it one can make out as similar anything that can be so assimilated, to everything to which it can be made similar, and expose anyone who tries to hide the fact that that is what he is doing.

PHAEDRUS: What do you mean by that?

SOCRATES: I think it will become clear if we look at it this way. Where is deception most likely to occur—regarding things that differ much or things that differ little from one another?

PHAEDRUS: Regarding those that differ little.

SOCRATES: At any rate, you are more likely to escape detection, as you shift from one thing to its opposite, if you proceed in small steps rather than in large ones.

PHAEDRUS: Without a doubt.

SOCRATES: Therefore, if you are to deceive someone else and to avoid deception yourself, you must know precisely the respects in which things are similar and dissimilar to one another.

---

[82] The Eleatic Palamades is Zeno of Elea, the author of the famous paradoxes about motion (see *Parmenides* 127d–8a).

PHAEDRUS: Yes, you must.

SOCRATES: And is it really possible for someone who doesn't know what each thing truly is to detect a similarity—whether large or small—between something he doesn't know and anything else?

PHAEDRUS: That is impossible.

SOCRATES: Clearly, therefore, the state of being deceived and holding beliefs contrary to what is the case comes upon people by reason of certain similarities.

PHAEDRUS: That is how it happens.

SOCRATES: Could someone, then, who doesn't know what each thing is ever have the art to lead others little by little through similarities away from what is the case on each occasion to its opposite? Or could he escape this being done to himself?

PHAEDRUS: Never.

SOCRATES: Therefore, my friend, the art of a speaker who doesn't know the truth and chases opinions instead is likely to be a ridiculous thing—not an art at all!

PHAEDRUS: So it seems.

SOCRATES: So, shall we look for instances of what we called the artful and the artless in the speech of Lysias you carried here and in our own speeches?

PHAEDRUS: That's the best thing to do—because, as it is, we are talking quite abstractly, without enough examples.

SOCRATES: In fact, by some chance the two speeches do, as it seems, contain an example of the way in which someone who knows the truth can toy with his audience and mislead them. For my part, Phaedrus, I hold the local gods responsible for this—also, perhaps, the messengers of the Muses who are singing over our heads may have inspired me with this gift: certainly I don't possess any art of speaking.

PHAEDRUS: Fine, fine. But explain what you mean.

SOCRATES: Come, then—read me the beginning of Lysias' speech.

PHAEDRUS: "You understand my situation: I've told you how good it would be for us, in my opinion, if we could work this out. In any case, I don't think I should lose the chance to get what I am asking for, merely because I don't happen to be in love with you. A man in love will wish he had not done you any favors—"

SOCRATES: Stop. Our task is to say how he fails and writes artlessly.   5
Right?

PHAEDRUS: Yes.   **263a**

SOCRATES: Now isn't this much absolutely clear: We are in accord
with one another about some of the things we discourse about and in
discord about others?

PHAEDRUS: I think I understand what you are saying; but, please,
can you make it a little clearer?   5

SOCRATES: When someone utters the word "iron" or "silver,"
don't we all think of the same thing?

PHAEDRUS: Certainly.

SOCRATES: But what happens when we say "just" or "good"?
Doesn't each one of us go in a different direction? Don't we differ
with one another and even with ourselves?   10

PHAEDRUS: We certainly do.

SOCRATES: Therefore, we agree about the former and disagree
about the latter.   263b

PHAEDRUS: Right.

SOCRATES: Now in which of these two cases are we more easily
deceived? And when does rhetoric have greater power?

PHAEDRUS: Clearly, when we wander in different directions.   5

SOCRATES: It follows that whoever wants to acquire the art of rhetoric must first make a systematic division and grasp the particular character of each of these two kinds of thing, both the kind where most
people wander in different directions and the kind where they do not.

PHAEDRUS: What a splendid thing, Socrates, he will have under-
stood if he grasps *that!*   263c

SOCRATES: Second, I think, he must not be mistaken about his
subject; he must have a sharp eye for the class to which whatever he is
about to discuss belongs.   5

PHAEDRUS: Of course.

SOCRATES: Well, now, what shall we say about love? Does it belong
to the class where people differ or to that where they don't?

PHAEDRUS: Oh, surely the class where they differ. Otherwise, do
you think you could have spoken of it as you did a few minutes ago,

10   first saying that it is harmful both to lover and beloved and then immediately afterward that it is the greatest good?

263d   SOCRATES: Very well put. But now tell me this—I can't remember
at all because I was completely possessed by the gods: Did I define
love at the beginning of my speech?

PHAEDRUS: Oh, absolutely, by Zeus, you most certainly did.

SOCRATES: Alas, how much more artful with speeches the
5   Nymphs, daughters of Achelous,[83] and Pan, son of Hermes,[84] are, according to what you say, than Lysias, son of Cephalus![85] Or am I
wrong? Did Lysias too, at the start of his love-speech, compel us to
assume that love is the single thing that he himself wanted it to be?
Did he then complete his speech by arranging everything in relation
263e   to that? Will you read its opening once again?

PHAEDRUS: If you like. But what you are looking for is not there.

5   SOCRATES: Read it, so that I can hear it in his own words.

PHAEDRUS: "You understand my situation: I've told you how
good it would be for us, in my opinion, if we could work this out. In
any case, I don't think I should lose the chance to get what I am ask-
264a   ing for, merely because I don't happen to be in love with you. A man
in love will wish he had not done you any favors, once his desire dies
down—"

SOCRATES: He certainly seems a long way from doing what we
wanted. He doesn't even start from the beginning but from the end,
5   making his speech swim upstream on its back. His first words are what
a lover would say to his boy as he was concluding his speech. Am I
wrong, Phaedrus, dear heart?

264b   PHAEDRUS: Well, Socrates, that was the end for which he gave the
speech!

SOCRATES: And what about the rest? Don't the parts of the speech
appear to have been thrown together at random? Is it evident that the

---

[83] See 230b7 note.

[84] Pan was a god, half man and half goat, associated with the pastoral world, and
with the Nymphs. Hermes, the son of Zeus and the nymph Maia, is, above all,
the messenger god, who carries out the orders of Zeus.

[85] See 227a2 note.

second point had to be made second for some compelling reason? Is that so for any of the parts? I at least—of course I know nothing   5
about such matters—thought the author said just whatever came to mind next, though not without a certain noble willfulness. But you, do you know any principle of speech-composition compelling him to place these things one after another in this order?

PHAEDRUS: It's very generous of you to think that I can understand his reasons so clearly.   264c

SOCRATES: But surely you will admit at least this much: Every speech must be put together like a living creature, with a body of its own; it must be neither without head nor without legs; and it must have a middle and extremities that are fitting both to one another and to the whole work.   5

PHAEDRUS: How could it be otherwise?

SOCRATES: But look at your friend's speech: Is it like that or is it otherwise? Actually, you'll find that it's just like the epigram people say is inscribed on the tomb of Midas the Phrygian.[86]

PHAEDRUS: What epigram is that? And what's the matter with it?   264d

SOCRATES: It goes like this:

> A maid of bronze am I, on Midas' tomb I lie
> As long as water flows, and trees grow tall
> Shielding the grave where many come to cry   5
> That Midas rests here I say to one and all.

I'm sure you notice that it makes no difference at all which of its verses comes first, and which last.   264e

PHAEDRUS: You are making fun of our speech, Socrates.

SOCRATES: Well, then, if that upsets you, let's leave that speech aside—even though I think it has plenty of very useful examples, pro-   5
vided one tries to emulate them as little as possible—and turn to the others. I think it is important for students of speechmaking to pay attention to one of their features.

PHAEDRUS: What do you mean?   **265a**

---

[86] Legendary eighth-century BCE king of Phrygia, famous for his golden touch.

SOCRATES: They were in a way opposite to one another. One claimed that one should give one's favors to the lover; the other, to the non-lover.

PHAEDRUS: Most manfully, too.

SOCRATES: I thought you were going to say "madly," which would have been the truth, and is also just what I was looking for: We did say, didn't we, that love is a kind of madness?

PHAEDRUS: Yes.

265b   SOCRATES: And that there are two kinds of madness, one produced by human illness, the other by a divinely inspired release from normally accepted behavior?

PHAEDRUS: Certainly.

SOCRATES: We also distinguished four parts within the divine kind and connected them to four gods. Having attributed the inspiration of the prophet to Apollo, of the mystic to Dionysus, of the poet to the Muses, and the fourth part of madness to Aphrodite and to Love, we said that the madness of love is the best. We used a certain sort of image to describe love's passion; perhaps it had a measure of truth in it, though it may also have led us astray. And having whipped up a not altogether implausible speech, we sang playfully, but also appropri-
265c   ately and respectfully, a storylike hymn to my master and yours, Phaedrus—to Love, who watches over beautiful boys.

PHAEDRUS: And I listened to it with the greatest pleasure.

SOCRATES: Let's take up this point about it right away: How was the speech able to proceed from censure to praise?

PHAEDRUS: What exactly do you mean by that?

SOCRATES: Well, everything else in it really does appear to me to have been spoken in play. But part of it was given with Fortune's guidance, and there were in it two kinds of things the nature of which
265d   it would be quite wonderful to grasp by means of a systematic art.

PHAEDRUS: Which things?

SOCRATES: The first consists in seeing together things that are scattered about everywhere and collecting them into one kind, so that by defining each thing we can make clear the subject of any instruction we wish to give. Just so with our discussion of love: Whether its definition was or was not correct, at least it allowed the speech to proceed clearly and consistently with itself.

PHAEDRUS: And what is the other thing you are talking about, Socrates?

SOCRATES: This, in turn, is to be able to cut up each kind according to its species along its natural joints, and to try not to splinter any part, as a bad butcher might do. In just this way, our two speeches placed all mental derangements into one common kind. Then, just as each single body has parts that naturally come in pairs of the same name (one of them being called the right-hand and the other the left-hand one), so the speeches, having considered unsoundness of mind to be by nature one single kind within us, proceeded to cut it up—the first speech cut its left-hand part, and continued to cut until it discovered among these parts a sort of love that can be called "left-handed," which it correctly denounced; the second speech, in turn, led us to the right-hand part of madness; discovered a love that shares its name with the other but is actually divine; set it out before us, and praised it as the cause of our greatest goods.

PHAEDRUS: You are absolutely right.

SOCRATES: Well, Phaedrus, I am myself a lover of these divisions and collections, so that I may be able to think and to speak; and if I believe that someone else is capable of discerning a single thing that is also by nature capable of encompassing many,[87] I follow "straight behind, in his tracks, as if he were a god."[88] God knows whether this is the right name for those who can do this correctly or not, but so far I have always called them "dialecticians."[89] But tell me what I must call them now that we have learned all this from Lysias and you. Or is it just that art of speaking that Thrasymachus and the rest of them use, which has made them masters of speechmaking and capable of producing others like them—anyhow those who are willing to bring them gifts and to treat them as if they were kings?

PHAEDRUS: They may behave like kings, but they certainly lack the knowledge you're talking about. No, it seems to me that you are right in calling the sort of thing you mentioned dialectic; but, it seems to me, rhetoric still eludes us.

SOCRATES: What are you saying? Could there be anything valuable which is independent of the methods I mentioned and is still grasped

265e

266a

5

266b

5

266c

5

266d

---

[87] Reading *pephukos* with some manuscripts.

[88] Adapted from Homer, *Odyssey* 2.406.

[89] See Introduction, pp. xv–xvi.

by art? If there is, you and I must certainly honor it, and we must say what part of rhetoric it is that has been left out.

PHAEDRUS: Well, there's quite a lot, Socrates: everything, at any rate, written up in the books on the art of speaking.

SOCRATES: You were quite right to remind me. First, I believe, there is the Preamble with which a speech must begin. This is what you mean, isn't it—the fine points of the art?

266e PHAEDRUS: Yes.

SOCRATES: Second come the Statement of Facts and the Evidence of Witnesses concerning it; third, Indirect Evidence; fourth, Claims to Plausibility. And I believe at least that excellent Byzantine word-wizard adds Confirmation and Supplementary Confirmation.

PHAEDRUS: You mean the worthy Theodorus?[90]

SOCRATES: Quite. And he also adds Refutation and Supplementary Refutation, to be used both in prosecution and in defense. Nor must we forget the most excellent Evenus of Paros,[91] who was the first to discover Covert Implication and Indirect Praise and who—some say—has even arranged Indirect Censures in verse as an aid to memory: a wise man indeed! And Tisias[92] and Gorgias?[93] How can we leave them out when it is they who realized that what is likely must be held in higher honor than what is true; they who, by the power of their language, make small things appear great and great things small; they who express modern ideas in ancient garb, and ancient ones in modern dress; they who have discovered how to argue both concisely and at infinite length about any subject? Actually, when I told Prodicus[94] this last, he laughed and said that only he had discovered the art of proper speeches: What we need are speeches that are neither long nor short but of the right length.

---

[90] See 261c3 note.

[91] Active as a sophist toward the end of the fifth century BCE. He is mentioned elsewhere in Plato (*Apology* 20b; *Phaedo* 60c–61c), but only a few tiny fragments of his works survive.

[92] A fifth-century teacher of rhetoric from Syracuse.

[93] See 261c2 note.

[94] A fifth-century teacher of rhetoric from Ceos, with an interest in fine distinctions of meaning (*Protagoras* 337a–c) and the correctness of names (*Cratylus* 384a8–c2).

PHAEDRUS: Brilliantly done, Prodicus!

SOCRATES: And what about Hippias[95] How can we omit him? I am sure our friend from Elis would cast his vote with Prodicus.

PHAEDRUS: Certainly.

SOCRATES: And what shall we say of the whole gallery of terms Polus[96] set up—speaking with Reduplication, Speaking in Maxims, Speaking in Images—and of the terms Licymnius[97] gave him as a present to help him explain Good Diction?

PHAEDRUS: But didn't Protagoras[98] actually use similar terms?

SOCRATES: Yes, Correct Diction, my boy, and other wonderful things. As to the art of making speeches bewailing the evils of poverty and old age, the prize, in my judgment, goes to the mighty Chalcedonian.[99] He it is also who knows best how to inflame a crowd and, once they are inflamed, how to hush them again with his words' magic spell, as he says himself. And let's not forget that he is as good at producing slander as he is at refuting it, whatever its source may be.

As to the way of ending a speech, everyone seems to be in agreement, though some call it Recapitulation and others by some other name.

PHAEDRUS: You mean, summarizing everything at the end and reminding the audience of what they've heard?

SOCRATES: That's what I mean. And if you have anything else to add about the art of speaking—

PHAEDRUS: Only minor points, not worth making.

SOCRATES: Well, let's leave minor points aside. Let's hold what we do have closer to the light so that we can see precisely the power of the art these things produce.

10

267c

5

267d

5

268a

---

[95] A contemporary of Socrates from Elis, who claimed expertise in astronomy, physics, grammar, poetry, and other subjects. Two Platonic dialogues are named after him; he also appears in the *Protagoras* (315b, 337c–8b).

[96] A pupil of Gorgias, who appears in the dialogue named for his master.

[97] A dithyrambic poet and teacher of rhetoric from Chios.

[98] A famous, early sophist (c. 490–420 BCE) from Abdera. See Introduction, p. xiv.

[99] Thrasymachus; see 261c2 note.

PHAEDRUS: A very great power, Socrates, especially in front of a crowd.

SOCRATES: Quite right. But now, my friend, look closely: Do you
5   think, as I do, that its fabric is a little threadbare?

PHAEDRUS: Can you show me?

SOCRATES: All right, tell me this. Suppose someone came to your friend Eryximachus or his father Acumenus[100] and said: "I know
268b   treatments to raise or lower (whichever I prefer) the temperature of people's bodies; if I decide to, I can make them vomit or make their bowels move, and all sorts of things. On the basis of this knowledge, I claim to be a physician; and I claim to be able to make others physicians as well by imparting it to them." What do you think they would
5   say when they heard that?

PHAEDRUS: What could they say? They would ask him if he also knew to whom he should apply such treatments, when, and to what extent.

SOCRATES: What if he replied, "I have no idea. My claim is that
268c   whoever learns from me will manage to do what you ask on his own"?

PHAEDRUS: I think they'd say the man's mad if he thinks he's a doctor just because he read a book or happened to come across a few potions; he knows nothing of the art.

SOCRATES: And suppose someone approached Sophocles[101] and
5   Euripides[102] and claimed to know how to compose the longest passages on trivial topics and the briefest ones on topics of great importance, that he could make them pitiful if he wanted, or again, by contrast, terrifying and menacing, and so on. Suppose further that he believed that by teaching this he was imparting the knowledge of
268d   composing tragedies—

PHAEDRUS: Oh, I am sure they too would laugh at anyone who thought a tragedy was anything other than the proper arrangement of

---

[100] See *Symposium* 175a4 note.

[101] Playwright from Colonus (c. 496–408 BCE). Author of *Antigone*, *Oedipus Tyrannus*, and other plays.

[102] Playwright from Athens (c. 480–406 BCE). Author of the *Bacchae*, *Medea*, and many other plays.

these things: They have to fit with one another and with the whole work.   5

SOCRATES: But I am sure they wouldn't reproach him rudely. They would react more like a musician confronted by a man who thought he had mastered harmony because he was able to produce the highest and lowest notes on his strings. The musician would not say fiercely, "You stupid man, you are out of your mind!" As befits   268e his calling, he would speak more gently: "My friend, though that too is necessary for understanding harmony, someone who has gotten as far as you have may still know absolutely nothing about the subject. What you know is what it's necessary to learn before you study harmony, but not harmony itself."   5

PHAEDRUS: That's certainly right.

SOCRATES: So Sophocles would also tell the man who was showing off to them that he knew the preliminaries of tragedy, but not the art   269a of tragedy itself. And Acumenus would say his man knew the preliminaries of medicine, but not medicine itself.

PHAEDRUS: Absolutely.

SOCRATES: And what if the "honey-tongued Adrastus"[103] (or perhaps Pericles)[104] were to hear of all the marvelous techniques we just   5 discussed—Speaking Concisely and Speaking in Images and all the rest we listed and proposed to examine under the light? Would he be angry or rude, as you and I were, with those who write of those tech-   269b niques and teach them as if they are rhetoric itself, and say something coarse to them? Wouldn't he—being wiser than we are—reproach us as well and say, "Phaedrus and Socrates, you should not be angry with these people—you should be sorry for them. The reason they   5 cannot define rhetoric is that they are ignorant of dialectic. It is their ignorance that makes them think they have discovered what rhetoric is when they have mastered only what it is necessary to learn as preliminaries. So they teach these preliminaries and imagine their pupils   269c have received a full course in rhetoric, thinking the task of using each of them persuasively and putting them together into a whole

---

[103] Described in the *Iliad* as a former king of Sicyon (2.572), leader of the first Argive expedition against Thebes. His name became a byword for eloquence. The quotation is from the early Spartan poet, Tyrtaeus, fragment 9.8.

[104] See *Symposium* 215e4 note.

speech is a minor matter, to be worked out by the pupils from their
5   own resources"?

PHAEDRUS: Really, Socrates, the art these men present as rhetoric
in their courses and handbooks is no more than what you say. In my
judgment, at least, your point is well taken. But how, from what
source, could one acquire the art of the true rhetorician, the really
269d   persuasive speaker?

SOCRATES: Well, Phaedrus, becoming good enough to be an accomplished competitor is probably—perhaps necessarily—like everything else. If you have a natural ability for rhetoric, you will become
a famous rhetorician, provided you supplement your ability with
5   knowledge and practice. To the extent that you lack any one of them,
to that extent you will be less than perfect. But, insofar as there is an
art of rhetoric, I don't believe the right method for acquiring it is to
be found in the direction Lysias and Thrasymachus have followed.

PHAEDRUS: Where can we find it then?

SOCRATES: My dear friend, maybe we can see now why Pericles
269e   was in all likelihood the greatest rhetorician of all.

PHAEDRUS: How is that?

SOCRATES: All the great arts require endless talk and ethereal spec-
ulation about nature: This seems to be what gives them their lofty
270a   point of view and universal applicability. That's just what Pericles
mastered—besides having natural ability. He came across Anaxagoras,
who was just that sort of man, got his full dose of ethereal specula-
5   tion, and understood the nature of mind and mindlessness—just the
subject on which Anaxagoras had the most to say.[105] From this, I
think, he drew for the art of rhetoric what was useful to it.

PHAEDRUS: What do you mean by that?

SOCRATES: Well, isn't the method of medicine in a way the same as
270b   the method of rhetoric?

---

[105] Anaxogoras of Clazomenae (c. 500–428 BCE) settled in Athens (c. 456), where
he remained until he fled to Lampsacus to escape indictment for impiety (c. 436).
The indictment may have been motivated, at least in part, by political hostility to
Pericles, whose patronage he enjoyed. In his philosophical speculations, Anaxagoras accorded a fundamental cosmological role to (divine) Mind. His views are
criticized at *Phaedo* 97b8–99d2.

PHAEDRUS: How so?

SOCRATES: In both cases we need to determine the nature of something—of the body in medicine, of the soul in rhetoric. Otherwise, all we'll have will be an empirical and artless practice. We won't be able to supply, on the basis of an art, a body with the medicines and diet that will make it healthy and strong, or a soul with the reasons and customary rules for conduct that will impart to it the convictions and virtues we want.

PHAEDRUS: That is most likely, Socrates.

SOCRATES: Do you think, then, that it is possible to reach a serious understanding of the nature of the soul without understanding the nature of the world as a whole?

PHAEDRUS: Well, if we're to listen to Hippocrates, Asclepius' descendant,[106] we won't even understand the body if we don't follow that method.

SOCRATES: He speaks well, my friend. Still, Hippocrates aside, we must consider whether argument supports that view.

PHAEDRUS: I agree.

SOCRATES: Consider, then, what both Hippocrates and true argument say about nature. Isn't this the way to think systematically about the nature of anything? First, we must consider whether the object regarding which we intend to become experts and capable of transmitting our expertise is simple or complex. Then, if it is simple, we must investigate its power: What things does it have what natural power of acting upon? By what things does it have what natural disposition to be acted upon? If, on the other hand, it takes many forms, we must enumerate them all and, as we did in the simple case, investigate how each is naturally able to act upon what and how it has a natural disposition to be acted upon by what.

PHAEDRUS: It seems so, Socrates.

SOCRATES: Proceeding by any other method would be like walking with the blind. Conversely, whoever studies anything on the basis of an art must never be compared to the blind or the deaf. On the

270c

5

10

270d

5

270e

---

[106] Hippocrates, a contemporary of Socrates, was the famous doctor whose name is given to the Hippocratic Oath. Asclepius is the god of healing.

contrary, it is clear that someone who teaches another to make speeches as an art will demonstrate precisely the essential nature of that to which speeches are to be applied. And that, surely, is the soul.

PHAEDRUS: Of course.

SOCRATES: This is therefore the object toward which the speaker's whole effort is directed, since it is in the soul that he attempts to produce conviction. Isn't that so?

PHAEDRUS: Yes.

SOCRATES: Clearly, therefore, Thrasymachus and anyone else who teaches the art of rhetoric seriously will, first, describe the soul with absolute precision and enable us to understand what it is: whether it is one and homogeneous by nature or takes many forms, like the shape of bodies, since, as we said, that's what it is to demonstrate the nature of something.

PHAEDRUS: Absolutely.

SOCRATES: Second, he will explain how, in virtue of its nature, it acts and is acted upon by certain things.

PHAEDRUS: Of course.

SOCRATES: Third, he will classify the kinds of speech and of soul there are, as well as the various ways in which they are affected, and explain what causes each. He will then coordinate each kind of soul with the kind of speech appropriate to it. And he will give instructions concerning the reasons why one kind of soul is necessarily convinced by one kind of speech while another necessarily remains unconvinced.

PHAEDRUS: This, I think, would certainly be the best way.

SOCRATES: In fact, my friend, no speech will ever be a product of art, whether it is a model or one actually given, if it is delivered or written in any other way—on this or on any other subject. But those who now write *Arts of Rhetoric*—we were just discussing them[107]—are cunning people: they hide the fact that they know very well everything about the soul. Well, then, until they begin to speak and write in this way, we mustn't allow ourselves to be convinced that they write on the basis of the art.

---

[107] See 266c ff.

PHAEDRUS: What way is that?   5

SOCRATES: It's very difficult to speak the actual words, but as to how one should write in order to be as artful as possible—that I am willing to tell you.

PHAEDRUS: Please do.

SOCRATES: Since the nature of speech is in fact to direct the soul, whoever intends to be a rhetorician must know how many kinds of soul there are. Their number is so-and-so many; each is of such-and-   271d
such a sort; hence some people have such-and-such a character and others have such-and-such. Those distinctions established, there are, in turn, so-and-so many kinds of speech, each of such-and-such a sort. People of such-and-such a character are easy to persuade by speeches of such-and-such a sort in connection with such-and-such   5
an issue for this particular reason, while people of such-and-such another sort are difficult to persuade for those particular reasons.

The orator must learn all this well, then put his theory into practice and develop the ability to discern each kind clearly as it occurs in the actions of real life. Otherwise he won't be any better off than he was   271e
when he was still listening to those discussions in school. He will now not only be able to say what kind of person is convinced by what kind of speech; on meeting someone he will be able to discern what he is like and make clear to himself that the person actually standing in front of him is of just this particular sort of character he had learned about in school—to that he must now apply speeches of such-and-   272a
such a kind in this particular way in order to secure conviction about such-and-such an issue. When he has learned all this—when, in addition, he has grasped the right occasions for speaking and for holding back; and when he has also understood when the time is right for Speaking Concisely or Appealing to Pity or Exaggeration or for any   5
other of the kinds of speech he has learned and when it is not—then, and only then, will he have finally mastered the art well and completely. But if his speaking, his teaching, or his writing lacks any one of these elements and he still claims to be speaking with art, you'll be   272b
better off if you don't believe him.

"Well, Socrates and Phaedrus," the author of this discourse might say, "do you agree? Could we accept an art of speaking presented in any other terms?"

PHAEDRUS: That would be impossible, Socrates. Still, it's evidently   5
rather a major undertaking.

SOCRATES: You're right. And that's why we must turn all our arguments every which way and try to find some easier and shorter route to the art: we don't want to follow a long rough path for no good reason when we can choose a short smooth one instead.

272c

Now, try to remember if you've heard anything helpful from Lysias or anybody else. Speak up.

5   PHAEDRUS: It's not for lack of trying, but nothing comes to mind right now.

SOCRATES: Well, then, shall I tell you something I've heard people say who care about this topic?

PHAEDRUS: Of course.

10   SOCRATES: We do claim, after all, Phaedrus, that it is fair to give the wolf's side of the story as well.

272d   PHAEDRUS: That's just what you should do.

SOCRATES: Well, these people say that there is no need to be so solemn about all this and stretch it out to such lengths. For the fact is, as we said ourselves at the beginning of this discussion, that one who intends to be an able rhetorician has no need to know the truth about

5   the things that are just or good or yet about the people who are such either by nature or upbringing. No one in a lawcourt, you see, cares at all about the truth of such matters. They only care about what is con-

272e   vincing. This is called "the likely," and that is what a man who intends to speak according to art should concentrate on. Sometimes, in fact, whether you are prosecuting or defending a case, you must not even say what actually happened, if it was not likely to have happened— you must say something that is likely instead. Whatever you say, you

5   should pursue what is likely and leave the truth aside: the whole art
273a   consists in cleaving to that throughout your speech.

PHAEDRUS: That's an excellent presentation of what people say who profess to be expert in speeches, Socrates. I recall that we raised this issue briefly earlier on, but it seems to be their single most impor-

5   tant point.

SOCRATES: No doubt you've churned through Tisias' book[108] quite carefully. Then let Tisias tell us this also: By "the likely" does he mean
273b   anything but what is accepted by the crowd?

---

[108] See 267a6 note.

PHAEDRUS: What else?

SOCRATES: And it's likely it was when he discovered this clever and artful technique that Tisias wrote that if a weak but spunky man is taken to court because he beat up a strong but cowardly one and stole his cloak or something else, neither one should tell the truth. The coward must say that the spunky man didn't beat him up all by him-self, while the latter must rebut this by saying that only the two of them were there, and fall back on that well-worn plea, "How could a man like me attack a man like him?" The strong man, naturally, will not admit his cowardice, but will try to invent some other lie, and may thus give his opponent the chance to refute him. And in other cases, speaking as the art dictates will take similar forms. Isn't that so, Phaedrus?

PHAEDRUS: Of course.

SOCRATES: Phew! Tisias—or whoever else it was and whatever name he pleases to use for himself—seems to have discovered an art which he has disguised very well! But now, my friend, shall we or shall we not say to him—

PHAEDRUS: What?

SOCRATES: This: "Tisias, some time ago, before you came into the picture, we were saying that people get the idea of what is likely through its similarity to the truth. And we just explained that in every case the person who knows the truth knows best how to determine similarities. So, if you have something new to say about the art of speaking, we shall listen. But if you don't, we shall remain convinced by the explanations we gave just before: No one will ever possess the art of speaking, to the extent that any human being can, unless he ac-quires the ability to enumerate the sorts of characters to be found in any audience, to divide everything according to its kinds, and to grasp each single thing firmly by means of one form. And no one can ac-quire these abilities without great effort—a laborious effort a sensible man will make not in order to speak and act among human beings, but so as to be able to speak and act in a way that pleases the gods as much as possible. Wiser people than ourselves, Tisias, say that a rea-sonable man must put his mind to being pleasant not to his fellow slaves (though this may happen as a side effect) but to his masters, who are wholly good. So, if the way round is long, don't be astonished: we must make this detour for the sake of things that are very important,

5

273c

5

10

273d

5

273e

5

274a

not for what you have in mind. Still, as our argument asserts, if that is
what you want, you'll get it best as a result of pursuing our own goal.

PHAEDRUS: What you've said is wonderful, Socrates—if only it
could be done!

SOCRATES: Yet surely whatever one must go through on the way
to an honorable goal is itself honorable.

PHAEDRUS: Certainly.

SOCRATES: Well, then, that's enough about artfulness and artless-
ness in connection with speaking.

PHAEDRUS: Quite.

SOCRATES: What's left, then, is aptness and ineptness in connection
with writing: What feature makes writing good, and what inept?
Right?

PHAEDRUS: Yes.

SOCRATES: Well, do you know how best to please god when you
either use words or discuss them in general?

PHAEDRUS: Not at all. Do you?

SOCRATES: I can tell you what I've heard the ancients said, though
they alone know the truth. However, if we could discover that ourselves, would we still care about the speculations of other people?

PHAEDRUS: That's a silly question. Still, tell me what you say
you've heard.

SOCRATES: Well, this is what I've heard. Among the ancient gods
of Naucratis[109] in Egypt there was one to whom the bird called the
ibis is sacred. The name of that divinity was Theuth,[110] and it was he
who first discovered number and calculation, geometry and astronomy, as well as the games of checkers and dice, and, above all else,
writing.

Now the king of all Egypt at that time was Thamus, who lived in
the great city in the upper region that the Greeks call Egyptian

---

[109] A Greek trading colony.

[110] Theuth (or Thoth) was the Egyptian god of writing, measuring, and calculation, represented on early monuments as an ibis. The Greeks identified him with
Hermes (see 263d6 note).

Thebes; Thamus is what they call Ammon.[111] Theuth came to exhibit
his arts to him and urged him to disseminate them to all the Egyp-   5
tians. Thamus asked him about the usefulness of each art, and while
Theuth was explaining it, Thamus praised him for whatever he
thought was right in his explanations and criticized him for whatever
he thought was wrong.   274e

The story goes that Thamus said much to Theuth, both for and
against each art, which it would take too long to repeat. But when
they came to writing, Theuth said: "O King, here is something that,
once learned, will make the Egyptians wiser and will improve their   5
memory; I have discovered a potion[112] for memory and for wisdom."
Thamus, however, replied: "O most expert Theuth, one man can
give birth to the elements of an art, but only another can judge how
they can benefit or harm those who will use them.[113] And now, since
you are the father of writing, your affection for it has made you describe its effects as the opposite of what they really are. In fact, it will   **275a**
introduce forgetfulness into the soul of those who learn it: they will
not practice using their memory because they will put their trust in
writing, which is external and depends on signs that belong to others,
instead of trying to remember from the inside, completely on their
own. You have not discovered a potion for remembering, but for reminding; you provide your students with the appearance of wisdom,   5
not with its reality. Your invention will enable them to hear many
things without being properly taught, and they will imagine that they
have come to know much while for the most part they will know
nothing. And they will be difficult to get along with, since they will   275b
merely appear to be wise instead of really being so."

PHAEDRUS: Socrates, you're very good at making up stories from
Egypt or wherever else you want!

SOCRATES: But, my friend, the priests of the temple of Zeus at
Dodona say that the first prophecies were the words of an oak. Every-   5
one who lived at that time, not being as wise as you young ones are

---

[111] Reading *Thamoun* (for *theon*) with Postgate. Ammon, king of the Egyptian
gods, is identified by the Egyptians with the sun god Ra, and by the Greeks (who
call him Thamus) with Zeus.

[112] See 230d6 note.

[113] See *Republic* 601c–602a.

today, found it rewarding enough in their simplicity to listen to an
oak or even a stone, so long as it was telling the truth, while it seems
to make a difference to you, Phaedrus, who is speaking and where he
275c   comes from. Why, though, don't you just consider whether what he
says is right or wrong?

PHAEDRUS: I deserved that, Socrates. And I agree that the Theban
king was correct about writing.

SOCRATES: Well, then, those who think they can leave written in-
5   structions for an art, as well as those who accept them, thinking that
writing can yield results that are clear or certain, must be quite naive and
truly ignorant of Ammon's prophetic judgment: otherwise, how could
they possibly think that words that have been written down can do
275d   more than remind those who already know what the writing is about?

PHAEDRUS: Quite right.

SOCRATES: You know, Phaedrus, writing shares a strange feature
5   with painting. The offspring of painting stand there as if they are
alive, but if anyone asks them anything, they remain most solemnly
silent. The same is true of written words. You'd think they were
speaking as if they had some understanding, but if you question anything that has been said because you want to learn more, it continues
to signify just that very same thing forever. When it has once been
275e   written down, every discourse roams about everywhere, reaching in-
discriminately those with understanding no less than those who have
no business with it, and it doesn't know to whom it should speak and
to whom it should not. And when it is faulted and attacked unfairly,
it always needs its father's support; alone, it can neither defend itself
5   nor come to its own support.

PHAEDRUS: You are absolutely right about that, too.

SOCRATES: Now tell me, can we discern another kind of dis-
276a   course, a legitimate brother of this one? Can we say how it comes
about, and how it is by nature better and more capable?

PHAEDRUS: Which one is that? How do you think it comes about?

SOCRATES: It is a discourse that is written down, with knowledge,
5   in the soul of the listener; it can defend itself, and it knows for whom
it should speak and for whom it should remain silent.

PHAEDRUS: You mean the living, breathing discourse of the man
who knows, of which the written one can be fairly called an image.

SOCRATES: Absolutely right. And tell me this. Would a sensible   276b
farmer, who cared about his seeds and wanted them to yield fruit,
plant them in all seriousness in the gardens of Adonis in the middle of
the summer and enjoy watching them bear fruit within seven days?[114]
Or would he do this as an amusement and in honor of the holiday, if
he did it at all? Wouldn't he use his knowledge of farming to plant the   5
seeds he cared for when it was appropriate and be content if they bore
fruit seven months later?

PHAEDRUS: That's how he would handle those he was serious
about, Socrates, quite differently from the others, as you say.   276c

SOCRATES: Now what about the man who knows what is just,
noble, and good? Shall we say that he is less sensible with his seeds
than the farmer is with his?   5

PHAEDRUS: Certainly not.

SOCRATES: Therefore, he won't be serious about writing them in
ink, sowing them, through a pen, with words that are as incapable of
speaking in their own defense as they are of teaching the truth adequately.

PHAEDRUS: That wouldn't be likely.   10

SOCRATES: Certainly not. When he writes, it's likely he will sow   276d
gardens of letters for the sake of amusing himself, storing up reminders for himself "when he reaches forgetful old age"[115] and for
everyone who wants to follow in his footsteps, and will enjoy seeing
them sweetly blooming. And when others turn to different amuse-   5
ments, watering themselves with drinking parties and everything else
that goes along with them, he will rather spend his time amusing
himself with the things I have just described.

PHAEDRUS: Socrates, you are contrasting a vulgar amusement with
the very noblest—with the amusement of a man who can while away   276e
his time telling stories of justice and the other matters you mentioned.

---

[114] A divine personage apparently associated with the seasons and with agricul-
ture, Adonis spent eight months of the year with Aphrodite, goddess of sexual
love, and the four winter months with Persephone, goddess of the Underworld.
Gardens of Adonis were pots or window-boxes used for forcing seeds during the
Athenian midsummer festival of Adonis. The seeds quickly germinated in the hot
sun, but the young plants withered there just as quickly.
[115] Apparent quotation. Source unknown.

SOCRATES: That's just how it is, Phaedrus. But it is much nobler to
5 be serious about these matters, and use the art of dialectic. The dia-
lectician chooses a proper soul and plants and sows within it discourse
accompanied by knowledge—discourse capable of helping itself as
277a well as the man who planted it, which is not barren but produces a
seed from which more discourse grows in the character of others.
Such discourse makes the seed forever immortal and renders the man
who has it as happy as any human being can be.

5 PHAEDRUS: What you describe is really much nobler still.

SOCRATES: And now that we have agreed about this, Phaedrus, we
are finally able to decide the issue.

PHAEDRUS: What issue is that?

SOCRATES: The issue which brought us to this point in the first
place: We wanted to examine the attack made on Lysias on account of
10 his writing speeches, and to ask which speeches are written artfully
277b and which not. Now, I think that we have answered that question
clearly enough.

PHAEDRUS: So it seemed; but remind me again how we did it.

SOCRATES: First, you must know the truth concerning everything
5 you are speaking or writing about; you must learn how to define each
thing in itself; and, having defined it, you must know how to divide it
into kinds until you reach something indivisible. Second, you must
understand the nature of the soul, along the same lines; you must de-
277c termine which kind of speech is appropriate to each kind of soul,
prepare and arrange your speech accordingly, and offer a complex
and elaborate speech to a complex soul and a simple speech to a simple one. Then, and only then, will you be able to use speech artfully,
to the extent that its nature allows it to be used that way, either in
5 order to teach or in order to persuade. This is the whole point of the
argument we have been making.

PHAEDRUS: Absolutely. That is exactly how it seemed to us.

277d SOCRATES: Now how about whether it's noble or shameful to give
or write a speech—when it could be fairly said to be grounds for reproach, and when not? Didn't what we said just a little while ago
make it clear—

5 PHAEDRUS: What was that?

SOCRATES: That if Lysias or anybody else ever did or ever does write—privately or for the public, in the course of proposing some law—a political document which he believes to embody clear knowledge of lasting importance, then this writer deserves reproach, whether anyone says so or not. For to be unaware of the difference between a dream-image and the reality of what is just and unjust, good and bad, must truly be grounds for reproach even if the crowd praises it with one voice.

10

277e

PHAEDRUS: It certainly must be.

SOCRATES: On the other hand, take a man who thinks that a written discourse on any subject can only be a great amusement, that no discourse worth serious attention has ever been written in verse or prose, and that those that are recited in public without questioning and explanation, in the manner of the rhapsodes, are given only in order to produce conviction. He believes that at their very best these can only serve as reminders to those who already know. And he also thinks that only what is said for the sake of understanding and learning, what is truly written in the soul concerning what is just, noble, and good can be clear, perfect, and worth serious attention: Such discourses should be called his own legitimate children, first the discourse he may have discovered already within himself and then its sons and brothers who may have grown naturally in other souls insofar as these are worthy; to the rest, he turns his back. Such a man, Phaedrus, would be just what you and I both would pray to become.

5

278a

5

278b

PHAEDRUS: I wish and pray for things to be just as you say.

5

SOCRATES: Well, then: our playful amusement regarding discourse is complete. Now you go and tell Lysias that we came to the spring which is sacred to the Nymphs and heard words charging us to deliver a message to Lysias and anyone else who composes speeches, as well as to Homer and anyone else who has composed poetry either spoken or sung, and third, to Solon[116] and anyone else who writes political documents that he calls laws: If any one of you has composed these things with a knowledge of the truth, if you can defend your writing when you are challenged, and if you can yourself make the argument that

278c

5

---

[116] See 258c1 note.

your writing is of little worth, then you must be called by a name derived not from these writings but rather from those things that you
278d are seriously pursuing.

PHAEDRUS: What name, then, would you give such a man?

SOCRATES: To call him wise, Phaedrus, seems to me too much, and proper only for a god. To call him wisdom's lover—a philosopher—
5 or something similar would fit him better and be more seemly.

PHAEDRUS: That would be quite appropriate.

SOCRATES: On the other hand, if a man has nothing more valuable than what he has composed or written, spending long hours twisting it around, pasting parts together and taking them apart—wouldn't you
278e be right to call him a poet or a speech writer or an author of laws?

PHAEDRUS: Of course.

SOCRATES: Tell that, then, to your friend.

PHAEDRUS: And what about you? What shall you do? We must
5 surely not forget your own friend.

SOCRATES: Whom do you mean?

PHAEDRUS: The beautiful Isocrates.[117] What are you going to tell him, Socrates? What shall we say he is?

10 SOCRATES: Isocrates is still young, Phaedrus. But I want to tell you
279a what I foresee for him.

PHAEDRUS: What is that?

SOCRATES: It seems to me that by his nature he can outdo anything that Lysias has accomplished in his speeches; and he also has a
5 nobler character. So I wouldn't be at all surprised if, as he gets older and continues writing speeches of the sort he is composing now, he makes everyone who has ever attempted to compose a speech seem like a child in comparison. Even more so if such work no longer satisfies him and a higher, divine impulse leads him to more important
279b things. For nature, my friend, has placed the love of wisdom in his mind.

---

[117] An Athenian teacher and orator (436–338 BCE) whose school was more famous in its day than Plato's Academy. Most scholars take the praise that follows to be ironic.

That is the message I will carry to my beloved, Isocrates, from the gods of this place; and you have your own message for your Lysias.   5

PHAEDRUS: So it shall be. But let's be off, since the heat has died down a bit.

SOCRATES: Shouldn't we offer a prayer to the gods here before we leave?

PHAEDRUS: Of course.

SOCRATES: O dear Pan[118] and all the other gods of this place, grant that I may be beautiful inside. Let all my external possessions be in friendly harmony with what is within. May I consider the wise man rich. As for gold, let me have as much as a moderate man could bear   279c
and carry with him.

Do we need anything else, Phaedrus? I believe my prayer is enough for me.

PHAEDRUS: Make it a prayer for me as well. Friends have everything in common.

SOCRATES: Let's be off.

---

[118] See 263d6 note.

ALCIBIADES

103a SOCRATES: I was the first man to fall in love with you, son of Clinias, and now that the others have stopped pursuing you I suppose you're wondering why I'm the only one who hasn't given up—and also why, when the others pestered you with conversation, I never even spoke to you all these years. Human causes didn't enter into it; I

5 was prevented by some daimonic being,[1] the effect of which you'll hear about later on. But now it no longer prevents me, so here I am.

103b I'm confident it won't prevent me in future either.

I've been observing you all this time, and I've got a pretty good idea how you treated all those men who pursued you: they held themselves in high esteem, but you were even more arrogant and sent

5 them packing, every single one of them. I'd like to explain the reason

104a why you felt yourself so superior.

You say you don't need anybody for anything, since your own qualities, from your body right up to your soul, are so great there's nothing you lack. In the first place, you fancy yourself the tallest and

5 best-looking man around—and it's quite plain to see you're not wrong about that. Next, you think that yours is the leading family in your city, which is the greatest city in Greece: on your father's side

104b you have plenty of aristocratic friends and relations, who would be of service to you if there was any need; and on your mother's side your connections are no worse and no fewer. And you have Pericles son of

5 Xanthippus,[2] whom your father left as a guardian to you and your brother; you think he's a more powerful ally than all those people I mentioned put together—he can do whatever he likes, not only in this city, but anywhere in Greece, and also in many important foreign countries. I will also mention your wealth, but I think that's the least

104c of the reasons you hold yourself in high esteem. You bragged about all those things and got the better of your suitors; they didn't measure up and came off the worse. You knew what was going on.

Translated by D. S. Hutchinson

[1] See *Symposium* 202d13 note.

[2] See *Symposium* 215e4 note.

And so I'm sure you're wondering what I could possibly have in mind—why don't I give up on you? The others have all been sent packing, so what do I hope to achieve by persisting?

ALCIBIADES: Yes, Socrates, perhaps you don't realize that you've just taken the words out of my mouth. I had already decided to come and ask you that very question: what could you have in mind? What do you hope to achieve by bothering me, always making so sure you're there wherever I am? Yes, I really do wonder what you might be up to, and I'd be very glad to find out.

SOCRATES: So then you'll probably be eager to give me your full attention, since, as you say, you're keen to know what I have in mind. I take it that you'll listen carefully?

ALCIBIADES: Yes, of course—just tell me.

SOCRATES: Watch out—I wouldn't be at all surprised if I found it as hard to stop as it was to start.

ALCIBIADES: Tell me, please. I will pay attention.

SOCRATES: Speak I must, then. It's not easy to play the role of suitor with a man who doesn't give in to suitors; nevertheless, I must summon up my courage and say what's on my mind.

Alcibiades, if I saw that you were content with the advantages I just mentioned and thought that this was the condition in which you should live out the rest of your life, I would have given up my love long ago; at least that's what I persuade myself. But I'm going to prove to you in person what very different plans you actually have in mind. Then you'll realize how constantly I've been thinking about you.

Suppose one of the gods asked you, "Alcibiades, would you rather live with what you now have, or would you rather die on the spot if you weren't permitted to acquire anything greater?" I think you'd choose to die. What then *is* your real ambition in life? I'll tell you. You think that as soon as you present yourself before the Athenian people—as indeed you expect to in a very few days—by presenting yourself you'll show them that you deserve to be honored more than Pericles or anyone else who ever was. Having shown that, you'll be the most influential man in the city, and if you're the greatest here, you'll be the greatest in the rest of Greece, and not only in Greece, but also among the foreigners who live on the same continent as we do.

And if that same god were then to tell you that you should have absolute power in Europe, but that you weren't permitted to cross over

105c   into Asia or get mixed up with affairs over there, I think you'd rather
        not live with only that to look forward to; you want your reputation
        and your influence to saturate all mankind, so to speak. I don't think
        you regard anybody as ever having been much to speak of, except
5   perhaps Cyrus and Xerxes.³ I'm not guessing that this is your ambi-
        tion—I'm sure of it.

        Since you know that what I say is true, maybe you'll say, "Well
        then, Socrates, what's this got to do with your point? You said you
105d   were going to tell me why you haven't given up on me."⁴ Yes, I will
        tell you, my dear son of Clinias and Dinomache. It is impossible to
        put any of these ideas of yours into effect without me—that's how
5   much influence I think I have over you and your business. I think this
        is why the god hasn't allowed me to talk to you all this time; and I've
        been waiting for the day he allows me.

105e   I'm hoping for the same thing from you⁵ as you are from the Athe-
        nians: I hope to exert great influence over you by showing you that
        I'm worth the world to you and that nobody is capable of providing
        you with the influence you crave, neither your guardian nor your rel-
5   atives, nor anybody else except me—with the god's help, of course.
        When you were younger, before you were full of such ambitions, I
        think the god didn't let me talk to you because the conversation
        would have been pointless. But now he's told me to, because now you
106a   will listen to me.

        ALCIBIADES: Really, Socrates, now that you've started talking you
        seem much more bizarre to me than when you followed me in si-
        lence, though you were very bizarre to look at then, too. Well, on the
        question of whether or not these are my ambitions, you seem to have
5   made up your mind already, and no denial of mine will do anything
        to convince you otherwise. Fine. But supposing I really do have these
        ambitions, how will you help me achieve them? What makes you in-
        dispensable? Have you got something to say?

106b   SOCRATES: Are you asking if I can say some long speech like the
        ones you're used to hearing? No, that sort of thing's not for me. But I
        do think I'd be able to show you that what I said is true, if only you
        were willing to grant me just one little favor.

---

³ Great, empire-building kings in the sixth and fifth centuries BCE.

⁴ Retaining the bracketed phrase in d1.

⁵ Omitting d7–e2 *endeixasthai . . . dunêsesthai.*

ALCIBIADES: Well, as long as you mean a favor that's not hard to grant, I'm willing.

5

SOCRATES: Do you think it's hard to answer questions?

ALCIBIADES: No, I don't.

SOCRATES: Then answer me.

ALCIBIADES: Ask me.

10

SOCRATES: My question is whether you have in mind what I say you have in mind.

106c

ALCIBIADES: Let's say I do, if you like, so I can find out what you're going to say.

SOCRATES: Right then; you plan, as I say, to come forward and advise the Athenians some time soon. Suppose I stopped you as you were about to take the podium and asked, "Alcibiades, what are the Athenians proposing to discuss? You're getting up to advise them because it's something you know better than they do, aren't you?" What would you reply?

5

ALCIBIADES: Yes, I suppose I would say it was something that I know better than they do.

106d

SOCRATES: So it's on matters you know about that you're a good adviser.

ALCIBIADES: Of course.

SOCRATES: Now the only things you know are what you've learned from others or found out for yourself; isn't that right?

5

ALCIBIADES: What else could I know?

SOCRATES: Could you ever have learned or found out anything without wanting to learn it or work it out for yourself?

ALCIBIADES: No, I couldn't have.

SOCRATES: Is that right? Would you have wanted to learn or work out something that you thought you understood?

10

ALCIBIADES: Of course not.

SOCRATES: So there was a time when you didn't think you knew what you now understand.

106e

ALCIBIADES: There must have been.

SOCRATES: But I've got a pretty good idea what you've learned. Tell me if I've missed anything: as far as I remember, you learned writing and lyre-playing and wrestling, but you didn't want to learn flute-playing.[6] These are the subjects that you understand—unless perhaps you've been learning something while I wasn't looking; but I don't think you have been, either by night or by day, on your excursions from home.

ALCIBIADES: No, those are the only lessons I took.

107a   SOCRATES: Well then, is it when the Athenians are discussing how to spell a word correctly that you'll stand up to advise them?

ALCIBIADES: Good God, I'd never do that!

SOCRATES: Then is it when they're discussing the notes on the lyre?

ALCIBIADES: No, never.

SOCRATES: But surely they're not in the habit of discussing wrestling in the Assembly.[7]

ALCIBIADES: Certainly not.

SOCRATES: Then what will they be discussing? I presume it won't be building.

ALCIBIADES: Of course not.

SOCRATES: Because a builder would give better advice on these matters than you.

107b   ALCIBIADES: Yes.

SOCRATES: Nor will they be discussing divination, will they?

ALCIBIADES: No.

SOCRATES: Because then a diviner would be better at giving advice than you.

ALCIBIADES: Yes.

SOCRATES: Regardless of whether he's tall or short, or handsome or ugly, or even noble or common.

---

[6] See *Symposium* 176e7 note.

[7] The ultimate decision-making power in the Athenian democracy, consisting of all the adult male citizens.

ALCIBIADES: Of course.[8]   b8

SOCRATES: And when the Athenians are discussing measures for
public health, it will make no difference to them if their counsellor is
rich or poor, but they will make sure that their adviser is a doctor.   107c

ALCIBIADES: Of course.   b11

SOCRATES: I suppose that's because advice on any subject is the
business not of those who are rich but of those who know it.   b10

ALCIBIADES: Quite reasonably so.   c3

SOCRATES: Then what *will* they be considering when you stand up
to advise them, assuming you're right to do so?   c5

ALCIBIADES: They'll be discussing their own business, Socrates.

SOCRATES: You mean their shipbuilding business—what sorts of
ships they should be building?

ALCIBIADES: No, Socrates, I don't.

SOCRATES: I suppose that's because you don't understand ship-
building. Am I right, or is there some other reason?   10

ALCIBIADES: No, that's it.

SOCRATES: So what kind of 'their own business' do you think they'll   107d
be discussing?

ALCIBIADES: War, Socrates, or peace, or anything else which is the
business of the city.

SOCRATES: Do you mean they'll be discussing who they should
make peace with and who they should go to war with and how?   5

ALCIBIADES: Yes.

SOCRATES: But shouldn't they do that with the ones with whom
it's better to?

ALCIBIADES: Yes.

SOCRATES: And when it's better?   107e

ALCIBIADES: Certainly.

---

[8] In the manuscripts, Alcibiades' reply and the next speech of Socrates are pre-
ceded by the following reply-speech pair; the translation follows a conjectural
transposition of b8–10 and b11–c2.

SOCRATES: And for as long a time as it's better?

ALCIBIADES: Yes.

SOCRATES: Now supposing the Athenians were discussing who
5   they should wrestle with and who they should spar with and how,
who would be a better adviser, you or the trainer?

ALCIBIADES: The trainer, I guess.

SOCRATES: And can you tell me what the trainer has in view when
10   he advises you who you should or shouldn't wrestle with, and when,
and how? I mean, for example, that one should wrestle with those
with whom it's better to wrestle, isn't that right?

ALCIBIADES: Yes.

108a   SOCRATES: And as much as is better?

ALCIBIADES: That's right.

SOCRATES: And when it's better, right?

ALCIBIADES: Certainly.

SOCRATES: Let's take another example: when you're singing, you
5   should sometimes accompany the song with lyre-playing and dancing.

ALCIBIADES: Yes, you should.

SOCRATES: You should do so when it's better to, right?

ALCIBIADES: Yes.

10   SOCRATES: And as much as is better.

ALCIBIADES: I agree.

SOCRATES: Really? Since you used the term 'better' in both
108b   cases—in wrestling and in playing the lyre while singing—what do
you call what's better in lyre-playing, as I call what's better in
wrestling 'athletic'? What do you call that?

ALCIBIADES: I don't get it.

SOCRATES: Then try to follow my example. My answer was, I
5   think, 'what is correct in every case'—and what is correct, I presume,
is what takes place in accordance with the skill,[9] isn't it?

ALCIBIADES: Yes.

---

[9] *Technê*; also "art," "craft," "expertise."

SOCRATES: Wasn't the skill athletics?

ALCIBIADES: Of course.   10

SOCRATES: I said that what's better in wrestling, was 'athletic'.   108c

ALCIBIADES: That's what you said.

SOCRATES: Wasn't that well said?

ALCIBIADES: I think so, anyway.   5

SOCRATES: Come on then, it's your turn; it's partly up to you, surely, to keep our conversation going well. First of all, tell me what the skill is for singing and dancing and playing the lyre correctly. What is it called as a whole? . . . Aren't you able to tell me yet?

ALCIBIADES: No, I can't.   10

SOCRATES: Well, try it this way. Who are the goddesses to whom the skill belongs?

ALCIBIADES: Do you mean the Muses, Socrates?

SOCRATES: I do indeed. Don't you see? What's the name of the skill that's named after them?   108d

ALCIBIADES: I think you mean music.

SOCRATES: Yes, I do. Now what is "correctly" for what takes place in accordance with this skill? In the other case I told you what "correctly" is for what takes place in accordance with the skill, so now it's   5
your turn to say something similar in this case. *How* does it take place?

ALCIBIADES: Musically, I think.

SOCRATES: A good answer. Come on now, what do you call what's better in both going to war and keeping the peace? In these last   10
two examples you said that what was better was more musical and   108e
more athletic, respectively. Now try to tell me what's better in this case, too.

ALCIBIADES: I really can't do it.

SOCRATES: But surely it's disgraceful if when you're speaking and   5
giving advice about food—saying that a certain kind is better than another, and better at a certain time and in a certain quantity—and someone should ask you, "What do you mean by 'better', Alcibiades?" you could tell him in that case that 'better' was 'healthier', though you don't even pretend to be a doctor; and yet in a case where you do pretend to understand and are going to stand up and give   **109a**

advice as though you knew, if you aren't able, as seems likely, to answer the question in this case, won't you be embarrassed? Won't that seem disgraceful?

ALCIBIADES: Yes, certainly.

SOCRATES: Then think about it, and try to tell me what the better
5   tends toward, in keeping the peace or in waging war with the right people.

ALCIBIADES: I'm thinking, but I can't get it.

SOCRATES: But suppose we're at war with somebody—surely you know what treatment we accuse each other of when we enter into a
10   war, and what we call it.

ALCIBIADES: I do—we say that they're playing some trick on us, or
109b attacking us or taking things away from us.

SOCRATES: Hold on—*how* do we suffer from each of these treatments? Try to tell me how one way differs from another way.

5   ALCIBIADES: When you say 'way', Socrates, do you mean 'justly' or 'unjustly'?

SOCRATES: Precisely.

ALCIBIADES: But surely that makes all the difference in the world.

SOCRATES: Really? Who will you advise the Athenians to wage war on? Those who are treating us unjustly, or those who are treating
10   us justly?

ALCIBIADES: That's a hard question you're asking. Even if someone
109c thought it was necessary to wage war on people who were treating us justly, he wouldn't admit it.

SOCRATES: Because I think that wouldn't be lawful.

5   ALCIBIADES: It certainly wouldn't.

SOCRATES: Nor would it be considered a proper thing to do.

ALCIBIADES: No.[10]

SOCRATES: So you would also frame your speech in these terms.

ALCIBIADES: I'd have to.

---

[10] Attributing *oude ge kalon dokei einai* in c5 to Socrates, and accepting the conjectured reply *ou* from Alcibiades.

SOCRATES: Then this 'better' I was just asking you about—when it comes to waging war or not, on whom to wage war and on whom not to, and when and when not to—this 'better' turns out to be the same as 'more just', doesn't it? 10

ALCIBIADES: It certainly seems so.

SOCRATES: But how could it, my dear Alcibiades? Don't you real- 109d ize that this is something you don't understand? Or perhaps, when I wasn't looking, you've been seeing some teacher who taught you how to tell the difference between the more just and the less just. Have you? . . . Well, who is he? Tell me who he is so that you can sign me up with him as well. 5

ALCIBIADES: Stop teasing me, Socrates.

SOCRATES: I'm not—I'll swear by Friendship,[11] yours and mine. I'd never perjure myself by him. So tell me who he is, if you can.

ALCIBIADES: And what if I can't? Don't you think I might know about justice and injustice some other way? 109e

SOCRATES: Yes, you might—if you found it out.

ALCIBIADES: Well, don't you think I might find it out?

SOCRATES: Yes, of course—if you investigate the matter. 5

ALCIBIADES: And don't you think I might investigate it?

SOCRATES: Yes, I do—if you thought you didn't know.

ALCIBIADES: And didn't I once think that?

SOCRATES: A fine answer. Can you tell me when this was, when you didn't think you knew about justice and injustice . . . Well, was it 110a last year that you were looking into it and didn't think you knew? Or did you think you knew? . . . Answer me truthfully, or else our con-versation will be a waste of time.

ALCIBIADES: Yes, I thought I knew.

SOCRATES: Didn't you think the same thing two years ago, and three years ago, and four? 5

ALCIBIADES: I did.

---

[11] One of the aspects under which Zeus was worshipped was as the god of friend-ship.

SOCRATES: But surely before that you were a boy, weren't you?

ALCIBIADES: Yes.

10   SOCRATES: Well now, at that point I'm sure you thought you knew.

ALCIBIADES: How can you be sure of that?

110b   SOCRATES: When you were a boy I often observed you, at school and other places, and sometimes when you were playing knuckle-bones or some other game,[12] you'd say to one or another of your playmates, very loudly and confidently—not at all like someone who was at a loss about justice and injustice—that he was a lousy cheater and
5   wasn't playing fairly. Isn't that true?

ALCIBIADES: But what was I to do, Socrates, when somebody cheated me like that?

SOCRATES: Do you mean, what should you have done if you did-
10   n't actually know then whether or not you were being cheated?

110c   ALCIBIADES: But I *did* know, by Zeus! I saw clearly that they were cheating me.

SOCRATES: So it seems that even as a child you thought you understood justice and injustice.

5   ALCIBIADES: Yes, and I *did* understand.

SOCRATES: At what point did you find it out? Surely it wasn't when you thought you knew.

ALCIBIADES: Of course not.

SOCRATES: Then when did you think you didn't know? Think
10   about it—you won't find any such time.

ALCIBIADES: By Zeus, Socrates, I really can't say.

110d   SOCRATES: So it isn't by finding it out that you know it.

ALCIBIADES: That's not very likely.

SOCRATES: But surely you just finished saying that it wasn't by being taught, either, that you knew it. So if you neither found it out nor were taught it, how and where did you come to know it?

5   ALCIBIADES: Maybe I gave you the wrong answer when I said I knew it by finding it out myself.

---

[12] See *Lysis* 206e5 note.

SOCRATES: Then how did it happen?

ALCIBIADES: I suppose I learned it in the same way as other people.

SOCRATES: That brings us back to the same argument: from whom? Do tell me. 10

ALCIBIADES: From people in general. 110e

SOCRATES: When you give the credit to 'people in general', you're falling back on teachers who are no good.

ALCIBIADES: What? Aren't they capable of teaching?

SOCRATES: No, they can't even teach you what moves to make or not make in knucklebones. And yet that's a trivial matter, I suppose, 5 compared with justice . . . What? Don't you agree?

ALCIBIADES: Yes.

SOCRATES: So although they can't teach trivial things, you say they can teach more serious things. 10

ALCIBIADES: I think so; at any rate, they can teach a lot of things that are more important than knucklebones.

SOCRATES: Like what?

ALCIBIADES: Well, for example, I learned how to speak Greek from them; I couldn't tell you who my teacher was, but I give the 111a credit to the very people you say are no good at teaching.

SOCRATES: Yes, my noble friend, people in general are good teachers of that, and it would be only fair to praise them for their 5 teaching.

ALCIBIADES: Why?

SOCRATES: Because they have what it takes to be good teachers of the subject.

ALCIBIADES: What do you mean by that? 10

SOCRATES: Don't you see that somebody who is going to teach anything must first know it himself? Isn't that right? 111b

ALCIBIADES: Of course.

SOCRATES: And don't people who know something agree with each other, not disagree?

ALCIBIADES: Yes. 5

SOCRATES: If people disagree about something, would you say that they know it?

ALCIBIADES: Of course not.

SOCRATES: Then how could they be teachers of it?

10 ALCIBIADES: They couldn't possibly.

SOCRATES: Well then, do you think that people in general disagree about what wood or stone is? If you ask them, don't they give the same answers? Don't they reach for the same things when they want 111c to get some wood or some stone? And similarly for all other such cases; I suppose this is pretty much what you mean by understanding Greek, isn't it?

5 ALCIBIADES: Yes.

SOCRATES: So they agree with each other in these cases, as we said, and with themselves when acting privately. But don't they also agree in public? Cities don't disagree with each other and use different words for the same thing, do they?

10 ALCIBIADES: No.

SOCRATES: So it's likely that they would make good teachers of these things.

111d ALCIBIADES: Yes.

SOCRATES: So if we wanted somebody to know these things, we'd be right to send him to lessons given by these people in general.

5 ALCIBIADES: Certainly.

SOCRATES: Now if we wanted to know not just what men or horses are like, but which of them could and couldn't run, would people in general be able to teach this as well?

10 ALCIBIADES: Of course not.

SOCRATES: Isn't the fact that they disagree with each other about 111e these things enough to show you that they don't understand them, and are not 'four-square teachers' of them?

ALCIBIADES: Yes, it is.

SOCRATES: Now if we wanted to know not just what men are like, 5 but what sick and healthy men are like, would people in general be able to teach us?

ALCIBIADES: Of course not.

SOCRATES: And if you saw them disagreeing about it, that would show you that they were bad teachers of it.

ALCIBIADES: Yes, it would.   10

SOCRATES: Very well, then—does it seem to you that people in general actually agree among themselves or with each other about just and unjust people and actions?   **112a**

ALCIBIADES: Not in the slightest, Socrates.

SOCRATES: Really? Do they disagree a huge amount about these things?

ALCIBIADES: Very much so.   5

SOCRATES: I don't suppose you've ever seen or heard people disagreeing so strongly about what is healthy and unhealthy that they fight and kill each other over it, have you?

ALCIBIADES: Of course not.

SOCRATES: But I know you've seen this sort of dispute over questions of justice and injustice; or even if you haven't seen it, at least   10
you've heard about it from many other people—especially Homer,   112b
since you've heard the *Iliad* and the *Odyssey*, haven't you?

ALCIBIADES: I certainly have, of course, Socrates.

SOCRATES: Aren't these poems all about disagreements over justice and injustice?   5

ALCIBIADES: Yes.

SOCRATES: It was over this sort of disagreement that the Achaeans and the Trojans fought battles and lost their lives, as did Odysseus and the suitors of Penelope.[13]

ALCIBIADES: You're right.   112c

SOCRATES: I suppose the same is true of those Athenians and Spartans and Boeotians who died at Tanagra, and later at Coronea, including your own father.[14] The disagreement that caused those battles and

---

[13] See *Phaedrus* 261b6 note. Penelope is Odysseus' wife, whose princely suitors he killed on his return from the Trojan Wars.

[14] In both these battles of the Peloponnesian War—Tanagra in 458 BCE with the Spartans and Coronea in 447 with the Boeotians and Lochrians—the Athenians were beaten by the Spartans. See Thucydides 1.108.1, 1.113.2.

5 those deaths was none other than a disagreement over justice and injustice, wasn't it?

ALCIBIADES: You're right.

SOCRATES: Are we to say that people understand something if they
112d disagree so much about it that in their disputes with each other they resort to such extreme measures?

ALCIBIADES: Obviously not.

SOCRATES: But aren't you giving credit to teachers of this sort
5 who, as you yourself admit, have no knowledge?

ALCIBIADES: I guess I am.

SOCRATES: Well then, given that your opinion wavers so much, and given that you obviously neither found it out yourself nor learned it from anyone else, how likely is it that you know about justice and injustice?

10 ALCIBIADES: From what you say anyway, it's not very likely.

112e SOCRATES: See, there you go again, Alcibiades, that's not well said!

ALCIBIADES: What do you mean?

SOCRATES: You say that *I* say these things.

ALCIBIADES: What? Aren't you saying that I don't understand jus-
5 tice and injustice?

SOCRATES: No, not at all.

ALCIBIADES: Well, am *I*?

SOCRATES: Yes.

ALCIBIADES: How?

10 SOCRATES: Here's how. If I asked you which is more, one or two, would you say two?

ALCIBIADES: I would.

SOCRATES: By how much?

ALCIBIADES: By one.

15 SOCRATES: Then which of us is saying that two is one more than one?

ALCIBIADES: I am.

SOCRATES: Wasn't I asking and weren't you answering?

ALCIBIADES: Yes.

SOCRATES: Who do you think is saying these things—me, the questioner, or you, the answerer?   **113a**

ALCIBIADES: I am.

SOCRATES: And what if I asked you how to spell 'Socrates', and you told me? Which of us would be saying it?   5

ALCIBIADES: I would.

SOCRATES: Come then, give me the general principle. When there's a question and an answer, who is the one saying things—the questioner or the answerer?

ALCIBIADES: The answerer, I think, Socrates.   10

SOCRATES: Wasn't I the questioner in everything just now?   **113b**

ALCIBIADES: Yes.

SOCRATES: And weren't you the answerer?

ALCIBIADES: I certainly was.

SOCRATES: Well then, which of us said what was said?   5

ALCIBIADES: From what we've agreed, Socrates, it seems that I did.

SOCRATES: And what was said was that Alcibiades, the handsome son of Clinias, doesn't understand justice and injustice—though he thinks he does—and that he is about to go to the Assembly to advise the Athenians on what he doesn't know anything about. Wasn't that it?   10

ALCIBIADES: Apparently.   **113c**

SOCRATES: Then it's just like in Euripides,[15] Alcibiades; 'you heard it from yourself, not from me.'[16] I'm not the one who says these things—*you* are—don't try to blame me. And furthermore, you're quite right to say so. This scheme you have in mind—teaching what   5
you don't know and haven't bothered to learn—your scheme, my good fellow, is crazy.

ALCIBIADES: Actually, Socrates, I think the Athenians and the other Greeks rarely discuss which course is more just or unjust. They   **113d**
think that sort of thing is obvious, so they skip over it and ask which

---

[15] See *Phaedrus* 268c5 note.

[16] Cf. Euripides, *Hippolytus* 350–3.

5 one would be advantageous to do. In fact, though, what's just is not the same, I think, as what's advantageous; many people have profited by committing great injustices, and others, I think, got no advantage from doing the right thing.

SOCRATES: So? Even if just and advantageous things happen to be
113e completely different, surely you don't think you know what's advantageous for people, and why, do you?

ALCIBIADES: What's to stop me, Socrates?—unless you're going to ask me all over again who I learned it from or how I found it out myself.

SOCRATES: What a way of carrying on! If you say something
5 wrong, and if there's a previous argument that can prove that it was wrong, you think you ought to be given some new and different proof, as if the previous one were a worn-out scrap of clothing that you
114a refuse to wear again. No, you want an immaculate, brand-new proof.

I'll pass over your anticipation of my argument and ask you, all the same, 'How did you come to understand what is advantageous? Who was your teacher?', and in my one question ask everything I asked you before. Clearly this will put you in the same position again—you
5 won't be able to prove that you know what is advantageous, either by finding it out or by learning it.

But since you've got a delicate stomach and wouldn't enjoy another taste of the same argument, I'll pass over this question of whether or not you know what is advantageous for the Athenians. But why don't
114b you prove whether the just and the advantageous are the same or different? You can question me, if you like, as I questioned you—or else work it out yourself, in your own argument.

ALCIBIADES: No, Socrates, I don't think I'd be able to work it out
5 in front of you.

SOCRATES: Well then, my good sir, imagine that I'm the Assembly and the people gathered there; even there, you know, you'll have to persuade them one by one. Isn't that right?

ALCIBIADES: Yes.

SOCRATES: If somebody knows something, don't you think he can
114c persuade people about it one by one, as well as all together? Take the schoolteacher—don't you think he persuades people about letters individually, as well as collectively?

ALCIBIADES: Yes.

SOCRATES: And won't the same person be able to persuade people about numbers individually, as well as in groups?   5

ALCIBIADES: Yes.

SOCRATES: He would be a mathematician, someone who knows about numbers.

ALCIBIADES: Certainly.

SOCRATES: So won't you also be able to persuade an individual person about the things you can persuade a group of people about?   10

ALCIBIADES: Probably.

SOCRATES: Obviously these are things you know about.

ALCIBIADES: Yes.

SOCRATES: Is there any difference between an orator speaking to the people and an orator speaking in this sort of conversation, except insofar as the former persuades them all together while the latter per-   114d
suades them one by one?

ALCIBIADES: I guess not.

SOCRATES: Well then, since it's plain that the same person can per-suade individuals as well as groups, practice on me, and try to prove   5
that what is just is sometimes not advantageous.

ALCIBIADES: Stop pushing me around, Socrates!

SOCRATES: No, in fact I'm going to push you around and persuade you of the *opposite* of what you're not willing to show me.

ALCIBIADES: Just try it!   10

SOCRATES: Just answer my questions.

ALCIBIADES: No, you do the talking yourself.   114e

SOCRATES: What?! Don't you want to be completely convinced?

ALCIBIADES: Absolutely, I'm sure.

SOCRATES: Wouldn't you be completely convinced if you yourself said, 'Yes, that's how it is'?   5

ALCIBIADES: Yes, I think so.

SOCRATES: Then answer my questions. And if you don't hear yourself say that just things are also advantageous, then don't believe anything else I say.

ALCIBIADES: No, I'm sure I won't. But I'd better answer—I don't
10   think I'll come to any harm.

SOCRATES: You're quite a prophet. Now tell me—are you saying
115a   that some just things are advantageous while others are not?

ALCIBIADES: Yes.

SOCRATES: Really? Are some of them admirable and others not
admirable?

5   ALCIBIADES: What do you mean by that question?

SOCRATES: Have you ever thought that someone was doing something that was both just and contemptible?

ALCIBIADES: No, I haven't.

SOCRATES: So all just things are admirable.

10   ALCIBIADES: Yes.

SOCRATES: Now what about admirable things? Are they all good,
or are some good and others not good?

ALCIBIADES: What I think, Socrates, is that some admirable things
are bad.

SOCRATES: And some contemptible things are good?

ALCIBIADES: Yes.

115b   SOCRATES: Are you thinking of this sort of case? Many people get
wounded and killed trying to rescue their friends and relatives in battle, while those who don't go to rescue them, as they should, escape
safe and sound. Is this what you're referring to?

ALCIBIADES: Exactly.

5   SOCRATES: Now you call a rescue of this sort admirable, in that it's
an attempt to help the people whom you should help, and this is what
courage is; isn't that what you're saying?

ALCIBIADES: Yes.

SOCRATES: But you call it bad, in that it involves wounds and
death, don't you?

10   ALCIBIADES: Yes.

SOCRATES: Now courage is one thing, and death is something else,
115c   right?

ALCIBIADES: Certainly.

SOCRATES: So it's not on the same basis that rescuing your friends is admirable and bad, is it?

ALCIBIADES: Apparently not.   5

SOCRATES: Now let's see whether, insofar as it's admirable, it's also good, as indeed it is. You agreed that the rescue is admirable, in that it's courageous. Now consider this very thing—courage. Is it good or bad? Look at it like this: which would you rather have, good things or bad things?   10

ALCIBIADES: Good things.

SOCRATES: Namely the greatest goods?   115d

ALCIBIADES: Very much so.[17]

SOCRATES: And wouldn't you be least willing to be deprived of such things?

ALCIBIADES: Of course.

SOCRATES: What would you say about courage? How much would you have to be offered to be deprived of that?   5

ALCIBIADES: I wouldn't even want to go on living if I were a coward.

SOCRATES: So you think that cowardice is the worst thing in the world.

ALCIBIADES: I do.

SOCRATES: On a par with death, it would seem.   10

ALCIBIADES: That's what I say.

SOCRATES: Aren't life and courage the extreme opposites of death and cowardice?

ALCIBIADES: Yes.

SOCRATES: And wouldn't you want the former most and the latter   115e
least?

ALCIBIADES: Yes.

SOCRATES: Is that because you think that the former are best and the latter are worst?

ALCIBIADES: Certainly.   5

---

[17] Assigning *malista* (d1) to Alcibiades, and rejecting the supplement *nai* (d2).

SOCRATES: Would you say that courage ranks among the best things and death among the worst?

ALCIBIADES: I would say so.

SOCRATES: So you called rescuing your friends in battle admirable, insofar as it is admirable, in that it does something good, being courageous.

ALCIBIADES: I think so, anyway.

SOCRATES: But you called it bad, in that it does something bad, being fatal.[18]

ALCIBIADES: Yes.

SOCRATES: Now since you call this act bad insofar as it produces something bad, wouldn't you also, in all fairness, have to call it good insofar as it produces something good?

ALCIBIADES: I think so.

SOCRATES: Isn't it also admirable insofar as it's good, and contemptible insofar as it's bad?

ALCIBIADES: Yes.

SOCRATES: Then when you say that rescuing one's friends in battle is admirable but bad, you mean exactly the same as if you'd called it good but bad.

ALCIBIADES: I suppose you're right, Socrates.

SOCRATES: So nothing admirable, to the extent that it's admirable, is bad, and nothing contemptible, to the extent that it's contemptible, is good.

ALCIBIADES: Apparently not.

SOCRATES: Now then, let's take a new approach. People who do what's admirable do things well, don't they?

ALCIBIADES: Yes.

SOCRATES: And don't people who do things well live successful[19] lives?

ALCIBIADES: Of course.

---

[18] Omitting *ge* in e13.

[19] *Eudaimones*; also "happy."

SOCRATES: Aren't they successful because they've got good things?

ALCIBIADES: Certainly.

SOCRATES: And they get good things by acting properly and admirably.

ALCIBIADES: Yes.   10

SOCRATES: So it is good to act properly.

ALCIBIADES: Of course.

SOCRATES: And good conduct is admirable.

ALCIBIADES: Yes.

SOCRATES: So we've seen once again that the very thing that is admirable is also good.   116c

ALCIBIADES: Apparently.

SOCRATES: So if we find that something is admirable, we'll also find that it's good—according to this argument, at least.   5

ALCIBIADES: We'll have to.

SOCRATES: Well then, are good things advantageous, or not?

ALCIBIADES: Advantageous.

SOCRATES: Do you remember what we agreed about doing just things?   10

ALCIBIADES: I think we agreed that someone who does what's just must also be doing what's admirable.

SOCRATES: And didn't we also agree that someone who does what's admirable must also be doing what's good?

ALCIBIADES: Yes.

SOCRATES: And that what's good is advantageous?   116d

ALCIBIADES: Yes.

SOCRATES: So, Alcibiades, just things are advantageous.

ALCIBIADES: So it seems.

SOCRATES: Well then, am I not the questioner and are you not the answerer?   5

ALCIBIADES: It appears I am.

SOCRATES: So if someone who believed that he knew what is just and unjust were to stand up to advise the Athenians, or even the

Peparethians,[20] and said that sometimes just things are bad,[21] what
could you do but laugh at him? After all, as you yourself say, the same
things are just and also advantageous.

ALCIBIADES: I swear by the gods, Socrates, I have no idea what I
mean—I must be in some absolutely bizarre condition! When you ask
me questions, first I think one thing, and then I think something else.

SOCRATES: And are you unaware, my dear fellow, of what this
feeling is?

ALCIBIADES: Completely.

SOCRATES: Well, if someone asked you whether you had two eyes
or three eyes, or two hands or four hands, or something else like that,
do you think you'd give different answers at different times, or would
you always give the same answer?

ALCIBIADES: I'm quite unsure of myself at this point, but I think
I'd give the same answer.

SOCRATES: Because you know it—isn't that the reason?

ALCIBIADES: I think so.

SOCRATES: So if you gave conflicting answers about something,
without meaning to, then it would be obvious that you didn't know it.

ALCIBIADES: Probably.

SOCRATES: Well then, you tell me that you're wavering about what
is just and unjust, admirable and contemptible, good and bad, and advantageous and disadvantageous. Isn't it obvious that the reason you
waver about them is that you don't know about them?

ALCIBIADES: Yes, it is.

SOCRATES: Would you also say that whenever someone doesn't
know something, his soul will necessarily waver about it?

ALCIBIADES: Of course.

SOCRATES: Really? Do you know any way of ascending to the stars?

ALCIBIADES: I certainly don't.

---

[20] Peparethus, an otherwise insignificant Aegean island, was embroiled in conflict
in the late 360s.

[21] As Alcibiades did at 113d.

SOCRATES: Does your opinion waver on this question, too?

ALCIBIADES: Of course not.

SOCRATES: Do you know the reason, or shall I tell you?

ALCIBIADES: Tell me.   10

SOCRATES: It's because, my friend, you don't understand it and you don't think you understand it.

ALCIBIADES: And what do you mean by that?   117c

SOCRATES: Let's look at it together. Do you waver about what you realize you don't understand? For example, you know, I think, that you don't know how to prepare a fine meal, right?

ALCIBIADES: Quite right.   5

SOCRATES: So do you have your own opinions about how to prepare it, and waver about it; or do you leave it to someone who knows how?

ALCIBIADES: The latter.

SOCRATES: Well, if you were sailing in a ship, would you be out there wondering whether to put the helm to port or starboard, and wavering because you didn't know? Or would you leave it to the   117d
skipper and take it easy?

ALCIBIADES: I'd leave it to the skipper.

SOCRATES: So you don't waver about what you don't know, if in fact you know that you don't know.   5

ALCIBIADES: Apparently not.

SOCRATES: Don't you realize that the errors in our conduct are caused by this kind of ignorance, of thinking that we know when we don't know?

ALCIBIADES: What do you mean by that?   10

SOCRATES: Well, we don't set out to do something unless we think we know what we're doing, right?

ALCIBIADES: Right.

SOCRATES: But when people don't think they know how to do something, they hand it over to somebody else, right?   117e

ALCIBIADES: Of course.

SOCRATES: So the sort of people who don't think they know how to do things make no mistakes in life, because they leave those things to other people.

ALCIBIADES: You're right.

SOCRATES: Well, who are the ones making the mistakes? Surely not the ones who know?

ALCIBIADES: Of course not.

SOCRATES: Well, since it's not those who know, and it's not those who don't know and know they don't know, is there anyone left except those who don't know but think they do know?

ALCIBIADES: No, they're the only ones left.

SOCRATES: So this is the ignorance that causes bad things; this is the most disgraceful sort of stupidity.

ALCIBIADES: Yes.

SOCRATES: And isn't it most harmful and most contemptible when it is ignorance of the most important things?

ALCIBIADES: Very much so.

SOCRATES: Well, can you name anything more important than what's just and admirable and good and advantageous?

ALCIBIADES: No, I really can't.

SOCRATES: But aren't those the things you say you're wavering about?

ALCIBIADES: Yes.

SOCRATES: So, if you're wavering, it's obvious from what we've said that not only are you ignorant about the most important things, but you also think you know what you don't know.

ALCIBIADES: I guess that's right.

SOCRATES: Good God, Alcibiades, what a sorry state you're in! I hesitate to call it by its name, but still, since we're alone, it must be said. You are wedded to stupidity, my good fellow, stupidity in the highest degree—our discussion and your own words convict you of it. This is why you're rushing into politics before you've got an education. You're not alone in this sad state—you've got most of our city's politicians for company. There are only a few exceptions, among them, perhaps, your guardian, Pericles.

ALCIBIADES: Yes, Socrates, and people do say that he didn't acquire his expertise[22] all by himself; he kept company with many experts like Pythoclides[23] and Anaxagoras.[24] Even now, despite his advanced age, he consults with Damon[25] for the same purpose.

SOCRATES: Really? Have you ever seen any expert who is unable to make others expert in what he knows? The person who taught you how to read and write—he had expertise in his field, and he made you and anybody else he liked expert as well, didn't he?

ALCIBIADES: Yes.

SOCRATES: And will you, having learned from him, be able to teach somebody else?

ALCIBIADES: Yes.

SOCRATES: And isn't it the same with the music teacher and the gymnastics teacher?

ALCIBIADES: Certainly.

SOCRATES: I think we can be pretty sure that someone understands something when he can show that he has made someone else understand it.

ALCIBIADES: I agree.

SOCRATES: Well then, can you tell me who Pericles has made into an expert? Shall we start with his sons?

ALCIBIADES: But Socrates, both of his sons turned out to be idiots!

SOCRATES: What about Clinias, your brother?

ALCIBIADES: There's no point talking about *him*—he's a madman!

SOCRATES: Well then, since Clinias is mad and Pericles' sons were idiots, what shall we say is the reason that he allowed *you* to be in the state you're in?

ALCIBIADES: I suppose it's because I didn't really pay attention.

---

[22] *Sophos*; also "wisdom."

[23] Teacher of music and sophist from Ceos, also mentioned at *Protagoras* 316e3.

[24] See *Phaedrus* 270a6 note.

[25] Pioneering fifth-century BCE musicologist, who had views on the psychological and political significance of music. Cf. *Republic* 400b1, c4, 424c6.

SOCRATES: But can you name any other Athenian or any
119a foreigner—slave or free—who became any more of an expert by
keeping company with Pericles? After all, I can name Pythodorus, son
of Isolochus, and Callias, son of Calliades,[26] who became wise
5 through their association with Zeno[27]; they paid him a hundred minas
each and became famous experts.

ALCIBIADES: I can't think of anyone, by Zeus.

SOCRATES: Very well. What do you propose for yourself? Do you
intend to remain in your present condition, or practice some self-
cultivation?

ALCIBIADES: Let's discuss it together, Socrates. You know, I do see
119b what you're saying and actually I agree—it seems to me that none of
our city's politicians has been properly educated, except for a few.

SOCRATES: And what does that mean?

5 ALCIBIADES: Well, if they were educated, then anyone who wanted
to compete with them would have to get some knowledge and go
into training, like an athlete. But as it is, since they entered politics as
amateurs, there's no need for me to train and go to the trouble of
119c learning. I'm sure my natural abilities will be far superior to theirs.

SOCRATES: Good God, my dear boy, what a thing to say—how
unworthy of your good looks and your other advantages!

ALCIBIADES: What in the world do you mean, Socrates? What are
you getting at?

5 SOCRATES: I'm furious with you and with my infatuation for you!

ALCIBIADES: Why?

SOCRATES: Because you stoop to compete with these people.

ALCIBIADES: Who else have I got to compete with?

SOCRATES: That's a fine sort of question, from a man who thinks
119d he holds himself in high esteem!

ALCIBIADES: What do you mean? Aren't they my competitors?

SOCRATES: Look here, if you were intending to steer a ship into
5 battle, would you be content to be the best sailor at steering? Granted

---

[26] Prominent fifth-century Athenian politicians.

[27] See *Phaedrus* 261d8 note.

that's necessary, but wouldn't you keep your eye on your real oppo-
nents and not on your comrades, as you're doing now? Surely you
ought to be so far superior to them that they're happy to be your   119e
humble comrades in the struggle, and wouldn't dream of competing
with you. I'm assuming that you do really intend to distinguish yourself with some splendid deed worthy of you and your city.

ALCIBIADES: Yes, that's certainly what I intend to do.

SOCRATES: Dear me, how very proper it is for you to be satisfied
with being better than the soldiers—how proper not to keep an eye   5
on the leaders of the opposing camp, so that you can some day become better than them by training and scheming against them!

ALCIBIADES: Who are you talking about, Socrates?   **120a**

SOCRATES: Don't you know that our city is at war from time to
time with the Spartans and with the Great King of Persia?

ALCIBIADES: You're right.

SOCRATES: So since you plan to be leader of this city, wouldn't it be 5
right to think that your struggle is with the kings of Sparta and Persia?

ALCIBIADES: That may well be true.

SOCRATES: But no sir, you've got to keep an eye on Midias[28] the
cockfighter and such people—people who try to run the city's affairs 120b
with their 'slave-boy hair styles' (as the women say) still showing on
their boorish minds. They set out to flatter the city with their outlandish talk, not to rule it. These are the people, I'm telling you,   5
you've got to keep your eyes on. So relax, don't bother to learn what
needs to be learned for the great struggle to come, don't train yourself
for what needs training—go ahead and go into politics with your
complete and thorough preparation.   120c

ALCIBIADES: No, Socrates, I think you're right. But still I don't
think the Spartan generals or the Persian king are any different from
anybody else.   5

SOCRATES: But what sort of a notion is that? Think about it.

ALCIBIADES: About what?

---

[28] An Athenian politician mocked by the comic playwrights (see Aristophanes,
Birds 1297–8).

SOCRATES: In the first place, when do you think you'd cultivate yourself: if you feared them and thought they were formidable, or if you didn't?

ALCIBIADES: Obviously if I thought they were formidable.

SOCRATES: Surely you don't think that cultivating yourself will do you any harm, do you?

ALCIBIADES: Not at all. In fact, it would be a big help.

SOCRATES: So that's one flaw in this notion of yours, a big flaw, isn't it?

ALCIBIADES: You're right.

SOCRATES: Now the second flaw is that it's also false, judging by the probabilities.

ALCIBIADES: What do you mean?

SOCRATES: Is it likely that natural talents will be greatest among noble families, or in other families?

ALCIBIADES: In noble families, obviously.

SOCRATES: Those who are well born will turn out to be perfectly virtuous, if they're well brought up, won't they?

ALCIBIADES: They certainly will.

SOCRATES: So let's compare our situation with theirs, and consider, first of all, whether the Spartan and Persian kings are of humbler descent. We know, of course, that the Spartan kings are descended from Heracles,[29] and the Persian kings are descended from Achaemenes,[30] and that the families of Heracles and Achaemenes go right back to Perseus, son of Zeus.[31]

ALCIBIADES: Mine too, Socrates—my family goes back to Eurysaces[32] and Eurysaces' goes back to Zeus.

---

[29] See *Lysis* 205c7 note.

[30] Founder of the Achaemenid dynasty, which ruled Persia until its conquest by Alexander the Great.

[31] Heracles, a son of Zeus, was also the son of Alcmene, daughter of Electryon, son of Perseus, son of Zeus. The Persians, as descendents of Perses, Perseus' son, are therefore his relatives.

[32] According to legend, Eurysaces, king of Salamis, was great-grandson of Aeacus, son of Zeus.

SOCRATES: So does mine too, noble Alcibiades, mine goes back to Daedalus[33] and Daedalus' goes back to Hephaestus,[34] son of Zeus. Starting with those kings, though, and tracing backwards, every one of them is a king all the way back to Zeus—kings of Argos and Sparta, and kings of Persia in eternity, and sometimes of Asia, too, as they are now. But you and I are private citizens, as were our fathers. And if you had to show off your ancestors and Salamis, the native land of Eurysaces, to Artaxerxes, son of Xerxes—or Aegina, the native land of Aeacus the ancestor of Eurysaces—don't you realize how much you'd be laughed at? But you think we're the equal of those men in the dignity of our descent, as well as in our upbringing.

Haven't you noticed what a commanding position the Spartan kings enjoy? Their wives are guarded at public expense by the ephors,[35] so as to ensure, as far as possible, that their kings are descended from the family of the Heraclidae alone. And as for the Persian king, his position is so supreme that nobody so much as *suspects* his heir of being fathered by anybody but him; that's why his queen is left unguarded except by fear. When the eldest son and heir to the throne is born, all the king's subjects have a feast day. Then, in the years that follow, the whole of Asia celebrates that day, the king's birthday, with further sacrifice and feasting. But when *we* are born, Alcibiades, "even the neighbors hardly notice it," as the comic poet says.[36]

Then the boy is brought up—not by some nanny of no account, but by the most highly respected eunuchs in the royal household. They attend to all the needs of the infant child, and are especially concerned to make him as handsome as possible, shaping and straightening his infant limbs; and for this they are held in great esteem. When the boys reach seven years of age they take up horseback riding with their instructors, and begin to hunt wild game.

When he is twice seven years, the boy is entrusted to people called the "royal tutors." These are four Persians of mature age who have

---

[33] Socrates' father, Sophroniscus, is alleged to have been a sculptor or stone carver (Diogenes Laertius 2.18). Some of statues on the Acropolis may have been attributed to Socrates himself (Pausanias 1.22). Daedalus was a legendary sculptor of great skill, to whom sculptors traced their ancestry. See *Euthyphro* 11b–d.

[34] See *Symposium* 192d3 note.

[35] Spartan officials.

[36] A line of the comic poet Plato, fragment 204 (Kock).

been selected as the best: the wisest, the justest, the most self-controlled, and the bravest. The first of them instructs him in the worship of their gods, the Magian lore of Zoroaster, son of Horomazes,[37] and also in what a king should know. The justest man teaches him to be truthful his whole life long. The most self-controlled man teaches him not to be mastered by even a single pleasure, so that he can get accustomed to being a free man and a real king, whose first duty is to rule himself, not be a slave to himself. The bravest man trains him to be fearless and undaunted, because fear is slavery.

But for you, Alcibiades, Pericles chose from among his household Zopyrus the Thracian,[38] a tutor so old he was perfectly useless. I could tell you about all the rest of the upbringing and education of your competitors, but it would be a long story and, besides, you can probably imagine the later stages from what I've told you so far. But, Alcibiades, your birth, your upbringing, and your education—or that of any other Athenian—is of no concern to anybody, to tell the truth—nobody, that is, except perhaps some man who may happen to be in love with you.

Again, if you care to consider the wealth of the Persians, the splendor, the clothes and trailing robes, the anointings with myrrh, the throng of servants-in-waiting, and all their other luxuries, you'd be ashamed of your circumstances, because you'd see how inferior they are to theirs.

Again, if you care to consider the self-control and the decorum of the Spartans, their confidence and their composure, their self-esteem and their discipline, their courage and their fortitude, and their love of hardship, victory, and honor, you'd consider yourself a mere child in all these respects.

Again, we'd better discuss your wealth, Alcibiades, if you're to see where you stand. *You* may devote yourself to it and think it makes you something, but if you care to look at the wealth of the Spartans you'd realize that it greatly exceeds ours in Athens. They have land of their own and in Messene[39] that not a single one of our estates could

---

[37] Zoroaster (thirteenth or fourteenth century BCE) was the founder of Persian religion. Horomazes was not, in fact, his father, but the good one of the two conflicting divinities in which he believed.

[38] Otherwise unknown.

[39] A neighbor of Sparta, and subject to it in this period.

compete with—not in size, nor in quality, nor in slaves—especially
Helots[40]—nor even in horses, nor in the other livestock grazing in
Messene. But I'll pass over all that.   122e

There is more gold and silver in Sparta in private hands than in the
rest of Greece put together. It's been coming in to them for many
generations, pouring in from all of Greece's cities, and often from foreign cities, too, and it never goes out again. It's just like what the fox   5
says to the lion in Aesop's fable[41]—you can clearly see the tracks of
the money going in toward Sparta, but the tracks coming out are   **123a**
nowhere to be seen. So you can be sure that the Spartans are the richest of the Greeks in gold and silver, and that the king is the richest of   5
all the Spartans, because the greatest share of these revenues goes to
him. Furthermore, he receives a considerable sum from the Spartans
by way of royal tribute.

But great as they are when compared with other Greek cities, the
Spartan fortunes are nothing compared with the fortunes of the Per-   **123b**
sians and their king. I once spoke with a reliable man who traveled
over to the Persian court, and he told me that he crossed a very large
and rich tract of land, nearly a day's journey across, which the locals   5
called "the Queen's girdle." There's another one called "the Queen's
veil," as well as many others, all fine and rich properties, each one   **123c**
named for a part of the Queen's wardrobe, because each one is set
aside to pay for the Queen's finery.

Now suppose someone were to say to Amestris, the king's mother
and the widow of Xerxes,[42] "The son of Dinomache intends to chal-   5
lenge your son; her wardrobe is worth only fifty minas at best, and her
son has less than three hundred acres of land at Erchia."[43] I think she'd
be wondering what this Alcibiades had up his sleeve to think of competing against Artaxerxes. I think she'd say, "I don't see what this   **123d**

---

[40] The serf population of Sparta.

[41] A lion lay in a cave, too old and ill to hunt. When other animals came to visit
him, he ate them. Then a vixen came, but stayed at the entrance. When the lion
asked her why she didn't come in, she said, "Because I see lots of tracks going in,
but none coming out."

[42] King of Persia (c. 486–465 BCE) who invaded Greece in the second Persian
War (begun in 480).

[43] The Attic "acre" was 874 square meters, so Alcibiades' holding was less than 26
hectares (65 modern acres).

fellow could be relying on, except diligence and wisdom—the Greeks don't have anything else worth mentioning."

But if she heard that this Alcibiades who is making this attempt is, in the first place, hardly twenty years old yet, and, secondly, entirely uneducated, and furthermore, when his lover tells him to study and cultivate himself and discipline himself so that he can compete with the king, he says he doesn't want to and that he's happy with the way he is—if she heard all that, I think she'd ask in amazement, "What in the world could this youngster be relying on?" Suppose we were to reply, "Good looks, height, birth, wealth, and native intelligence." Then, Alcibiades, considering all that they have of these things as well, she'd conclude that we were stark raving mad. Again, I think that Lampido, the daughter of Leotychides, wife of Archidamus and mother of Agis, who were all Spartan kings, would be similarly amazed if you, with your bad upbringing, proposed to compete with her son, considering all his advantages.

And yet, don't you think it's disgraceful that even our enemies' *wives* have a better appreciation than we do of what it would take to challenge them? No, my excellent friend, trust in me and in the Delphic inscription and "know thyself."[44] These are the people we must defeat, not the ones you think, and we have no hope of defeating them unless we act with both diligence and skill. If you fall short in these, then you will fall short of achieving fame in Greece as well as abroad; and that is what I think you're longing for, more than anyone else ever longed for anything.

ALCIBIADES: Well, Socrates, what kind of self-cultivation do I need to practice? Can you show me the way? What you said really sounded true.

SOCRATES: Yes—but let's discuss together how we can become as good as possible. You know, what I've said about the need for education applies to me as well as to you—we're in the same condition, except in one respect.

ALCIBIADES: What?

SOCRATES: My guardian is better and wiser than Pericles, your guardian.

ALCIBIADES: Who's that, Socrates?

---

[44] See *Phaedrus* 229e6 note.

SOCRATES: God, Alcibiades; it was a god who prevented me from talking with you before today.[45] I put my faith in him, and I say that your glory will be entirely my doing.   10

ALCIBIADES: You're teasing me, Socrates.   124d

SOCRATES: Maybe; but I'm right in saying that we stand in need of self-cultivation. Actually, every human being needs self-cultivation, but *especially* the two of us.

ALCIBIADES: You're right about me.

SOCRATES: And about me.   5

ALCIBIADES: So what should we do?

SOCRATES: There must be no giving up, my friend, and no slacking off.

ALCIBIADES: No, Socrates, that really wouldn't do.

SOCRATES: No it wouldn't. So let's work it out together. Tell me—we say that we want to be as good as possible, don't we?   124e

ALCIBIADES: Yes.

SOCRATES: In what respect?

ALCIBIADES: In what good men do, obviously.

SOCRATES: Good at what?   5

ALCIBIADES: Taking care of things, obviously.

SOCRATES: What sorts of things? Horses?

ALCIBIADES: Of course not.

SOCRATES: In that case, we'd consult a horse expert.

ALCIBIADES: Yes.   10

SOCRATES: Well, do you mean sailing?

ALCIBIADES: No.

SOCRATES: In that case, we'd consult a sailing expert.

ALCIBIADES: Yes.

SOCRATES: Well, what sorts of things? Whose business is it?   15

ALCIBIADES: The leading citizens of Athens.

---

[45] Cf. 103a5 and note.

125a   SOCRATES: By 'leading citizens' do you mean clever men or stupid men?

ALCIBIADES: Clever.

SOCRATES: But isn't everybody good at what they're clever at?

5   ALCIBIADES: Yes.

SOCRATES: And bad at what they're not?

ALCIBIADES: Of course.

SOCRATES: And is the shoemaker clever at making shoes?

10   ALCIBIADES: Certainly.

SOCRATES: Then he's good at it.

ALCIBIADES: That's right.

SOCRATES: Well now, isn't the shoemaker stupid at making clothes?

15   ALCIBIADES: Yes.

125b   SOCRATES: So he's bad at that.

ALCIBIADES: Yes.

SOCRATES: So the same person is both good and bad, at least by this argument.

5   ALCIBIADES: Apparently.

SOCRATES: Do you mean to say that *good men* are also bad?

ALCIBIADES: Of course not.

SOCRATES: So which ones *do* you say are good men?

ALCIBIADES: I mean those with the ability to rule in the city.

10   SOCRATES: But not, I presume, over horses.

ALCIBIADES: No, of course not.

SOCRATES: Over people?

ALCIBIADES: Yes.

SOCRATES: When they're sick?

15   ALCIBIADES: No.

SOCRATES: When they're at sea?

ALCIBIADES: No.

SOCRATES: When they're harvesting?

ALCIBIADES: No.

SOCRATES: When they're doing nothing? Or when they're doing something?   125c

ALCIBIADES: Doing something.

SOCRATES: Doing what? Try to make it clear for me.

ALCIBIADES: It's when they're helping each other and dealing with each other, as we do in our urban way of life.   5

SOCRATES: So you mean ruling over men who deal with men.

ALCIBIADES: Yes.

SOCRATES: Over the boatswains who deal with rowers?

ALCIBIADES: Of course not.   10

SOCRATES: That's what the pilot is good at.

ALCIBIADES: Yes.

SOCRATES: Do you mean ruling over flute-players, who direct the singers and deal with the dancers?   125d

ALCIBIADES: Of course not.

SOCRATES: Again, that's what the chorus-master is good at.

ALCIBIADES: Certainly.

SOCRATES: So what *do* you mean by being able to "rule over men   5
who deal with men"?

ALCIBIADES: I mean ruling over the men in the city who take part in citizenship and who make a mutual contribution.

SOCRATES: Well, what skill is this? Suppose I asked you the same thing again—what skill makes men understand how to rule over men   10
who take part in sailing?

ALCIBIADES: The pilot's.

SOCRATES: And what knowledge did we say enables them to rule   125e
over those who take part in singing?

ALCIBIADES: The chorus-master's, as you just said.

SOCRATES: Well now, what do you call the knowledge that enables you to rule over those who take part in citizenship?   5

ALCIBIADES: I call it the knowledge of good advice, Socrates.

SOCRATES: But then do you think the pilot's advice is bad advice?

ALCIBIADES: Of course not.

SOCRATES: Then is it good advice?

ALCIBIADES: I should think so; he has to ensure the safety of his
126a passengers.

SOCRATES: You're right. Well then, what's the purpose of this
good advice you're talking about?

ALCIBIADES: The safety and better management of the city.

5   SOCRATES: But what is present or absent when the city is safe and
better managed? If, for example, you asked me, "What is present or
absent in the body when it is safe and better managed?" I'd reply,
"Health is present and disease is absent." Wouldn't you agree?

126b   ALCIBIADES: Yes.

SOCRATES: And if you asked me again, "What is present in our
eyes when they are better cared for?" I'd say the same sort of thing—
"Sight is present and blindness is absent." Again, with our ears, deaf-
5   ness is absent and hearing is present when they're in better condition
and getting better treatment.

ALCIBIADES: You're right.

SOCRATES: Well then, what about a city? What is it that's present
or absent when it's in a better condition and getting better manage-
10   ment and treatment?

126c   ALCIBIADES: The way I look at it, Socrates, mutual friendship will
be present, and hatred and insurrection will be absent.

SOCRATES: When you say "friendship," do you mean agreement
or disagreement?

5   ALCIBIADES: Agreement.

SOCRATES: What skill is it that makes cities agree about numbers?

ALCIBIADES: Arithmetic.

SOCRATES: What about private citizens? Isn't it the same skill?

10   ALCIBIADES: Yes.

SOCRATES: And doesn't it also make each person agree with himself?

ALCIBIADES: Yes.

SOCRATES: And what skill is it that makes each of us agree with
himself about whether a hand's-width is larger than an arm's-length?
126d   It's measuring, isn't it?

ALCIBIADES: Of course.

SOCRATES: Doesn't it make both cities and private citizens agree?

ALCIBIADES: Yes.   5

SOCRATES: And isn't it the same with weighing?

ALCIBIADES: It is.

SOCRATES: Well, this agreement you're talking about, what is it? What's it about? What skill provides it? Doesn't the same skill make both a city and a private citizen agree, both with themselves and with others?   10

ALCIBIADES: That does seem quite likely.

SOCRATES: What is it then? Don't give up. . . . Try your best to tell me.   126e

ALCIBIADES: I suppose I mean the sort of friendship and agreement you find when a mother and father agree with a son they love, and when a brother agrees with his brother, and a woman agrees with her husband.

SOCRATES: Well, Alcibiades, do you think that a husband is able to agree with his wife about wool-working, when he doesn't understand   5
it and she does?

ALCIBIADES: Of course not.

SOCRATES: Nor does he have any need to, because that's for a woman to know about.

ALCIBIADES: That's right.   10

SOCRATES: And is a woman able to agree with her husband about military tactics, without having learned about it?   127a

ALCIBIADES: Of course not.

SOCRATES: I suppose you'd say that that's for a man to know about.

ALCIBIADES: I would.   5

SOCRATES: So, according to your argument, some subjects are women's subjects and some are men's subjects.

ALCIBIADES: Of course.

SOCRATES: So, in these areas at least, there's no agreement between men and women.   10

ALCIBIADES: No.

SOCRATES: Nor is there any friendship, since friendship was agreement.

ALCIBIADES: Apparently not.

15 SOCRATES: So women are not loved by men, insofar as they do their own work.

127b ALCIBIADES: It seems not.

SOCRATES: Nor are men loved by women, insofar as they do theirs.

ALCIBIADES: No.

5 SOCRATES: So neither are cities well governed when the different groups each do their own work.

ALCIBIADES: But I think they *are*, Socrates.

SOCRATES: What do you mean? In that case there's no friendship in cities, but we said friendship was present when cities are well governed, and not otherwise.

10 ALCIBIADES: But I think it's when each person does his own work that mutual friendship results.

SOCRATES: You've just changed your mind. What do you mean
127c now? Can there be friendship without agreement? Can there be any agreement when some know about the matter and others don't?

ALCIBIADES: There can't possibly.

5 SOCRATES: But when everyone does his own work, is everyone being just, or unjust?

ALCIBIADES: Just, of course.

SOCRATES: So when the citizens do what is just in the city, there is no friendship between them.

10 ALCIBIADES: Again, Socrates, I think there must be.

SOCRATES: Then what *do* you mean by this "friendship" and
127d "agreement" that we must be wise and good advisers in if we're to be good men? I can't figure out what it is, or who's got it. According to your argument, it seems that sometimes certain people have it and
5 sometimes they don't.

ALCIBIADES: Well, Socrates, I swear by the gods that I don't even know what I mean. I think I must have been in an appalling state for a long time, without being aware of it.

SOCRATES: But don't lose heart. If you were fifty when you realized it, then it would be hard for you to cultivate yourself, but now you're just the right age to see it. 127e

ALCIBIADES: Now that I've seen it, Socrates, what should I do about it?

SOCRATES: Answer my questions, Alcibiades. If you do that, then, 5 god willing—if we are to trust in my divination—you and I will be in a better state.

ALCIBIADES: Then we will be, if it depends on my answering.

SOCRATES: Well then, what does it mean to cultivate oneself?—I'm afraid we often think we're cultivating ourselves when we're not. 128a When does a man do that? Is he cultivating himself when he cultivates what he has?

ALCIBIADES: *I* think so, anyway.

SOCRATES: Really? When does a man cultivate or care for his feet? 5 Is it when he's caring for what belongs to his feet?

ALCIBIADES: I don't understand.

SOCRATES: Is there anything you'd say belonged to a hand? Take a ring, for example—could it belong anywhere else on a man but on his finger?

ALCIBIADES: Of course not. 10

SOCRATES: Similarly a shoe belongs nowhere but on the feet.

ALCIBIADES: Yes.

SOCRATES: Likewise cloaks and bedclothes belong to the rest of the body.

ALCIBIADES: Yes. 128b

SOCRATES: So when we cultivate or care for our shoes, are we caring for our feet?

ALCIBIADES: I don't really understand, Socrates.

SOCRATES: Surely, Alcibiades, you talk about taking proper care of one thing or another, don't you? 5

ALCIBIADES: Yes, I do.

SOCRATES: And when you make something better, you say you're taking proper care of it.

10   ALCIBIADES: Yes.

SOCRATES: What skill is it that makes shoes better?

ALCIBIADES: Shoemaking.

SOCRATES: So shoemaking is the skill by which we take care of shoes.

128c   ALCIBIADES: Yes.

SOCRATES: Do we use shoemaking to take care of our feet, too? Or do we use the skill that makes our feet better?

ALCIBIADES: The latter.

SOCRATES: Isn't the skill that makes the feet better the same as
5   what makes the rest of the body better?

ALCIBIADES: I think so.

SOCRATES: Isn't this skill athletics?

ALCIBIADES: Yes, absolutely.

SOCRATES: So while we take care of our feet with athletics, we
10   take care of what belongs to our feet with shoemaking.

ALCIBIADES: Certainly.

SOCRATES: And while we take care of our hands with athletics, we take care of what belongs to our hands with ring-making.

ALCIBIADES: Yes.

SOCRATES: And while we cultivate our bodies with athletics, we
15   take care of what belongs to our bodies with weaving and other skills.
128d

ALCIBIADES: That's absolutely right.

SOCRATES: So while we cultivate each thing with one skill, we cultivate what belongs to it with another skill.

5   ALCIBIADES: Apparently so.

SOCRATES: And so when you're cultivating what belongs to you, you're not cultivating yourself.

ALCIBIADES: Not at all.

SOCRATES: For it seems that cultivating yourself and cultivating what belongs to you require different skills.

10   ALCIBIADES: Apparently.

SOCRATES: Well then, what sort of skill could we use to cultivate ourselves?

ALCIBIADES: I couldn't say.

SOCRATES: But we've agreed on this much, at least—it's a skill that   128e
won't make anything that belongs to us better, but it will make *us* better.

ALCIBIADES: You're right.

SOCRATES: Now if we didn't know what a shoe was, would we
have known what skill makes a shoe better?   5

ALCIBIADES: No, we couldn't have.

SOCRATES: Nor would we have known what skill makes a ring
better if we didn't know what a ring was.

ALCIBIADES: True.

SOCRATES: Well then, could we ever know what skill makes us
better if we didn't know what *we* were?   10

ALCIBIADES: We couldn't.   **129a**

SOCRATES: Is it actually such an easy thing to know oneself? Was it
some simpleton who inscribed those words on the temple wall at
Delphi? Or is it difficult, and not for everybody?

ALCIBIADES: Sometimes I think, Socrates, that anyone can do it,   5
but then sometimes I think it's extremely difficult.

SOCRATES: But Alcibiades, whether it's easy or not, nevertheless
this is the situation we're in: if we know ourselves, then we might be
able to know how to cultivate ourselves, but if we don't know ourselves, we'll never know how.

ALCIBIADES: I agree.   10

SOCRATES: Tell me, how can we find out what *the itself* itself is?[46]   129b
Maybe this is the way to find out what our*selves* might be—maybe
it's the only possible way.

ALCIBIADES: You're right.

SOCRATES: Hold on, by Zeus—who are you speaking with now?
Anybody but me?   5

---

[46] Reading *auto to auto* in b1. The just itself (*auto to dikaion*) is the characteristic
that all just things share. Similarly, the itself, itself, is the characteristic that all
(it)selves, including myself and yourself, have in common. Such shared characteristics are forms (*eidê, ideai*), and "the F itself" is a common way of referring to the
form of F. See Introduction, pp. xiv–xvi.

ALCIBIADES: No.

SOCRATES: And I'm speaking with you.

ALCIBIADES: Yes.

10   SOCRATES: Is Socrates doing the talking?

ALCIBIADES: He certainly is.

SOCRATES: And is Alcibiades doing the listening?

ALCIBIADES: Yes.

SOCRATES: And isn't Socrates talking with words?

129c   ALCIBIADES: Of course.

SOCRATES: I suppose you'd say that talking is the same as using words?

ALCIBIADES: Certainly.

SOCRATES: But the thing being used and the person using it—
5   they're different, aren't they?

ALCIBIADES: What do you mean?

SOCRATES: A shoemaker, for example, cuts with a knife and a scraper, I think, and with other tools.

ALCIBIADES: Yes, he does.

10   SOCRATES: So isn't the cutter who uses the tools different from the tools he's cutting with?

ALCIBIADES: Of course.

SOCRATES: And likewise isn't the lyre-player different from what he's playing with?

15   ALCIBIADES: Yes.

SOCRATES: This is what I was just asking—doesn't the user of a
129d   thing always seem to be different from what he's using?

ALCIBIADES: It seems so.

SOCRATES: Let's think about the shoemaker again. Does he cut
5   with his tools only, or does he also cut with his hands?

ALCIBIADES: With his hands, too.

SOCRATES: So he uses his hands, too.

ALCIBIADES: Yes.

SOCRATES: And doesn't he use his eyes, too, in shoemaking?

ALCIBIADES: Yes. 10

SOCRATES: Didn't we agree that the person who uses something is different from the thing that he uses?

ALCIBIADES: Yes.

SOCRATES: So the shoemaker and the lyre-player are different from the hands and eyes they use in their work. 129e

ALCIBIADES: So it seems.

SOCRATES: Doesn't a man use his whole body, too?

ALCIBIADES: Certainly.

SOCRATES: And we agreed that the user is different from the thing being used. 5

ALCIBIADES: Yes.

SOCRATES: So a man is different from his own body.

ALCIBIADES: So it seems.

SOCRATES: Then what *is* a man?

ALCIBIADES: I don't know what to say. 10

SOCRATES: Yes, you do—say that it's what uses the body.

ALCIBIADES: Yes.

SOCRATES: What else uses it but the soul? **130a**

ALCIBIADES: Nothing else.

SOCRATES: And doesn't the soul rule the body?

ALCIBIADES: Yes.

SOCRATES: Now here's something I don't think anybody would disagree with. 5

ALCIBIADES: What?

SOCRATES: Man is one of three things.

ALCIBIADES: What things?

SOCRATES: The body, the soul, or the two of them together, the whole thing.

ALCIBIADES: Of course. 10

SOCRATES: But we agreed that man is that which rules the body.

ALCIBIADES: Yes, we did agree to that. 130b

SOCRATES: Does the body rule itself?

ALCIBIADES: It couldn't.

SOCRATES: Because we said it was ruled.

5   ALCIBIADES: Yes.

SOCRATES: So *this* can't be what we're looking for.

ALCIBIADES: Not likely.

SOCRATES: Well then, can the two of them together rule the body? Is this what man is?

10   ALCIBIADES: Yes, maybe that's it.

SOCRATES: No, that's the least likely of all. If one of them doesn't take part in ruling, then surely no combination of the two of them could rule.

ALCIBIADES: You're right.

130c   SOCRATES: Since a man is neither his body, nor his body and soul together, what remains, I think, is either that he's nothing, or else, if he *is* something, he's nothing other than his soul.

ALCIBIADES: Quite so.

5   SOCRATES: Do you need any clearer proof that the soul is the man?

ALCIBIADES: No, by Zeus, I think you've given ample proof.

SOCRATES: Well, if we've proven it fairly well, although perhaps not rigorously, that will do for us. We'll have a rigorous proof when we find out what we skipped over, because it would have taken quite
130d   a lot of study.

ALCIBIADES: What was that?

SOCRATES: What we mentioned just now, that we should first consider what *the itself* itself is. But in fact, we've been considering what a *particular itself*[47] is, instead of what *the* itself is. Perhaps that was
5   enough for us, for surely nothing about us has more authority than the soul, wouldn't you agree?

ALCIBIADES: Certainly.

SOCRATES: So the right way of looking at it is that, when you and
10   I talk to each other, one soul uses words to address another soul.

---

[47] Reading *auton hekaston* at d4.

ALCIBIADES: Very true.   130e

SOCRATES: That's just what we were saying a little while ago—that Socrates converses with Alcibiades not by saying words to his face, apparently, but by addressing his words to *Alcibiades*, in other words, to his soul.   5

ALCIBIADES: I see it now.

SOCRATES: So the command that we should know ourselves means that we should know our souls.

ALCIBIADES: So it seems.   **131a**

SOCRATES: And someone who knows about his body[48] knows not himself, but what belongs to him.

ALCIBIADES: That's right.

SOCRATES: So no doctor, to the extent he's a doctor, knows himself, and neither does any trainer, to the extent he's a trainer.   5

ALCIBIADES: It seems not.

SOCRATES: So farmers and other tradesmen are a long way from knowing themselves. It seems *they* don't even know what belongs to   10
them; their skills are about what's even further away than what belongs to them. They only know what belongs to the body and how to   131b
take care of it.

ALCIBIADES: You're right.

SOCRATES: If being self-controlled is knowing yourself, then their skills don't make any of them self-controlled.   5

ALCIBIADES: I don't think so.

SOCRATES: That's why we consider these skills to be beneath us, and not suitable for a gentleman to learn.

ALCIBIADES: You're quite right.

SOCRATES: Furthermore, if someone takes care of his body, then   10
isn't he caring for something that belongs to him, and not for himself?

ALCIBIADES: That seems likely.

SOCRATES: And isn't someone who takes care of his wealth caring neither for himself nor for what belongs to him, but for something even further away?   131c

---

[48] Omitting *ti* with some manuscripts.

ALCIBIADES: I agree.

SOCRATES: So the money-earner is not, in fact, doing his own work.

ALCIBIADES: Right.

5   SOCRATES: Now if there was someone who loved Alcibiades' body, he wouldn't be loving Alcibiades, only something that belonged to Alcibiades.

ALCIBIADES: That's right.

SOCRATES: But someone who loved you would love your soul.

10   ALCIBIADES: By our argument, I think he'd have to.

SOCRATES: Wouldn't someone who loves your body go off and leave you when your beauty is no longer in full bloom?

ALCIBIADES: Obviously.

SOCRATES: But someone who loves your soul will not leave you, as
131d   long as you're making progress.

ALCIBIADES: That's probably right.

SOCRATES: Well, I'm the one who won't leave you—I'm the one who will stay with you, now that your body has lost its bloom and
5   everyone else has gone away.

ALCIBIADES: I'm glad you are, Socrates, and I hope you never leave me.

SOCRATES: Then you must try to be as attractive as possible.

ALCIBIADES: I'll certainly try.

131e   SOCRATES: So this is your situation: you, Alcibiades, son of Clinias, have no lovers and never have had any, it seems, except for one only, and he is your darling[49] Socrates, son of Sophroniscus and Phaenarete.

5   ALCIBIADES: True.

SOCRATES: Remember when I first spoke to you? You said that you were just about to say something; you wanted to ask me why I was the only one who hadn't given up on you.[50]

---

[49] An echo of *Odyssey* ii.365.

[50] At 104c–d.

ALCIBIADES: That's right.

SOCRATES: Well, this is the reason: I was your only lover—the others were only lovers of what you had. While your possessions are passing their prime, *you* are just beginning to bloom. I shall never forsake you now, never, unless the Athenian people make you corrupt and ugly.[51] And that is my greatest fear, that a love of the common people might corrupt you, for many Athenian gentlemen have suffered that fate already. "The people of great-hearted Erechtheus"[52] might look attractive on the outside, but you need to scrutinize them in their nakedness, so take the precaution I urge.

132a

5

ALCIBIADES: What precaution?

SOCRATES: Get in training first, my dear friend, and learn what you need to know *before* entering politics. That will give you an antidote against the terrible dangers.

132b

ALCIBIADES: I think you're right, Socrates. But try to explain how exactly we should cultivate ourselves.

5

SOCRATES: Well, we've made one step forward anyway—we've pretty well agreed what we are; we were afraid that we might make a mistake about that and unwittingly cultivate something other than ourselves.

ALCIBIADES: That's right.

10

SOCRATES: And the next step is that we have to cultivate our soul and look to that.

132c

ALCIBIADES: Obviously.

SOCRATES: And let others take care of our bodies and our property.

5

ALCIBIADES: Quite so.

SOCRATES: Now, how can we get the clearest knowledge of our soul? If we knew that, we'd probably know ourselves as well . . . By the gods—that admirable Delphic inscription we just mentioned[53]—didn't we understand it?

10

ALCIBIADES: What's the point of bringing that up again, Socrates?

---

[51] Cf. *Republic* 491c–493d.

[52] An epithet for the people of Athens, in Homer, *Iliad* ii.547.

[53] "Know Thyself;" cf. 129a.

132d   SOCRATES: I'll tell you what I suspect that inscription means, and what advice it's giving us. There may not be many examples of it, except the case of sight.

ALCIBIADES: What do you mean by that?

SOCRATES: You think about it, too. If the inscription took our
5   eyes to be men and advised them, "See thyself," how would we understand such advice? Shouldn't the eye be looking at something in which it could see itself?

ALCIBIADES: Obviously.

10   SOCRATES: Then let's think of something that allows us to see both it
132e   and ourselves when we look at it.

ALCIBIADES: Obviously, Socrates, you mean mirrors and that sort of thing.

SOCRATES: Quite right. And isn't there something like that in the
5   eye, which we see with?

ALCIBIADES: Certainly.

SOCRATES: I'm sure you've noticed that when a man looks into an
133a   eye his face appears in it, like in a mirror. We call this the "pupil," for it's a sort of miniature of the man who's looking.[54]

ALCIBIADES: You're right.

5   SOCRATES: Then an eye will see itself if it observes an eye and looks at the best part of it, the part with which it can see.

ALCIBIADES: So it seems.

SOCRATES: But it won't see itself if it looks at anything else in a
10   man, or anything else at all, unless it's similar to the eye.

133b   ALCIBIADES: You're right.

SOCRATES: So if an eye is to see itself, it must look at an eye, and at that region of it in which the good activity of an eye actually occurs,
5   and this, I presume, is seeing.

ALCIBIADES: That's right.

SOCRATES: Then if the soul, Alcibiades, is to know itself, it must look at a soul, and especially at that region in which what makes a
10   soul good, wisdom, occurs, and at anything else which is similar to it.

---

[54] The Greek word for "pupil" also means "doll."

ALCIBIADES: I agree with you, Socrates.

SOCRATES: Can we say that there is anything about the soul which is more divine than that where knowing and understanding take place? 133c

ALCIBIADES: No, we can't.

SOCRATES: Then that region in it resembles the divine,[55] and someone who looked at that and grasped everything divine—vision[56] and understanding—would have the best grasp of himself as well.   5

ALCIBIADES: So it seems.[57]

SOCRATES: But we agreed that knowing oneself was the same as being self-controlled.

ALCIBIADES: Certainly.   10

SOCRATES: So if we didn't know ourselves and weren't self-controlled, would we be able to know which of the things that belong to us were good and which were bad?

ALCIBIADES: How could we know that, Socrates?

SOCRATES: No; I suppose it would seem impossible to you to know that what belongs to Alcibiades belongs to him, without know-   133d
ing Alcibiades.

ALCIBIADES: Quite impossible, I'm sure.

SOCRATES: And similarly we couldn't know that what belongs to us belongs to us, without knowing ourselves.   5

ALCIBIADES: How could we?

---

[55] Reading *theiôi* in c4.

[56] Accepting the emendation *thean* (vision) for *theon* (god) in c5.

[57] Omitting 133c8–17 (which seem to have been added by a later neo-Platonist scholar). The lines read:

> SOCRATES: Just as mirrors are clearer, purer, and brighter than the reflecting surface of the eye, isn't God both purer and brighter than the best part of our soul?
>
> ALCIBIADES: I would certainly think so, Socrates.
>
> SOCRATES: So the way that we can best see and know ourselves is to use the finest mirror available and look at God and, on the human level, at the virtue of the soul.
>
> Alcibiades: Yes.

SOCRATES: And if we didn't even know what belongs to us, how could we possibly know what belongs to our belongings?

ALCIBIADES: We couldn't.

10   SOCRATES: Then it wasn't quite right to agree, as we did a few minutes ago,[58] that some people know what belongs to them without knowing themselves, while others know what belongs to their belongings. It seems that it's the job of one man, and one skill, to know

133e all these things: himself, his belongings, and his belongings' belongings.

ALCIBIADES: That seems likely.

SOCRATES: And it follows that anyone who doesn't know his own

5   belongings probably won't know other people's belongings either.

ALCIBIADES: Quite so.

SOCRATES: And if he doesn't know other people's belongings, nor will he know what belongs to the city.

ALCIBIADES: He couldn't.

SOCRATES: So such a man couldn't become a statesman.

10   ALCIBIADES: Of course not.

SOCRATES: Nor could he even manage a household estate.

134a ALCIBIADES: Of course not.

SOCRATES: Nor indeed will he know what he's doing.

ALCIBIADES: Certainly not.

SOCRATES: And if he doesn't know what he's doing, won't he make mistakes?

5   ALCIBIADES: Certainly.

SOCRATES: Since he makes mistakes, won't he conduct himself badly, both publicly and privately?

ALCIBIADES: Of course.

SOCRATES: Since he conducts himself badly, won't he be a failure?

10   ALCIBIADES: Absolutely.

SOCRATES: What about the people he's working for?

ALCIBIADES: They will be too.

---

[58] At 131a–c.

SOCRATES: Then it's impossible for anyone to prosper unless he is self-controlled and good.

ALCIBIADES: Impossible.   134b

SOCRATES: So it's the bad men who are failures.

ALCIBIADES: Absolutely.

SOCRATES: And so the way to avoid being a failure is not by getting rich, but by being self-controlled.   5

ALCIBIADES: Apparently.

SOCRATES: So it's not walls or war-ships or shipyards that cities need, Alcibiades, if they are to prosper, nor is it numbers or size, without virtue.

ALCIBIADES: Definitely.   10

SOCRATES: So if you are to manage the city's business properly and well, you must impart virtue to the citizens.   134c

ALCIBIADES: Of course.

SOCRATES: Is it possible to impart something you haven't got?

ALCIBIADES: How could you?

SOCRATES: Then you, or anyone else who is to be ruler and trustee,   5
not only of himself and his private business, but also the city and the city's business, must first acquire virtue himself.

ALCIBIADES: You're right.

SOCRATES: So what you need to get for yourself and for the city isn't political power, nor the authority to do what you like; what you need is justice and self-control.   10

ALCIBIADES: Apparently.[59]

---

[59] Accepting a conjectural deletion of 134d1–e7 (which seem to have been added by a later neo-Platonist scholar). The lines read:

> SOCRATES: And if you and the city act with justice and self-control, you and the city will be acting in a way that pleases God.
>
> ALCIBIADES: That seems likely.
>
> SOCRATES: And, as we were saying before, you will be acting with a view to what is divine and bright.
>
> ALCIBIADES: Apparently.
>
> SOCRATES: Of course, if you keep that in view, you will see and understand yourselves and your own good.

134e8   SOCRATES: Because my dear Alcibiades, when an individual or a city with no intelligence is at liberty to do what he or it wants, what do you think the likely result will be? For example, if he's sick and has

10   the power to do whatever he likes—without any medical insight but

135a   with such a dictator's power that nobody criticizes him—what's going to happen? Isn't it likely his health will be ruined?

ALCIBIADES: You're right.

5   SOCRATES: And in a ship, if someone were free to do what he liked, but was completely lacking in insight and skill in navigation, don't you see what would happen to him and his fellow sailors?

ALCIBIADES: I do indeed; they would all die.

SOCRATES: Likewise, if a city, or any ruler or administrator, is

135b   lacking in virtue, then bad conduct will result.

ALCIBIADES: It must.

SOCRATES: Well then, my good Alcibiades, if you are to prosper, it

5   isn't supreme power you need to get for yourself or the city, but virtue.

ALCIBIADES: You're right.

SOCRATES: But before one acquires virtue it's better to be ruled by somebody superior than to rule; this applies to men as well as to boys.

10   ALCIBIADES: So it seems.

SOCRATES: And isn't what is better also more admirable?

ALCIBIADES: Yes.

SOCRATES: And isn't what is more admirable more appropriate?

135c   ALCIBIADES: Of course.

ALCIBIADES: Yes.

SOCRATES: And you will act properly and well.

ALCIBIADES: Yes.

SOCRATES: And if you act that way, I'm prepared to guarantee your prosperity.

ALCIBIADES: And I trust your guarantee.

SOCRATES: But if you act unjustly, with your eyes on what is dark and godless, as is likely, your conduct will also be dark and godless, because you don't know yourself.

ALCIBIADES: That's likely.

SOCRATES: So it's appropriate for a bad man to be a slave, since it's better.

ALCIBIADES: Yes.

SOCRATES: And vice is appropriate for a slave.

ALCIBIADES: Apparently. 5

SOCRATES: And virtue is appropriate for a free man.

ALCIBIADES: Yes.

SOCRATES: Well, my friend, shouldn't we avoid whatever is appropriate for slaves?

ALCIBIADES: Yes, as much as possible, Socrates.

SOCRATES: Can you see what condition you're now in? Is it appropriate for a free man or not? 10

ALCIBIADES: I think I see only too clearly.

SOCRATES: Then do you know how to escape from your present state?—let's not call a handsome young man by *that* name.

ALCIBIADES: I do. 135d

SOCRATES: How?

ALCIBIADES: It's up to you, Socrates.

SOCRATES: That's not well said, Alcibiades.

ALCIBIADES: Well, what should I say? 5

SOCRATES: That it's up to god.

ALCIBIADES: Then that's what I say. And furthermore I say this as well: we're probably going to change roles, Socrates. I'll be playing yours and you'll be playing mine, for from this day forward I will never fail to attend on you, and you will always have me as your attendant. 10

SOCRATES: Then my love for you, my excellent friend, will be just like a stork: after hatching a winged love in you, it will be cared for by it in return. 135e

ALCIBIADES: Yes, that's right. I'll start to cultivate justice in myself right now. 5

SOCRATES: I should like to believe that you will persevere, but I'm afraid—not because I distrust your nature, but because I know how powerful the city is—I'm afraid it might get the better of both me and you.

REPUBLIC

Selections

In the following passage from Republic 3, *Socrates discusses the sort of* paiderasteia *appropriate to the Guardians and Philosopher-Rulers of his ideally just and happy city—Kallipolis.*

SOCRATES: Can you think of any pleasure that is greater or keener **403a** 5 than sexual pleasure?

GLAUCON: No, I cannot—or of a more insane one either.

SOCRATES: But isn't the right sort of passion a naturally moderate and musically-educated passion for order and beauty?

GLAUCON: Yes.

10 **SOCRATES:** Then nothing insane and nothing akin to dissoluteness can be involved in the right love?

GLAUCON: No, they cannot.

403b **SOCRATES:** Then sexual pleasure must not be involved, must it, and the lover and the boy who passionately love and are loved in the right way must have no share in it?

GLAUCON: No, by Zeus, Socrates, it must not be involved.

SOCRATES: It seems, then, that you will lay it down as a law in the city we are founding that a lover—if he can persuade his boyfriend to let him—may kiss him, be with him, and touch him, as a father would 5 a son, for the sake of beautiful things. But, in all other respects, his association with the one he cares about must never seem to go any **403c** further than this. Otherwise, he will be reproached as untrained in music, and as lacking in appreciation for beautiful things.

GLAUCON: That's right.

In this very brief second passage, also from Republic 3, *Socrates is explicit, as he is in the* Lysis *as well, that love is, in an important sense, a self-interested emotion. We desire the happiness or welfare of those we love because their welfare contributes to our own.*

Translated by C. D. C. Reeve

SOCRATES: But a person would care most for what he loved. (412d2)

GLAUCON: Necessarily.

SOCRATES: And he would love something most if he thought that the same things were advantageous both for it and for himself, and if he thought that when it did well, he would do well too, and that if it didn't, the opposite would happen. 5

GLAUCON: That's right.

In this passage from Republic 4, Socrates introduces his tri-partite soul, consisting of reason (the charioteer in the Phaedrus), spirit (the white horse), and appetite (the black horse), locating sexual passion (erôs) in the latter.

SOCRATES: Now we would say, wouldn't we, that some people are thirsty sometimes yet unwilling to drink? 439c3

GLAUCON: Many people often are.

SOCRATES: What, then, should one say about them? Isn't it that there is an element in their soul urging them to drink, and also one stopping them—something different that masters the one doing the urging. 5

GLAUCON: I certainly think so.

SOCRATES: Doesn't the element doing the stopping in such cases arise—when it does arise—from rational calculation, while the things that drive and drag are present because of feelings and diseases? 439d

GLAUCON: Apparently so.

SOCRATES: It would not be unreasonable for us to claim, then, that there are two elements, different from one another, and to call the element in the soul with which it calculates, the rationally calculating element, and the one with which it feels passion, hungers, thirsts, and is stirred by other appetites, the irrational and appetitive element, friend to certain ways of being filled and certain pleasures. 5

GLAUCON: No, it would not. Indeed, it would be a very natural thing for us to do. 439e

Some remarks from Republic 5 on the all-or-nothing nature of love, whether of boys, of honor, or of philosophy.

SOCRATES: Do I have to remind you, or do you recall, that when we say someone loves something, if the description is correct, it must be clear not just that he loves some part of it but not another, but, on the contrary, that he cherishes the whole of it? 474c10

GLAUCON: You will have to remind me, it seems. I do not recall
the point at all.

SOCRATES: I did not expect you to give that response, Glaucon. A
passionate man should not forget that *all* boys in the bloom of youth
somehow manage to sting and arouse a passionate lover of boys, and
seem to merit his attention and passionate devotion. Isn't that the way
you people behave to beautiful boys? One, because he is snub-nosed,
you will praise as "cute"; another is hook-nose you will say is "regal";
while the one in the middle you say is "well-proportioned." Dark
ones look "manly," and pale ones are "children of the gods." As for
the "honey-colored," do you think that this very term is anything but
the euphemistic coinage of a lover who found it easy to tolerate a sal-
low complexion provided it was accompanied by the bloom of youth?
In a word, you people find any excuse, and use any expression, to
avoid rejecting anyone who is flower is in full bloom.

GLAUCON: If you insist on taking *me* as your example of what
passionate men do, I will go along with you . . . for the sake of
argument!

SOCRATES: What about lovers of wine? Don't you observe them
behaving in just the same way? Don't they find any excuse to indulge
their passionate devotion to wine of any sort?

GLAUCON: They do, indeed.

SOCRATES: And you also observe, I imagine, that if honor-lovers
cannot become generals, they serve as lieutenants, and if they cannot
be honored by important people and dignitaries, they are satisfied
with being honored by insignificant and inferior ones, since it is
honor as a whole they are desirers of.

GLAUCON: Exactly.

SOCRATES: Then do you affirm this or not? When we say that
someone has an appetite for something, are we to say that he has an
appetite for everything of that kind, or for one part of it but not
another?

GLAUCON: Everything.

SOCRATES: Then in the case of the philosopher, too, won't we say
that he has an appetite for *wisdom*—not for one part and not another,
but for all of it?

GLAUCON: True.

SOCRATES: So, if someone is choosy about what he learns, especially if he is young and does not have a rational grasp of what is useful and what is not, we won't say that he is a lover of learning or a 475c philosopher—any more than we would say that someone who is choosy about his food is famished, or has an appetite for food, or is a lover of food rather than a picky eater.

GLAUCON: And we would be right not to say it. 5

SOCRATES: But someone who is ready and willing to taste every kind of learning, who turns gladly to learning and is insatiable for it, *he* is the one we would be justified in calling a philosopher. Isn't that so?

In his fascinating study of the psychopathology of the tyrant in Republic 9, *Plato gives us his fullest and most vivid discussion of what happens when unbridled sexual passion takes over a person's soul.*

SOCRATES: The tyrannical man himself remains to be investigated, 571a how he evolves from a democratic one, what he is like once he has come to exist, and whether the way he lives is wretched or blessedly happy.

ADEIMANTUS: Yes, he still remains.

SOCRATES: Do you know what else I still miss? 5

ADEIMANTUS: What?

SOCRATES: I do not think we have adequately distinguished the nature and number of our appetites. And if that subject is not adequately dealt with, our investigation will lack clarity. 571b

ADEIMANTUS: Well, isn't now as fine a time as any?

SOCRATES: It certainly is. So consider what I want to look at in them. It is this. Among unnecessary pleasures and appetites there are some that seem to me to be lawless. These are probably present in all 5 of us, but they are held in check by the laws and by our better appetites allied with reason. In a few people, they have been eliminated entirely or only a few weak ones remain, while in others they are stronger and more numerous. 571c

ADEIMANTUS: Which ones do you mean?

SOCRATES: The ones that wake up when we are asleep, whenever the rest of the soul—the rational, gentle, and ruling element—slumbers. Then the bestial and savage part, full of food or drink, comes 5 alive, casts off sleep and seeks to go and gratify its own characteristic instincts. You know it will dare to do anything in such a state, released and freed from all shame and wisdom. In fantasy, it does not shrink from trying to have sex with a mother or with anyone else, man, god, or beast. It will commit any foul murder and there is no food it refuses to eat. In a word, it does not refrain from anything, no matter how foolish or shameful.

571d

ADEIMANTUS: That's absolutely true.

5

SOCRATES: On the other hand, I suppose someone who keeps himself healthy and temperate will awaken his rational element before going to sleep and feast it on fine arguments and investigations, which he has brought to an agreed conclusion within himself. As for the appetitive element, he neither starves nor over-feeds it, so it will slumber and not disturb the best element with its pleasure or pain, but will leave it alone, just by itself and pure, to investigate and reach out for the perception of something—whether past, present, or future—that it does not know. He soothes the spirited element in a similar way, and does not get angry and fall asleep with his spirit still aroused. And when he has calmed these two elements and stimulated the third, in which wisdom resides, he takes his rest. You know this is the state in which he most readily grasps the truth and in which the visions appearing in his dreams are least lawless.

571e

572a

5

572b

ADEIMANTUS: I completely agree.

SOCRATES: Well, we have been led a bit astray and said a bit too much. What we want to pay attention to is this: there are appetites of a terrible, savage, and lawless kind in everyone—even in those of us who seem to be entirely moderate. This surely becomes clear in sleep. Do you think I am talking sense? Do you agree with me?

5

ADEIMANTUS: Yes, I do agree.

SOCRATES: Now recall what we said the democratic man is like.[1] He was the result, we presumed, of a childhood upbringing by a thrifty father, who honored only appetites that made money and despised the unnecessary ones whose objects are amusement and showing-off. Isn't that right?

10

572c

ADEIMANTUS: Yes.

5

---

[1] 558c–562a2.

SOCRATES: And by associating with more sophisticated men, who are full of the appetites we just described, he starts to indulge in every kind of arrogance and adopt their kind of behavior, because of his hatred of his father's thrift. But, since he has a better nature than his corrupters, he is pulled in both directions and settles in the middle between their two ways of life. And enjoying each in what he takes to be moderation, he lives a life that is neither illiberal nor lawless, transformed now from an oligarch to a democrat.   572d

ADEIMANTUS: Yes, that was—and still is—our belief about someone like that.

SOCRATES: Suppose, then, that this man has now in turn become older, and has a son who is also brought up in his father's way of life.   5

ADEIMANTUS: I will.

SOCRATES: Suppose, too, that the same things happen to him as happened to his father: He is led into all the kinds of lawlessness that those leading him call total freedom. His father and the rest of his   572e family come to the aid of the appetites that are in the middle, while the others help the opposite ones. And when these terrible enchanters and tyrant-makers have no hope of keeping hold of the young man in any other way, they contrive to implant a powerful passion (*erôta*) in   5 him as the popular leader of those idle and profligate appetites—a sort-of great winged drone. Or do you think passion is ever anything   **573a** else in such people?

ADEIMANTUS: I certainly do not think it is.

SOCRATES: And when the other appetites come buzzing around— filled with incense, perfumes, wreaths, wine, and all the other pleas-   5 ures found in such company, they feed the drone, make it grow as large as possible, and plant the sting of longing in it. Then this popular leader of the soul adopts madness as its bodyguard and is stung to frenzy. If it finds any beliefs or appetites in the man that are regarded   573b as good or are still moved by shame, it destroys them and throws them out, until it has purged him of temperance and filled him with imported madness.

ADEIMANTUS: You have perfectly described how a tyrannical man comes to exist.   5

SOCRATES: Is that, then, why Passion (*Erôs*) has long been called a tyrant?

ADEIMANTUS: Probably so.

SOCRATES: And hasn't a drunken man, my friend, something of a tyrannical cast of mind too?

573c

ADEIMANTUS: He has.

SOCRATES: And of course someone who is mad and deranged attempts to rule not only human beings but gods as well and expects to be able to rule them.

5 ADEIMANTUS: Of course.

SOCRATES: A man becomes tyrannical in the precise sense, then, you marvelous fellow, when his nature or his practices or both together lead him to drunkenness, passion, and melancholia.

10 ADEIMANTUS: Absolutely.

SOCRATES: So that, it seems, is how a tyrannical man comes to exist. Now what is his life like?

573d ADEIMANTUS: Why don't *you* tell *me*, as askers of riddles usually do.

SOCRATES: I will tell you. You see, I think someone in whom the tyrant of Passion dwells, and in whom it serves as captain of everything in the soul, next goes in for, revelries, festivities, luxuries, girlfriends, and all that sort of thing.

5 ADEIMANTUS: Inevitably.

SOCRATES: And don't lots of terrible appetites sprout up each day and night beside it, creating needs for all sorts of things?

ADEIMANTUS: Indeed they do.

10 SOCRATES: So any income someone like that has is soon spent.

ADEIMANTUS: Of course.

SOCRATES: And the next thing, surely, is borrowing and expenditure of capital.

573e

ADEIMANTUS: What else?

SOCRATES: And when everything is gone, won't the violent crowd of appetites that have nested within him inevitably shout in protest? And when people of this sort are driven by the stings of these other appetites but particularly of Passion itself, which leads all the others as if they were its bodyguard, stung to frenzy, don't they look to see who possesses anything that can be taken from him by deceit or force?

5

574a

ADEIMANTUS: Certainly.

SOCRATES: He must take it from every source, then, or live in great suffering and pain.

ADEIMANTUS: He must. 5

SOCRATES: And just as the late-coming pleasures within him do better than the older ones and steal away their satisfactions, won't he himself, young as he is, think he deserves to do better than his father and mother? And, if he has spent his own share, won't he try to take some of his father's wealth by converting it to his own use? 10

ADEIMANTUS: Of course.

SOCRATES: And if his parents resist him, won't he first try to steal it 574b and deceive them?

ADEIMANTUS: Certainly.

SOCRATES: And if he cannot, won't he next try to seize it by force? 5

ADEIMANTUS: I suppose so.

SOCRATES: And if, you amazing man, the old man and woman stand their ground and put up a fight would he take care and be reluctant to act like a tyrant?

ADEIMANTUS: I am not very optimistic about the parents of some- 10 one like that!

SOCRATES: But, in the name of Zeus, Adeimantus, do you really think that for the sake of his latest love, an unnecessary girlfriend, he would strike his mother, who is his oldest and necessary friend? Or that for the sake of his latest and unnecessary boyfriend, who is in the bloom of youth, he would strike his aged and necessary father, the 574c oldest of his friends, who is no longer in the bloom of youth? Or that he would enslave his parents to them, if he brought them into the same house? 5

ADEIMANTUS: Yes, by Zeus, he would.

SOCRATES: It seems to be a great blessing to produce a tyrannical son!

ADEIMANTUS: It certainly does!

SOCRATES: What happens to someone like that when the posses- sions of his father and mother give out and the swarm of pleasures 574d now inside him has grown dense? Won't he first try to break into someone's house or snatch the cloak of someone walking late at night? Next, won't he try to clean out some temple? And in the course of all that, his old childhood beliefs about fine or shameful things—beliefs 5 that are accounted just—are mastered by the new ones that have been released from slavery and, as the bodyguard of Passion, hold sway along with it. These are the ones that used to be freed in sleep as a dream, when he himself, since he was still subject to the laws and his father, had a democratic constitution within him. But under the tyranny of Passion, what he used to become occasionally in his dreams, he has now become permanently while awake, and so there is no terrible murder, no food, and no act from which he will refrain. On the contrary, Passion lives like a tyrant within him in complete anarchy and lawlessness as his sole ruler, and drives him, as if he were a city, to dare anything that will provide sustenance for itself and the unruly mob around it—some of which have come in from the outside as a result of his bad associates, while others have come from within, freed and let loose by his own bad habits. Isn't this the life such a man leads?

ADEIMANTUS: It is.

SOCRATES: And if there are only a few men like that in a city, and the majority of the others are temperate, they emigrate in order to become the bodyguard of some other tyrant or serve as paid auxiliaries if there happens to be a war somewhere. But if they chance to live in a time of peace and calm, they stay right there in the city and cause lots of little evils.

ADEIMANTUS: What sort of evils do you mean?

SOCRATES: They steal, break into houses, snatch purses, steal clothes, rob temples, and kidnap people. Sometimes, if they are capable speakers, they become sycophants[2] and bear false witness and accept bribes.

ADEIMANTUS: You mean they are small evils—provided there are only a few such people.

SOCRATES: Yes. After all, small evils are small by comparison to big ones. And when it comes to producing corruption and misery in a

---

[2] Athens had nothing corresponding to our public prosecutors. Private citizens prosecuted cases themselves. By the middle of the fifth century, some Athenians began to make a profession of bringing nuisance suits against others, which they dropped in exchange for a bribe. These people were called sycophants. A vivid sense of their power and importance is conveyed in L. B. Carter, *The Quiet Athenian* (Oxford: Clarendon Press, 1986).

city, all these evils together do not—as the saying goes—come within a mile of a tyrant. But when you get a large number of these people and their followers in a city, and they become aware of their numbers, they are the ones who—together with the foolishness of the people— create the tyrant out of the one among them who has in his soul the greatest and strongest tyrant of all.

ADEIMANTUS: Naturally, since he would be the most tyrannical.

SOCRATES: That's if they submit willingly. But if the city doesn't put itself in his hands, then, just as he once chastised his mother and father, he will now punish his fatherland in the same way, if he can, bringing in new friends and making and keeping his once beloved motherland—as the Cretans call it—or fatherland their slaves. And that is surely the end at which the appetites of a man like that aim.

ADEIMANTUS: It most certainly is.

SOCRATES: So isn't this what such men are like in private life, before they start to rule? In the first place, don't they associate with flatterers who are ready to do anything to serve them? Or if they need something from someone themselves, won't they grovel and willingly engage in any sort of posturing, the way slaves do? But once they get what they need, isn't it a different story altogether?

ADEIMANTUS: Yes, completely different.

SOCRATES: So those with a tyrannical nature live their entire lives without ever being friends with anyone, always a master to one man or a slave to another, but never getting a taste of freedom or true friendship.

ADEIMANTUS: Exactly.

SOCRATES: Wouldn't we be right to call people like that untrustworthy?

ADEIMANTUS: Of course.

SOCRATES: And as unjust as anyone can be—assuming we were right in our earlier conclusions about what justice is like.

ADEIMANTUS: And we certainly were right.

SOCRATES: Let's sum up the worst type of man, then. He is surely the one who, when awake, is like the dreaming person we described earlier.

575d

5

575e

576a

5

10
576b

LAWS
Selections

In this brief passage from Laws 1, *"natural" sexual activity and its attendant pleasures are distinguished from "unnatural" ones.*

ATHENIAN: . . . [Whether among human beings or beasts,] when what is by nature female enters into partnership with what are by nature males in procreation, you must bear in mind that the pleasure involved seems due to nature; but when males do so with males, or females with females, it seems against nature, and the recklessness of those who first engaged in it seems to have been caused by a lack of self-control where pleasure is concerned.

The following passage from Laws 8 *concerns the sort of legislation a city should enact to regulate sexual behavior. Cleinias is a Cretan, Megillus a Spartan.*

ATHENIAN: It isn't difficult to see how these and similar matters[1] should be put in legal order, or that making an amendment here or there won't help or harm a city very much. But there are other matters that are quite different, and about which it is difficult to persuade people. Indeed, it is a task for a god more than anyone else—were it somehow possible for the orders themselves to come from him. As things stand, however, it looks as though we need a daring human being, someone who values frankness above everything and declares what he thinks best for a city and its citizens; someone who, in the midst of corrupt souls, orders what is appropriate and in keeping with the entire constitution, speaks in opposition to the most powerful desires, and all alone, with no human help whatsoever, follows reason alone.

CLEINIAS: What reason are we talking about now, sir? We don't understand what you're getting at.

ATHENIAN: That's not surprising. I'll try to say what I mean more clearly. When, in the course of my discussion, I came to education, I

Translated by C. D. C. Reeve

[1] Various sorts of games, competitions, and military training.

envisaged young men and young women associating with one another on friendly terms. Naturally enough, I became alarmed when I   5
asked myself how one is to manage a city like this, in which young
men and young women are well nourished and free from the onerous
and slavish tasks that do the most to inhibit lewdness,² and where
everyone is occupied their whole life with religious sacrifices, festi-
vals, and choral dances. How, in such a city, will they ever avoid the   835e
desires that have frequently cast so many people down in ruin—the
desires that reason, in striving to become law, orders them to avoid? It
isn't surprising that the majority of desires are kept in check by the   5
legal requirements established earlier. For example, the proscription
of excessive wealth is no small benefit to temperance, and the entire   **836a**
system of education contains laws well designed for the same purpose.
In addition to this, there is the eye of the rulers, trained not to look
away, but to keep the young under constant surveillance. These measures are as adequate, then, as any human measure can be, to deal with
other desires. But what about sexual love for young people, whether   5
male or female, and that of women for men or men for women?
These have myriad effects on human beings individually and on   836b
whole cities. What precautions should one take against them? What
remedy³ can we devise to escape the risks of each? This is not at all
easy, Cleinias. Indeed, though in quite a few other cases the whole of
Crete, and Sparta as well, have given us quite considerable help in   5
framing laws that depart from common practices, when it comes to
sexual love—we can be frank since we're alone—they are entirely opposed to us. Suppose you follow nature and establish the law that was
in effect before Laius.⁴ You would say that it was correct not to have   836c
the sorts of sexual relations with adult males and boys that one has
with females. As evidence, you would cite what is natural for beasts,
pointing out that the males don't touch the males for such purposes
because it isn't natural to do so. Though your argument would per-   5
haps be found persuasive,⁵ it would not accord at all with your cities.⁶

---

² *Hubris.* See *Symposium* 181c4 note.

³ *Pharmakon:* See *Phaedrus* 230d6 note.

⁴ The father of Oedipus and supposedly the first man to have sex with another
male.

⁵ Reading *pithanôi* with the manuscripts. Many editors follow Badham's emendation *apithanô* ("unpersuaded").

⁶ Crete and Sparta.

There's an additional point, however. These practices are incompatible
with what we say must be the lawgiver's ever-present concern. For we
are always trying to find which enactments promote virtue and which
do not. So, then, suppose that we agreed to enact a law in the present
case declaring such practices noble, or at least in no way shameful. To
what extent would that help us promote virtue? Will a courageous
character be naturally engendered in the soul of the seduced person?
Or that of a temperate person in the seducer's? Would anyone ever be
seduced by such claims? Wouldn't he believe just the opposite?
Wouldn't everyone censure the utter softness[7] of the one who gives in
to these pleasures and lacks the fortitude to stand up to them, and reproach the one who plays the part of the female with his resemblance
to what he imitates? What person, then, would pass a law like that?
Hardly anyone—at least if he understands what a true law is. How,
then, do we establish that this is true? You have to examine the nature
of friendship, of desire, and of so-called "love affairs," if you want to
think correctly in these areas. For there are two kinds of them involved here, and a third kind that is based on both. Since one name is
applied to all of them, that causes total puzzlement and obscurity.

CLEINIAS: How so?

ATHENIAN: Surely, we call what is like to its like a "friend" in
point of virtue, and what is equal to its equal. Secondly, what is poor
is a "friend" to what is wealthy, these being *opposite* in kind. And
when either sort of friendship becomes intense, we call it a "love."

CLEINIAS: That's right.

ATHENIAN: Now, friendship based on opposition is a terrible and
savage thing, and among us is seldom reciprocated, while that deriving from likeness is gentle and reciprocated throughout life. As for the
third that is a mixture of these two—in the first place, it isn't easy to
discover what this third sort of lover wants for himself. Next, because
he is pulled in opposite directions by the two, he's puzzled himself,
with one telling him to pluck the young bloom, and the other forbidding him to do so. For the one that loves the body and hungers for its
bloom, as for ripe fruit, tells him to take his fill without consideration
for the soul of his beloved or his character; whereas the other considers desire for the body a by-product and puts admiring looks in place

---

[7] *Malakia*: See *Symposium* 173d8 note.

of sex. It desires what is really soul with what is really soul, and re-   5
gards the satisfaction of body by body as lewdness.[8] So, feeling simul-
taneous awe and reverence for temperance, courage, high-mindedness,
and wisdom, he will wish to remain always chaste with a beloved who
is chaste. This mixture of both of these is the third sort of love we   837d
mentioned just now. Well, since these are the sorts of love there are,
should the law forbid all of them and prevent them from arising
amongst us? Or isn't it obvious that the virtuous sort, the sort that desires a young man to become the best that he can, is the sort we   5
should want to have exist in our city, while, if possible, we forbid the
other two? What do you think, Megillus, my friend?

MEGILLUS: What you've said about these matters, sir, is in every
way finely put.   837e

ATHENIAN: It looks as though I find you in accord, my friend, just
as I expected. So, there is no need for me to inquire about the attitude
of your law[9] to such things; your agreement to the argument is sufficient. Later on I'll come back to these matters and try to charm
Cleinias into agreeing with me, too. So let's take it for now that   5
you've both given me your assent, and go through all the laws in detail.

MEGILLUS: All right.

ATHENIAN: I have at hand a device[10] for establishing this law[11] on a
firm footing. In one way, it's easy; in another, altogether as difficult as   **838a**
can be.

MEGILLUS: What do you mean?

ATHENIAN: We know, of course, that even as things are, most
human beings, lawless though they be, readily and strictly refrain   5
from having sex with people they find beautiful, and do so not *un*-
willingly, but as willingly as possible.

MEGILLUS: When do you mean?

ATHENIAN: When the beautiful person is a brother or a sister. And
in the case of a son or a daughter, too, the same law, unwritten
though it is, is very effective in preventing one from either openly or   838b

---

[8] *Hubris.* See *Symposium* 181c4 note.

[9] The law of Sparta.

[10] *Technê.*

[11] The law pertaining to unnatural or nonprocreative sex.

secretly sleeping with them, or having any other sort of sexual contact.
5   In fact, most people have no desire whatsoever for such intercourse.

MEGILLUS: That's true.

ATHENIAN: It's a small number of words, then, don't you think,
that quenches all such pleasures?

MEGILLUS: What words are those?

ATHENIAN: The ones that say that these acts are entirely unholy,
10 indeed hated by the gods and the most shameful of shameful things.
838c And they're efficacious because no one ever speaks of them in any
other way, but from the moment of birth each one of us hears these
things being always and everywhere said, not just in comedies, but
frequently in the speeches of serious tragedy, too, as when a Thyestes
5   is brought on stage, or some Oedipus or other, or a Macareus, who
had secret intercourse with his own sister, but when found out,
promptly committed suicide as just punishment for the crime?[12]

MEGILLUS: You're absolutely right about this, at least: when no one
838d ever attempts in any way to breathe a contrary word, the power of
solemn reports is amazing.

ATHENIAN: So, what we said just now is correct: when a lawgiver
wants to enslave some desire that is itself a preeminent enslaver of
5   people, it's easy for him to see, at least, the way he should handle it.
He will have succeeded in making this law as secure as possible if he
can get everyone—slaves, free citizens, children, women, the entire
city—to take such solemn reports about the matter as having a sacred-
838e ness to them.

MEGILLUS: Certainly. But how it will ever be possible for him to
make everyone willing to say such things—

ATHENIAN: I'm glad you have taken me up on this. You see, that
was precisely what I was getting at when I said that I had a device for
5   putting into effect this law of ours promoting the natural use of sexual intercourse in procreation, by abstaining from sex with men, and

---

[12] Thyestes, brother of Atreus (father of Agamemnon and Menelaus), raped his
daughter Pelopia while she slept, unaware of who she was. Oedipus unwittingly
killed his father and married his mother. In the play by Sophocles, he blinded
himself but did not commit suicide. In a lost play of Euripides, however,
Macareus did kill himself when incest with his sister Canace became known.

not deliberately killing off the human race, nor yet wasting sperm on rocks or stone where it will never take root and produce a natural off-spring, and by abstaining from any female "ground" in which you **839a** would not wish your sperm to take root. If this law is put on a per-manent and effective footing—and if, just as it is presently effective in the case of sex with parents, it should rightly be victorious in the other cases too—it would have a myriad of good effects. For, in the   5 first place, it is established in accord with nature, serving to prevent sexual distress and insanity, every sort of adultery, every sort of excess in eating and drinking, and ensuring that men are intimate friends to their own wives. And many other good things would also result if one   839b could make this law effective. Suppose, however, that a headstrong young man, full of a large quantity of sperm, heard us establishing this law. He would probably heap abuse on us for setting up foolish and impossible legal requirements, and fill the place with his outcries. This   5 was what I had in mind when I said that I had a device—in one way entirely easy, in another extremely difficult—that would help perma-   839c nently establish this law.[13] It is very easy to see both *that* it can be done and *in what way*: we maintain that if a legal requirement has been suf-ficiently imbued with sacredness, it will enslave every soul, filling each with a fear that will make it wholly obedient to the established laws.   5 Yet we have reached a point nowadays where people think it can't be done even so. It is just the same with the institution of common messes: people believe that it isn't possible for a whole city to keep up the practice in the long term. Yet this was refuted by the fact of its ex-istence among your people—although your cities still don't regard it   839d as a natural institution for women. It was because of this, because of the strength of this incredulity, that I described both these practices[14]   5 as very difficult to put on a permanent legal footing.

MEGILLUS: And you are certainly right about that.

ATHENIAN: Even so, would you two like me to give you both a somewhat persuasive argument that it isn't beyond human capacity to be done, but is in fact quite possible?

CLEINIAS: Certainly.   10

---

[13] See 838a.

[14] The practice of avoiding nonprocreative sex and that of having state-sponsored messes for citizens.

839e   ATHENIAN: Well, would someone more easily abstain from sex,
and be willing to do in a spirit of moderation as he is ordered in this
area, if his body is in good condition and properly trained, or if it is in
poor condition?

CLEINIAS: He would find it much easier, I imagine, if properly
trained.

ATHENIAN: Well, haven't we all heard about Iccus of Tarentum,
840a   who competed at Olympia and elsewhere? He was so eager for victory, and had such skill and such a mixture of courage and temperance in his soul, so the story goes, that he never touched a woman, or
a boy either, for that matter, during the entire period of his final
training. And essentially the same story is told about Crison, Astylus,
5   and Diopompus, and a great many others.[15] And yet, Cleinias, their
souls were much less well educated than those of your and my citi-
840b   zens, and in their bodies much lustier.

CLEINIAS: What you say is true: our ancient sources are quite definite that this is what really happened with these athletes.

ATHENIAN: Well then. For the sake of victory in wrestling, run-
5   ning, and the like, they had the courage to abstain from what most
people call sheer bliss. So, our young people will lack the fortitude
needed to win a much more noble victory?—the noblest one of all, as
840c   we shall tell them in stories or sayings from the time they are children,
and sing in songs, and surely charm them into believing.

CLEINIAS: What victory?

ATHENIAN: Victory over pleasures. If they conquer them, they will
5   live happily, but if they lose, the very opposite. Besides, can't we expect that the fear that this[16] is something utterly unholy will give them
the power to conquer what their inferiors have conquered?

10   CLEINIAS: It's likely, anyway.

ATHENIAN: Now that we have reached this point in regard to our
legal requirement, but because of the corrupt condition of most

---

[15] Iccus won the Olympic pentathlon and became a famous trainer (cf. *Protagoras*
316d); Crison of Himera was a famous Olympic runner (*ibid.* 335e); Astylus of
Crotona won victories in three successive Olympic games. Diopompus is otherwise unknown.

[16] Nonprocreative sex.

people, have fallen into perplexity, I say that our legal requirement   840d
about these matters simply must go forward, proclaiming that our
citizens mustn't be inferior to birds and also beasts, who are born into
large flocks and, until the time comes for them to breed, live celibate,   5
pure, and chaste lives. Then, when they reach that age, they pair off as
they please, male with female and female with male, and for the remaining time live in a pious and just manner, firmly committed to the
initial agreements constituting their friendship. So, our citizens must   840e
at least be better than these beasts. If, however, they are corrupted by
the majority of other Greeks and barbarians, through seeing and
hearing about the very great power that so-called "free" Love[17] has
among them, and so lack the fortitude to keep control, then the   5
Law-guardians, acting as Law-makers, will have to devise a second law
for them.

CLEINIAS: What further law do you advise them to establish, if the   841a
one being established now is beyond them?

ATHENIAN: Clearly, the one that is second to it, Cleinias.

CLEINIAS: Which one do you mean?   5

ATHENIAN: The one that is said to leave the strength of these pleasures no room for exercise, by using hard labor to divert what would
increase and nourish it to another part of the body. This is what
would happen if no one ever had sex without feeling shame. For
shame would make having it infrequent, and infrequency would make   841b
it a less tyrannical mistress. Let them, therefore, regard concealment in
sexual matters—though not complete abstinence—as the honorable
thing, sanctioned by a requirement that is embodied in people's habits
and in unwritten law; and openness as shameful. In that way, we shall
have a secondary legal standard of what is shameful and what is
honorable, one having a secondary sort of correctness. And those   5
whose natures have been corrupted, whom we describe as "weaker
than themselves,"[18] since they are all of one kind, will be hemmed in
by three kinds of influences and forcibly prevented from disobeying   841c
the law.

CLEINIAS: Which ones?

---

[17] *Atakton Aphroditên:* "disorderly" or "disobedient Aphrodite."
[18] That is, lacking in self-control. See 626e ff.

ATHENIAN: Reverence for the gods, love of honor, and the development of a desire not for bodies that have beautiful qualities, but for
5   souls that do. These things I am now mentioning are no doubt like prayerful wishes in a storybook; yet if they actually came to pass in any city, they would certainly have the very best effects. God willing, however, we might perhaps forcibly impose one or the other of the
841d following two rules of sexual conduct: either [1] that no one should dare to touch any well-born, free person other than the woman who is his wife, or sow unhallowed and illegitimate sperm in courtesans, or sterile seed in males in defiance of nature; or [2] that we could en-
5   tirely abolish sex between males; and, in the case of women, if any man has sex with any of them, other than those who enter his house with the sanction of the gods and holy matrimony, whether purchased or acquired in some other way, and fails to keep the affair con-
841e cealed from every man or woman, we would no doubt seem to be legislating correctly if we established a law barring him from all civic honors on the grounds that he is really an alien. Let this law, then, whether it ought to be called one law or two, be established to deal
5   with sexual matters and everything involving erotic love—and with the right and wrong sorts of ways we have of interacting with one
842a another as a result of such desires.

The following brief passage from Laws 9 *describes the laws that should govern rape.*

ATHENIAN: If someone sexually violates a free woman or boy, he
874c3 may be killed with impunity by the victim of the violence, or by the victim's father, brothers, or sons. If a husband discovers his wedded
5   wife being violated and kills the man who violated her, he will be innocent under the law.